THE ULTIMATE BOOK OF
FRESH &
DRIED
FLOWERS

THE ULTIMATE BOOK OF

FRESH &
DRIED &
FLOWERS

A COMPLETE GUIDE TO FLORAL ARRANGING

Fiona Barnett and Terence Moore

LORENZ BOOKS

FIRST PUBLISHED IN 1999 BY LORENZ BOOKS

© ANNESS PUBLISHING LIMITED 1999

LORENZ BOOKS IS AN IMPRINT OF
ANNESS PUBLISHING LIMITED
HERMES HOUSE
88–89 BLACKFRIARS ROAD
LONDON SE1 8HA

ISBN 0 7548 0084 9

A CIP CATALOGUE RECORD FOR THIS BOOK
IS AVAILABLE FROM THE BRITISH LIBRARY

PUBLISHER: JOANNA LORENZ
PROJECT EDITOR: FELICITY FORSTER
TEXT: FIONA BARNETT, ROGER EGERICKX AND
TERENCE MOORE
CONTRIBUTING EDITORS: JUDY COX AND JACKIE MATTHEWS
ADDITIONAL PROJECTS: DEENA BEVERLEY (PP 158, 434), KALLY
ELLIS AND ERCOLE MORONI (PP 134, 136, 200, 212, 238, 256, 260,
304, 332, 334–5, 372, 500), TESSA EVELEGH (PP 127, 180, 224, 247,
258, 262, 278–9, 283, 288–9, 322, 331, 338, 340, 344, 346–7, 404,
409), LUCINDA GANDERTON (P 291) AND GILLY LOVE (PP 264, 287)
DESIGNERS: NIGEL PARTRIDGE AND IAN SANDOM
JACKET DESIGNER: MABEL CHAN
PHOTOGRAPHERS: MICHELLE GARRETT AND
DEBBIE PATTERSON
ADDITIONAL PHOTOGRAPHY: ANDREW CAMERON,
JOHN FREEMAN AND POLLY WREFORD
EDITORIAL READER: KATE HENDERSON
PRODUCTION CONTROLLER: BEN WORLEY

PREVIOUSLY PUBLISHED AS TWO SEPARATE VOLUMES,
THE NEW FLOWER ARRANGER AND *NEW FLOWER DESIGN*

PRINTED AND BOUND IN GERMANY

1 3 5 7 9 10 8 6 4 2

AUTHOR ACKNOWLEDGEMENTS
FIONA BARNETT WOULD LIKE TO THANK ROGER EGERICKX AND
RICHARD KISS OF DESIGN AND DISPLAY (SALES LTD) FOR THEIR
GENEROUS PROVISION OF FACILITIES. WITH SPECIAL THANKS TO
JENNY BENNETT FOR ALL HER HARD WORK.

CONTENTS
· · ·

INTRODUCTION

Fresh flower displays are the perfect way to celebrate the arrival of the earliest flowers of the season, and dried flower arrangements provide year-round interest. From an intricate corsage to a simple tied posy, flower arranging requires care and consideration, and in the following pages advice is given on balance, scale, proportion and colour, to ensure beautiful and creative displays.

INTRODUCTION

· · ·

*Above: Lily and Hyacinth
Planted Basket*

*Below: Summer Basket
Display*

FRESH FLOWERS

The vagaries of fashion have had their impact on flower arranging just as they have on most other aspects of life. However, one discernible long-term trend has been a relaxation of the formal approach of 20 years or more ago when flowers sometimes looked as though they had been beaten into submission!

Nowadays, the strait-jacket of formality has been replaced by an emphasis on the flowers themselves, creating the impact in a natural way.

No longer restricted by a set of rigid rules, the flower arranger is free to take inspiration from anything that triggers the creative process: it may be the decor of a room or a particular type of container, but equally it could just be the mood of the moment or even the state of the weather!

Of course, modern flower arranging still relies on the basic principles of colour, scale, proportion and balance, but it uses these to create more adventurous designs in exciting colour combinations and textures. It is also concerned with simplicity, and today the flower arranger is as likely to create a successful display with daffodils in a jam jar as with an opulent arrangement on a pedestal.

Flower arranging has become the art of understanding the materials and getting the best out of them with the minimum complication.

Above: Fruit and Flower Swag

Left: Arum Lily Vase

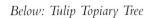

One of the single most important factors in allowing the flower arranger more creative freedom has been the enormous improvement in the availability and good quality of commercially grown cut flowers. The flower arranger is no longer restricted by the seasonal availability of the majority of popular cut blooms and has an ever-growing range of flowers to work with. Furthermore, modern growing techniques have improved the quality and increased the life span of cut flowers: for example the few days' cut life of sweet peas has been extended to a week or more.

All of these improvements give today's flower arranger more options in terms of choice of materials, colour palette and arranging techniques.

To some, flower arranging is an all-consuming passion, but to many it remains a mystery. In reality, it is an activity in which most people can, to a greater or lesser extent, successfully participate. All you need is a working knowledge of the contents of this book coupled with a little determination, some imagination and lots of practice. The important thing to remember is that flower arranging is a creative, not just a physical, process.

Right: Dried Flower Tussie Mussies

DRIED FLOWERS

Dried flowers used to be thought of chiefly as a winter substitute for unavailable fresh blooms. But improvements in the technology of preserving plant materials has resulted in an increase in types of dried flowers and the introduction of vibrant new colours. The astonishing range of materials and colours now available has heralded a new dawn of possibilities.

Today's approach to dried flower displays is to emphasize colour and texture by using massed materials so that the collective strength of their qualities creates the impact. Even where a number of varieties are incorporated in a display they should be used in clusters to extract the maximum effect. It is wise to avoid using individual stems of a particular material because this will make for rather bitty looking displays.

To get the best out of dried plant material, do not be afraid to integrate other materials with them: dried fruits, gourds, seashells, roots and driftwood can all add an extra dimension to a display. To create an opulent effect, bunches of dried herbs and spices, and varieties of dried and preserved mosses can be added and groups of filled terracotta pots may be attached. With all this choice today's dried

Above: Decorated Pot Display

Right: Crescent Moon Wreath

Above: Apple and Lavender Topiary Tree

Left: Peony and Apple Table Arrangement

flower display is a far cry from the fading brown and orange dust traps of the past.

Impressive though improvements in preserving plant materials may be, the ravages of time, sunlight, moisture and dust still take their toll on dried flowers. Do not make the mistake of believing dried arrangements will last for ever. A useful life of around six months is the best that can be expected before dried flowers begin to look dusty and faded.

However, by taking a few simple common sense precautions, the life of a dried arrangement can be maximized. To avoid fading, keep the arrangement out of direct sunlight. Do not allow dried flowers to become damp and particularly be aware of condensation in bathrooms and on window ledges. To prevent the build-up of dust give the arrangement an occasional blast with a hair-dryer set on slow and cool. When the arrangement is new, spray it with hair lacquer to help prevent the dropping of grass seeds and petals, but do not use hair-spray on dust-covered dried flowers.

A potentially rewarding aspect of dried flower arranging is drying and preserving the plant material yourself. It takes patience and organization but with application you will be able to preserve materials not commercially available and, since some dried flowers can be expensive, you will save yourself money.

There are different methods of preservation to suit different plant materials. In the following pages, these methods are clearly explained. There is also a list of materials with the appropriate drying method for each. The list is not exhaustive so if the material you want to preserve is not referred to, then assess its characteristics, find a similar type and try the method recommended for that.

Below: Rose and Starfish Wreath

BALANCE

Balance is very important in a flower display, both physically and visually.

Foremost, the flower arranger must ensure the physical stability of the display. This involves understanding the mechanics of the arrangement, the types and sizes of materials used, how they are positioned and in what type of container. Different types of floral displays require different strategies to ensure their stability.

A large arrangement to be mounted on a pedestal will need a heavy, stable container. The display materials should be distributed evenly around the container and the weight concentrated as near the bottom as possible. Make sure the longer flowers and foliage do not cause the display to become top-heavy.

A mantelpiece arrangement can be particularly difficult to stabilise since the display materials hanging down over the shelf will tend to pull it forward. So use a heavy container and position the flowers and foliage as far back in it as possible.

Check the stability of an arrangement at regular stages during its construction.

Achieving a visual balance in a flower arrangement involves scale, proportion and colour as well as creating a focal point in the display.

The focal point of an arrangement is an area to which the eye should be naturally drawn and from which all display materials should appear to flow. While the position of the focal point will vary according to the type of display, generally speaking it will be towards its centre. This is where the boldest colours and shapes should be concentrated, with paler colours around the outside.

Always think of the display in three dimensions, never forgetting that as well as a front, it will have sides and a back. This is not difficult to remember for a bouquet or a free-standing, pedestal-mounted display, but can be forgotten if a display is set against a wall. Even a flat-backed arrangement needs depth and shape. Recessing materials around the focal point will help give it depth and weight.

Balance in a floral display is the integration of all visual factors to create a harmonious appearance and with practice you will develop the ability to achieve this.

SCALE AND PROPORTION

Scale is a very important consideration when planning a floral display.

In order to create an arrangement which is pleasing to the eye, the sizes of different flower types used in the same display should not be radically different. For example, it would be difficult to make amaryllis look in scale with lily-of-the-valley.

The type of foliage used should be in scale with the flowers, the display itself must be in scale with its container, and the arrangement and its container must be in scale with its surroundings. A display in a large space in a public building must itself be appropriately large enough to make a statement, conversely a bedside table would require no more than an arrangement in a bud vase.

Proportion is the relationship of width, height and depth within a floral display and in this respect there are some rule-of-thumb guidelines worth bearing in mind.
❖ In a tied bouquet, the length of the stems below the binding point should be approximately one-third of the bouquet's overall height.

❖ In a trailing wedding bouquet, the focal point of the display will probably be about one-third of the overall length up from its lowest point.

❖ For a pedestal arrangement, the focal point will be approximately two-thirds of the overall height down from its top-most point.

❖ A vase with long-stemmed flowers such as lilies, should be around one-third the height of the flowers.

❖ The focal point of a corsage is about one-third the overall height up from the bottom.

However, remember that decisions on the scale and proportion of a floral display are a matter of personal taste and thus will vary from person to person.

The important thing is not simply to accept a series of rules on scale and proportion but to give these factors your consideration and develop your own critical faculties in this area.

COLOUR

The way in which colour is used can be vital to the success or failure of a display and there are several factors to bear in mind when deciding on a colour palette.

Though most people have an eye for colour, an understanding of the theory of colour is useful. Red, blue and yellow are the basic hues from which all other colours stem. Red, orange and yellow are warm colours which tend to create an exciting visual effect, while green, blue and violet are cooler and visually calmer.

Generally speaking, the lighter, brighter and hotter a colour, the more it will dominate an arrangement. White (which technically is the absence of colour) is also prominent in a display of flowers.

On the other hand, the darker and cooler the colour, the more it will visually recede into a display. It is important to bear this in mind when creating large displays to be viewed from a distance. In such circumstances blue and violet, in particular, can become lost in an arrangement.

Usually a satisfactory visual balance should be achieved if the stronger, bolder coloured flowers are positioned towards the centre of the display with the paler, more subtle colours around the outside.

Now armed with some basic knowledge of colour theory you can be braver in your choice of palette. "Safe" colour combinations such as creams with whites, or pinks with mauves have their place, but experiment with oranges and violets, yellows and blues, even pinks and yellows and you will add a vibrant dimension to your flower arranging.

Above: A contorted branch makes an unusual "trunk" for this dried topiary tree.

Top left: The heavy blossoms of white lilac are set against the darker stems of pussy willow and cherry.

Above: These bright yellow sunflowers are complemented by the brown contorted hazel twigs.

Left: The natural greens, yellows and mauves of these herbs blend perfectly together.

SECTION ONE

· · ·

GETTING STARTED: FLOWER BASICS

· · ·

There is an enormous range of materials and equipment available to the flower arranger, and this section offers a complete guide to getting started with your fresh and dried flower displays. There is information on caring for cut flowers, a guide to dried flower materials, equipment and containers, drying techniques, and the use of fruit and vegetables in displays. Wiring techniques are also fully explained, thereby enabling the reader to create beautiful flower displays with confidence.

CARE OF CUT FLOWERS

• • •

CONDITIONING

Conditioning is the term for the process of preparing flowers and foliage for use in arranging.

The general rules are: remove all lower leaves to ensure there is no soft material below the water level where it will rot, form bacteria and shorten the life of the arrangement; cut the stem ends at an angle to provide as large a surface area as possible for the take-up of water; and, finally, stand all materials in cold water for a couple of hours to encourage the maximum intake of water before use.

For many varieties of flower and foliage this treatment is perfectly adequate; for some, however, there are a number of additional methods to increase their longevity.

BOILING WATER

The woody stems of lilac, guelder rose and rhododendron, the sap-filled stems of milkweed (euphorbia) and poppy, even roses and chrysanthemums, will benefit from the shock treatment of immersing their stem ends in boiling water.

Remove all lower foliage, together with approximately 6 cm (2½ in) of bark from the ends of woody stems. Cut the stem ends at an angle of 45 degrees and, in the case of woody stems, split up to approximately 6 cm (2½ in) from the bottom. Wrap any flowerheads in paper to protect them from the hot steam.

Carefully pour boiling water into a heatproof container to a depth of

approximately 6 cm (2½ in) and plunge the bottoms of the stems into the hot water, leaving them for two to three minutes before removing and plunging them into deep cold water. The heat of the boiling water will have dispelled air from the stems to enable the efficient take-up of cold water. The boiling water will also have destroyed bacteria on the stem ends.

Wilted roses can also be revived by having their stems recut and given the boiling water treatment, and then left standing (with their heads wrapped up to their necks) in cold water for two hours.

The rose stripper (below) is invaluable when dealing with very thorny stems.

SEARING

Searing is a method of extending the lives of plants such as milkweed (euphorbia) and poppies which contain a milky sap, the release of which affects the water quality.

It involves passing the stem end through a flame until it is blackened, then placing it in tepid water. This forms a layer of charcoal to seal the stem end, preventing sap leakage but still allowing the take-up of water.

HOLLOW STEMS
Delphiniums, amaryllis and lupins have hollow stems and the best method of conditioning them is to turn them upside-down and literally fill them with water.

To keep the water in the stem, form a plug from cotton wool or tissue and carefully bung the open stem end. Tie a rubber band around the base of the stem to avoid splitting, then stand the stem in tepid water. The water trapped inside the stem will keep it firm and the cotton wool will help draw more water up into it.

FOLIAGE
Generally the rules for conditioning foliage are the same as for flowers. It is vital to strip the lower leaves and cut the stem base at an angle. Depending on the stem structure and size, other special techniques may well apply. It is also important to scrape the bark from the bottom 6 cm (2½ in) of the stem and split it to further encourage the take-up of water and thereby prolong the life of the foliage.

WRAPPING TO STRAIGHTEN STEMS
Some flowers, such as gerbera, have soft, flexible weak stems and other flowers may simply have wilted. There is a technique for strengthening such material: take a group of flowers and wrap the top three-quarters of their stems together in paper to keep them erect, then stand them in deep cool water for about two hours. The cells within the stems will fill with water and be able to stand on their own when the paper is removed.

ETHYLENE GAS
Ethylene is an odourless gas emitted by such things as rubbish (garbage), exhaust fumes, fungi and ripening fruit. It has the effect of accelerating the rate at which some flowers mature which in turn causes non-opening and dropping of buds and yellowing of leaves. Particularly susceptible are carnations, freesia, alstroemeria and roses. Be aware of this when using fruit in a flower arrangement.

FLOWER AVAILABILITY CHART

• • •

This list is an indication of current availability of the flowers from the Dutch market.
As development in production of individual varieties improve, this information may change.
❀❀❀ *good availability*   ❀❀ *some availability*   ❀ *limited availability*

FLOWER TYPE	JAN	FEB	MAR	APR	MAY	JUN	JUL	AUG	SEP	OCT	NOV	DEC	SPECIAL NOTES
Achillea			*	*	*			***	***				*Some varieties only available in Spring*
Aconitum (monkshood)					*			***	***				
Agapanthus	*	*						***	***	*	*	*	*Some varieties moderately available in Winter*
Ageratum		*			*			***	***	***	***		
Alchemilla (mollis)							*	*					
Allium					*			***	***				
Alstroemeria	***	**	**	***	***	***	***	***	***	***	***	***	*Some varieties not so available early Spring*
Amaranthus (red and green)	**						**	***	***	***	***	***	
Amaryllis (Belladonna)	**							**	**	***	***	***	
Ammi majus (white dill)	***	***	***	***	***	***	***	**	**	***	***	***	
Anemones	***	***	***	***	***	***	***			***	***	***	
Anethum graveolens (green dill)	**				**		**	**	***	***	***		
Anigozanthus (kangaroo paw)	**	**	**	**	**	**	**	**	**	*	**	**	*Some varieties not available mid-Spring*
Anthuriums	***	***	***	***	***	***	***	***	***	***	***	***	*Most colours available throughout the year*
Antirrhinum majus	***	***	*	***	***	***	***	***	***	***	***	***	*Most colours not available in early Spring*
Asclepias	**	***	**	**	**	***	***	***	***	***	***	***	*A. incarnata only available early Autumn*
Asters	***	***				***	***	***	***	***	***	***	*Some varieties only available late Autumn*
Astilbe					*	*	*	***	***	***	***	***	*A. 'Whasingthon' only available late Spring*
Astrantia								*	*	*	*		
Atriplex	**	***	***	***	***	**			**	**	**	**	
Bouvardia	***	***	***	***	***	***	***	***	***	***	***	***	*B. longiflorum not available in Spring*
Bupleurum griffithii	***	***	***	***	***	***	***	***	***	***	***	***	
Callistephus (China aster)			*	*	*			***	***	***	***	***	
Campanula					***	***	***						
Carthamus	**	**	**	**			**	***	***	***	***	***	
Celosia	**	**						**	***	***	***	***	
Centaurea cyanus (cornflower)								***	***	***	***		
Centaurea macrocephala								*	*				
Chamelaucium (waxflower)		**	**	**	**								
Chelone obliqua					**	**			***	***	***		
Chrysanthemum santini	***	***	***	***	***	***	***	***	***	***	***	***	
Chrysanthemum (Indicum gr.)	***	***	***	***	***	***	***	***	***	***	***	***	
Cirsium		**	**		**	***	***	***	***	***	***	***	
Convallaria majalis (lily-of-the-valley)	**	**	**	**	***	***	***	***	**	**	**	**	
Crocosmia (Montbretia)							***	***	***				
Cyclamen	***	***	***	***	***							***	
Cymbidium orchids	***	***	***	***	***	***	***	**		***	***	***	
Dahlias									***	***	***	***	
Delphinium ajacis (larkspur)	***	***	***	***	***	***	***	***	***	***	***	***	
Delphinium	**	**	**	**	**	***	***	***	***	***	***	**	
Dendrobium orchids	***	***	***	***	***	***	***	***	***	***	***	***	
Dianthus barbatus (sweet william)	*	*	***	***	***	***	***	***	*	*	*	*	
Dianthus (standard carnation)	***	***	***	***	***	***	***	***	***	***	***	***	
Dianthus (spray carnation)	***	***	***	***	***	***	***	***	***	***	***	***	
Echinops								***	***	***	***	***	
Eremurus stenophyllus (fox tail lily)						***	***	***	*	*	*		
Eryngium	***	***						***	***	***	***	***	
Eupatorium								***	***	***	***		
Euphorbia fulgens	***	***	***							***	***	***	
Eustoma russellianum	***	***					***	***	***	***	***	***	
Forsythia intermedia			***	***	***	***							
Freesia	***	***	***	***	***	***	***	***	***	***	***	***	
Gerbera	***	***	***	***	***	***	***	***	***	***	***	***	
Gladioli								***	***	***	***	***	

Flower Type	Jan	Feb	Mar	Apr	May	Jun	Jul	Aug	Sep	Oct	Nov	Dec	Special Notes
Gloriosa rothschildiana (glory lily)	✻✻✻	✻✻✻	✻✻	✻✻✻	✻✻✻	✻✻✻	✻✻✻	✻✻✻	✻✻✻	✻✻✻	✻✻✻	✻✻✻	
Godetia	✻✻✻			✻✻✻	✻✻✻	✻✻✻	✻✻✻	✻✻✻	✻✻✻	✻✻✻	✻✻✻	✻✻✻	
Gomphrena	✻✻	✻✻						✻✻	✻✻✻	✻✻✻	✻✻✻	✻✻✻	
Gypsophila	✻✻✻	✻✻✻	✻✻✻	✻✻✻	✻✻✻	✻✻✻	✻✻✻	✻✻✻	✻✻✻	✻✻✻	✻✻✻	✻✻✻	
Helenium								✻✻✻	✻✻✻	✻✻✻	✻✻✻	✻✻✻	
Helianthus (sunflower)						✻✻✻	✻✻✻	✻✻✻	✻✻✻	✻✻✻	✻✻✻	✻✻	
Heliconia	✻✻✻	✻✻✻	✻✻✻	✻✻✻	✻✻✻	✻✻✻	✻✻	✻✻✻	✻✻✻	✻✻✻	✻✻✻	✻✻✻	
Hippeastrum	✻✻✻	✻✻✻	✻✻✻	✻✻✻									
Hyacinths		✻✻	✻✻✻	✻✻✻	✻✻✻	✻✻✻	✻✻						
Hydrangea	✻✻	✻✻	✻✻	✻✻	✻✻	✻✻	✻✻	✻✻	✻✻✻	✻✻✻	✻✻✻	✻✻✻	
Hypericum	✻✻	✻✻						✻✻	✻✻	✻✻	✻✻	✻✻	
Iris	✻✻✻	✻✻✻	✻✻✻	✻✻✻	✻✻✻	✻✻✻	✻✻	✻✻✻	✻✻✻	✻✻✻	✻✻✻	✻✻✻	
Ixia					✻	✻							
Kniphofia (red hot pokers)						✻✻	✻✻	✻✻	✻	✻	✻	✻✻	
Lathyrus (sweet peas)			✻	✻	✻✻	✻✻	✻✻	✻✻✻					
Leucanthemum	✻✻✻	✻✻✻	✻✻✻	✻✻✻	✻✻✻	✻✻✻	✻✻✻	✻✻✻	✻✻✻	✻✻✻		✻✻✻	
Liatris	✻✻✻	✻✻✻	✻✻✻	✻✻✻	✻✻✻	✻✻✻	✻✻✻	✻✻✻	✻✻✻	✻✻✻	✻✻✻	✻✻✻	
Lilium	✻✻✻	✻✻✻	✻✻✻	✻✻✻	✻✻✻	✻✻✻	✻✻✻	✻✻✻	✻✻✻	✻✻✻	✻✻✻	✻✻✻	
Limonium (stratice)	✻✻✻	✻✻✻	✻✻✻	✻✻✻	✻✻✻	✻✻✻	✻✻✻	✻✻✻	✻✻✻	✻✻✻	✻✻✻	✻✻✻	
Lysimachia clethroides		✻✻✻	✻✻✻	✻✻✻	✻✻✻	✻✻✻	✻✻✻	✻✻✻	✻✻✻	✻✻✻	✻✻✻	✻✻✻	
Lysimachia vulgaris	✻✻	✻✻							✻✻	✻✻	✻✻	✻✻	
Matthiola incana (stocks)	✻	✻	✻	✻	✻✻✻	✻✻✻	✻✻✻	✻✻✻	✻✻	✻✻	✻✻	✻	*A white variety is available all year*
Mentha (flowering mint)									✻✻✻	✻✻✻	✻✻✻		
Molucella laevis (bells of Ireland)	✻✻✻	✻✻✻	✻✻✻	✻✻✻	✻✻✻	✻✻✻	✻✻✻	✻✻✻	✻✻✻	✻✻✻	✻✻✻	✻✻✻	
Muscari (grape hyacinth)	✻✻	✻✻✻	✻✻✻	✻✻✻	✻✻✻	✻✻✻	✻✻					✻✻	
Narcissi		✻✻✻	✻✻✻	✻✻✻	✻✻✻	✻✻✻							
Nerine	✻✻✻	✻✻✻	✻✻✻	✻✻✻	✻✻✻	✻✻✻	✻✻✻	✻✻✻	✻✻✻	✻✻✻	✻✻✻	✻✻✻	
Oenothera									✻✻✻				
Oncidium (golden showers orchid)	✻✻✻	✻✻✻	✻✻✻	✻✻✻	✻✻✻	✻✻✻	✻✻✻	✻✻✻	✻✻✻	✻✻✻	✻✻✻	✻✻✻	
Origanum								✻✻✻	✻✻✻	✻✻✻	✻✻✻	✻✻✻	
Ornithogalum arabicum (Moroccan chincherinchee)	✻✻	✻✻	✻✻	✻✻	✻✻	✻✻	✻✻	✻✻			✻✻	✻✻	
Ornithagalum thyrsoides (chincherinchee)	✻✻✻	✻✻✻	✻✻✻	✻✻✻	✻✻✻	✻✻✻		✻✻✻	✻✻✻	✻✻✻		✻✻✻	
Peonies						✻✻✻	✻✻✻	✻✻✻					
Papaver (poppy seed heads)								✻✻✻	✻✻✻	✻✻✻	✻✻✻	✻✻✻	
Paphiopedilum (orchid)	✻✻✻	✻✻✻	✻✻✻	✻✻		✻✻	✻✻	✻✻✻	✻✻✻	✻✻✻	✻✻✻	✻✻✻	
Phalaenopsis (orchid)	✻✻✻	✻✻✻	✻✻✻	✻✻✻	✻✻✻	✻✻✻	✻✻✻	✻✻✻	✻✻✻	✻✻✻	✻✻✻	✻✻✻	
Phlox	✻✻✻	✻✻✻	✻✻✻	✻✻✻	✻✻✻	✻✻✻	✻✻✻	✻✻✻	✻✻✻	✻✻✻	✻✻✻	✻✻✻	
Physostegia (obedient plant)								✻	✻	✻	✻		
Protea	✻✻✻	✻✻✻	✻✻✻			✻✻						✻✻✻	
Prunus	✻✻	✻✻✻	✻✻✻	✻✻✻	✻✻✻	✻✻							
Ranunculus		✻✻	✻✻✻	✻✻✻	✻✻✻	✻✻✻	✻✻✻						
Roses	✻✻✻	✻✻✻	✻✻✻	✻✻✻	✻✻✻	✻✻✻	✻✻✻	✻✻✻	✻✻✻	✻✻✻	✻✻✻	✻✻✻	
Saponaria									✻✻✻	✻✻✻	✻✻✻		
Scabious									✻✻✻	✻✻✻	✻✻✻		
Scilla (bluebells)		✻✻✻	✻✻✻	✻✻✻	✻✻✻								
Sedum spectabile									✻✻✻	✻✻✻	✻✻✻		
Solidago	✻✻✻	✻✻✻	✻✻✻	✻✻✻	✻✻✻	✻✻✻	✻✻✻	✻✻✻	✻✻✻	✻✻✻	✻✻✻	✻✻✻	
Strelitzia	✻✻✻	✻✻✻	✻✻✻	✻✻✻	✻✻✻	✻✻✻	✻✻✻	✻✻✻	✻✻✻	✻✻✻	✻✻✻	✻✻✻	
Symphoricarpos (snowberry)									✻✻✻	✻✻✻	✻✻✻	✻✻✻	
Syringa (lilac)	✻✻✻	✻✻✻	✻✻✻	✻✻✻	✻✻✻	✻✻						✻✻✻	
Tanacetum (feverfew)	✻✻✻	✻✻✻	✻✻✻	✻✻✻	✻✻✻	✻✻✻	✻✻✻	✻✻✻	✻✻✻	✻✻✻	✻✻✻	✻✻✻	
Trachelium	✻✻✻	✻✻✻	✻✻✻	✻✻✻	✻✻✻	✻✻✻	✻✻✻	✻✻✻	✻✻✻	✻✻✻	✻✻✻	✻✻✻	*White Trachelium not available early Spring*
Triteleia (Brodiaea)						✻✻✻	✻✻✻	✻✻✻	✻✻✻	✻✻✻	✻✻✻		
Tulips	✻✻	✻✻	✻✻	✻✻	✻✻	✻✻	✻✻					✻✻	
Veronica	✻✻✻	✻✻✻	✻✻✻	✻✻✻	✻✻✻	✻✻✻	✻✻✻	✻✻✻	✻✻✻	✻✻✻	✻✻✻	✻✻✻	
Viburnum opulus (guelder rose)	✻✻	✻✻	✻✻	✻✻	✻✻	✻✻	✻✻	✻✻					
Zantedeschia aethiopica (arum lily)	✻✻	✻✻	✻✻	✻✻	✻✻	✻✻	✻✻	✻✻✻	✻✻✻	✻✻✻	✻✻✻	✻✻	
Zantedeschia (calla lily)	✻✻✻	✻✻✻	✻✻✻	✻✻✻	✻✻✻	✻✻✻	✻✻✻	✻✻✻	✻✻✻	✻✻✻	✻✻✻	✻✻✻	
Zinnia								✻✻✻	✻✻✻	✻✻			

DRIED MATERIALS

· · ·

The range of dried flowers and materials is enormous and your local florist will be able to advise you.

BUYING MATERIALS

There are a few general rules to bear in mind when selecting materials. Make sure the stock is bright in colour and not too brittle. Check the flowers for moth damage, especially roses and peonies. Look inside the flowers for grubs or eggs. All dried flowers will lose some material when handled, but avoid any that drop a lot of petals.

If shop-bought flowers have dried out, hang them in a moist room such as the kitchen or bathroom for a day or two to absorb some moisture and make them much easier to work with. Don't leave them longer or they may become too damp and start to rot. If they feel too soft after a couple of days, reverse the process by placing them in a dry, warm airing cupboard.

USING FRESH MATERIALS

Branches, twigs and moss can be used fresh, in fact they are much easier to work with when a little damp. Displays using these items must be left in a warm, dry place to dry out.

DRYING MATERIALS

Air-drying is the easiest and most successful method, in a place with a constant flow of warm, dry air, such as an airing cupboard or a space above a slow-burning oven. Dry woody items on a wire rack; they may take some time. Flowers can be tied and hung upside-down and will take much less time. If the drying space is light, cover or wrap the materials with newspaper, making sure that air can still circulate around them. Experiment – even daffodils can be dried, producing wonderful results.

Ambrosina has a strong and attractive scent that is wonderful to work with.

ACHILLEA FILIPENDULINA
(Golden yarrow)

This mustard-yellow plant has been a favourite for many years. The large heads fill spaces quickly in any large, country-style arrangement. They are easy to keep dust-free.

ACHILLEA PTARMICA

Clusters of small, bright white flowers on dark green stems. Use with care; the bright white tends to stand out when combined with other materials. They have a very long life but need to be kept away from damp or the white will turn to pale brown very quickly.

ALCHEMILLA MOLLIS
(Lady's mantle)

This is a beautiful material to use; it can be added to all types of displays and gives a soft feel. However, in time, the colour will fade to a soft yellow-brown. Take care when using, as it tends to break quite readily. Alchemilla is very easy to grow.

AMARANTHUS
(Love-lies-bleeding)

Most commonly seen either in natural dark green or dyed dark red. May be long and upright, but also available as a long, soft tail. Be selective when choosing bunches; their thickness and

length vary tremendously. For small display work, use the thinner variety. *Amaranthus caudatus* is particularly attractive and has a pale green colour.

AMBROSINA

Widely available in two versions, short and long, this is a pale green plant. As with all green material, avoid strong light. In a centrally heated house it will dry out and become very fragile, so keep it away from the heat.

ANAPHALIS MARGARITACEA
(Pearl everlasting)

A fluffy white flower that is extremely easy to grow. The flowers dry in the garden on the stem. Make sure you pick them before they go to seed, or you will have a room full of fluff.

BUPLEURUM GRIFFITHII

This green plant is a useful filler. Care needs to be taken when using it in light conditions, because the green will fade fast. Each stem has a large number of heads with small seeds.

CARTHAMUS

Available with and without flowers; the dark ginger flower is used to make dye. A stunning addition to a display, the bunches tend to be fairly large and need to be split and wired. Choose flowers which have deep green leaves and dark orange flowers.

The greeny-yellow centre of anaphalis makes it match well with other materials.

CHINESE LANTERN
(Physalis)
The vivid orange colour of the paper-thin lanterns will not last if exposed to strong light. It is a fairly easy plant to grow in the garden.

COBRA LEAVES
These large preserved (dried) leaves are very useful for wrapping and also for coating containers. Other types of leaf are also available.

The globe-shaped heads of Echinops are a deep steely-blue at their best.

COPPER BEECH
(Fagus sylvatica)
The dark brown leaf makes a good backdrop. In their natural condition, the leaves tend to curl as they dry. They are best preserved (dried) and will then keep indefinitely and will be more easy to work with.

ECHINOPS RITRO
(Globe thistle)
Handle with care as the delicate blue heads are prone to break apart. The new season's stock handles much better. Echinops are quite expensive but are also very easy to grow in the right conditions.

ECHINOPS SPHAEROCEPHALUS
The same family but much larger, with spiky silvery-blue heads. They take spray colour very well. Handle with care.

Larkspur is a popular flower and is available in a range of attractive colours.

EUCALYPTUS
Available mostly as a preserved (dried) product, this wonderful leaf normally comes in two colours, green and brown. A joy to work with, because it gives off a beautiful scent when the stems and leaves are bruised. The scent will last for months. Ideal for large displays that require long stems.

EVERLASTING *see* Strawflower

GLOBE ARTICHOKE
(Cynara cardunculus)
These make a huge statement and deserve to be displayed alone. The outside comes in a range of green and purple; the centre is a mass of delicate mauve fronds. To dry them, hang them upside-down, wrapped in paper with the bottom open over a constant flow of warmth for 2–3 weeks.

GOLDEN MUSHROOMS
These are often found with ready-fixed stems; if yours have no stems add them with a glue gun. A light spray of clear florist's lacquer will bring out the rich colours.

GRASSES *see* Wheat

HOLLY OAK
(Banksia serrata)
This very large leaf is usually preserved (dried). It makes a good substitute for holly and will not lose its shape or dry out.

HYDRANGEA MACROPHYLLA
One of the most useful dried materials, in a range of colours from very dark pink through to a pale almost-grey and a variety of tones to dark blue. Can be dried very easily at home, in a light-free, warm area. The large heads have a very long life.

IMMORTELLE
(Xeranthemum)
Small, star-shaped, mostly purple or white flowers with an extremely long shelf life, these tolerate bright light very well. Often used as a filler because they are inexpensive, but the strong purple colour will dominate a display.

KUTCHI FRUIT
An exotic caramel-coloured seed pod with a vanilla aroma. It combines well with woodland materials.

LARKSPUR
(Consolida)
Very close to the delphinium, these flowers come in a range of colours but are most commonly blue, pink or white. If the bunches are a little crushed, revive them with very gentle steaming. Probably one of the most useful display flowers, it is a pretty flower and ideal for summer displays.

You can spray Holly Oak with paint or gild lightly with gold for a special look.

Not only does Lavender look and smell so attractively, but it is easy to work with.

LAVENDER
(Lavandula)

Dutch lavender is a pale-coloured lavender, with uniform stems and a strong scent. French lavender (*Lavandula stoechas*) is a magnificent rich blue. Take care when buying, because the quality often varies. Lavender is a popular display filler.

MARIGOLD
(Tagetes erecta)

Bright yellow or orange, this makes a spectacular splash of colour. Choose flowers with as little damage as possible. They look almost fresh and can even be arranged alone in a terracotta pot.

MARJORAM
(Origanum marjorana)

This dark purple and green herb works well with dried materials such as roses, peonies, nigella and lavender.

MINT
(Mentha)

This pale purple flower looks very uninspiring alone, but combined with other materials it makes a good partner. It gives off a lovely scent.

MINTOLA BALLS

These woody seed pods look similar to small coconuts. They are often supplied with wooden stakes.

MOSSES

The main types of moss used in this book are sphagnum, tillandsia, green wood, lichen and reindeer moss. Although all can be purchased dried, only tillandsia moss is really suitable for use in this condition; the other varieties are best used slightly damp then left to dry out in the display. You can also buy different coloured mosses to suit your display.

NICANDRA
(Physalodes)

This green seed pod is a smaller alternative to the orange Chinese lantern. The pale colour can be used with many other colours and the shape gives a distinctive texture to an arrangement. Keep it away from direct sunlight. In time, the green will turn dark brown but for a seed pod this is quite acceptable.

NIGELLA DAMASCENA
(Love-in-a-mist)

A real favourite, these seed pods combine purple and green colours with an unusual shape. However, they dislike bright light and will fade very fast. A good material for special-occasion displays. Enhance or change their colour using spray paints.

NIGELLA ORIENTALIS

The same family as love-in-a-mist, but a completely different shape. All-green, it is susceptible to loss of colour. Usually it has quite a short season, so is not always available.

OAK
(Quercus)

This leaf is used in a similar way to preserved (dried) copper beech. It tends to be a little thicker and will stand the test of time even better. It often has a little brown dye added to give a dark, rich colour.

OREGANO
(Origanum vulgare)

This well-loved herb makes a dried plant that can be used over and over again. It has a very unusual texture and a beautiful scent. The colour will keep indefinitely. Any unused pieces can be kept for a pot-pourri, mixed with lavender and rose petals.

PEONY
(Paeonia)

These have a very short season. Although expensive to buy, they are quite easy to dry at home, if you are careful. Mostly dark pink, they can also be a rich pinky-cream. Moths love peonies so make sure that there are no eggs in the flowers.

POPPY SEED HEAD
(Papaver)

Although these are very common, they range from dark powder-grey through to greeny-grey, and will suit most colour schemes. Avoid spraying them with clear florist's lacquer, which will destroy the powdery bloom. Do not use the seeds on food.

PROTEA COMPACTA
(Cape honey flower)

This woody head will last for ever and needs only a light dusting to maintain its good looks. A range of different sizes is available. Use a strong pair of cutters to cut the stems.

Nicandra have a pale colour and attractive rounded seed pods.

RAT'S-TAIL STATICE
(Psylliostachys suworwii)

These dark to pale pink flowers come in a huge variety of lengths. Although they will be fairly straight when fresh, they tend to drop after a time. They look their best in small bunches and add a distinctive texture to a display.

ROSA PALEANDER

These are the miniature version of the standard dried rose and not generally prone to moth attack. They are available in a huge range of colours. Watch out for the thorns. They look particularly good combined with the larger roses.

ROSES
(Rosa)

One of the most expensive of all dried flowers, they are also the most exquisite. A wide range of different colours is available. Always save them until last so that the rose heads do not get broken and so that they remain most central to your design. Most varieties will welcome a little steaming, which revitalizes them and releases a beautiful scent. Roses are prone to attack from moths and need to be inspected for eggs from time to time.

Pink roses are combined with preserved leaves here to create a warm effect.

Red roses make any arrangement special and are ideal for displays made as gifts.

SANFORDII

Small clusters of bright flowers. The golden yellow colour has a very long life, but the flowerheads need to be supported by other materials or their weight will bend the stems.

SEA HOLLY
(Eryngium)

Clusters of small blue thistles, this is a plant to be handled with gloves! Sea holly has a long life, with the colour lasting a long time. As it fades it becomes grey-green turning to pale brown. *Eryngium alpinum* has purplish-blue, cone-shaped flowerheads and a frilly "collar".

SILENE PENDULA
(Campion)

This tiny pink flower looks as though it is fresh, even when dried. It will lose some petals but not enough to matter. The colour keeps for a long time and you only need to add this flower in small quantities. The small flowerheads create a soft look in a display. Give the flowerheads some support, to stop them hanging down.

SOLIDASTER

A hybrid species made by crossing solidago and aster, this pale yellow flower keeps its colour well. Bunches are fairly large and each stem has dozens of flowers that can be wired into small bunches. A good filler.

STRAWFLOWER
(Helichrysum)

This is one of the best-known dried flowers and has slipped from favour with many arrangers. However, the range of colours is vast and it has a very long life. Used in bunches, it can look quite stunning.

SUNFLOWER
(Helianthus)

These popular large yellow flowers have only recently been added to the list of dried materials. The yellow petals tend to be quite small and to fade, but sunflowers are very good for large extravagant displays. The stems can easily be extended by pushing a cane up into the hollow stem.

TOLBOS
(Top brush)

A spiky form of protea that is becoming more widely available. It has a furry centre and usually bears a number of heads on each stem.

WHEAT

Wheat is only one of a number of grasses available. Although very attractive, these grasses need to be used with care. Unfortunately, their green colour has a very short life, and they have given dried displays a bad reputation as their colour quickly fades to brown.

Strawflowers look striking in small groups and are long-lasting.

FRESH FLOWER ARRANGEMENTS: EQUIPMENT

. . .

The flower arranger can get by with the minimum of equipment when he or she is just starting out. However, as he or she becomes more adventurous, a selection of specialized tools and equipment will be useful. This section itemizes those pieces of equipment used in the projects contained in the book.

CELLOPHANE (PLASTIC WRAP)

As wrapping for a bouquet, cellophane (plastic wrap) can transform a bunch of flowers into a lovely gift, and it has a more practical use as a waterproof lining for containers. Also, it can look very effective scrunched up in a vase of water to support flower stems.

FLORIST'S ADHESIVE

This very sticky glue is supplied in a pot and is the forerunner to the hot, melted adhesive of the glue gun. It is necessary when attaching synthetic ribbons or other materials which might be adversely affected by the heat of a glue gun.

FLORIST'S ADHESIVE TAPE

This is a strong adhesive tape used to secure plastic foam in containers. Although it will stick under most circumstances, avoid getting it too wet as this will limit its adhesive capability.

PLASTIC FOAM

Plastic foam comes in a vast range of shapes, sizes and densities, and is available for both dry and fresh flowers. While the rectangular brick is the most familiar, other shapes are available for specific purposes.

Plastic foam is lightweight, convenient to handle and very easy to cut and shape with just a knife. A brick of plastic foam for fresh flowers soaks up water very quickly

Before starting to build a design make sure you have all the materials close to hand.

(approximately 1½ minutes) but must not be resoaked as the structure alters and its effectiveness will be reduced. Plastic foam for dried flowers can seem too hard for the delicate stems of some flowers but a softer version is available, so consider which type you need before starting the design.

FLORIST'S SCISSORS

A strong, sharp pair of scissors are the flower arranger's most important tool. As well as cutting all those things you would expect, the scissors must also be sturdy enough to cut woody stems and even wires.

FLORIST'S TAPE (STEM-WRAP TAPE)

This tape is not adhesive, but the heat of your hands will help secure it to itself as it is wrapped around a stem

The tape is used to conceal wires and seal stem ends. It is made either from plastic or crêpe paper and it will stretch to provide a thin covering. The tape is available in a range of colours although green is normally used on fresh flowers.

FLORIST'S WIRE

Wire is used to support, control and secure materials, also to extend stems and to replace them where weight reduction is required. The wire tends to be sold in different lengths. Most of the projects in this book use 36 cm (14 in) lengths. Always use the lightest gauge of wire you can while still providing sufficient support. The most popular gauges are:

1.25mm (18g)	0.28mm (31g)
0.90mm (20g)	0.24mm (32g)
0.71mm (22g)	Silver reel
0.56mm (24g)	*(rose) wires:*
0.46mm (26g)	0.56mm (24g)
0.38mm (28g)	0.32mm (30g)
0.32mm (30g)	0.28mm (32g)

Make sure that the wires are kept in a dry place because any moisture will cause them to rust.

GLOVES

While some flower arranging processes would be impeded by gloves, it makes sense to protect your hands whenever necessary, especially if handling materials with sharp thorns or sap which might irritate the skin. So keep some domestic rubber gloves and heavy-duty gardening gloves in your florist's workbox.

GLUE GUN

The glue gun is an electrically powered device fed by sticks of glue, which it melts to enable the user to apply glue via a trigger action. In floristry it is a relatively recent development but invaluable in allowing the arranger to attach dried or fresh materials to swags, garlands or circlets securely, cleanly and efficiently.

The glue and the tip of the gun are extremely hot, so take care at all times when using a glue gun. Never leave a hot glue gun unattended.

PAPER RIBBON

Paper ribbon is an alternative to satin and synthetic ribbon and is available in a large range of mostly muted, soft

colours. It is sold twisted and rolled up. Cut the length of ribbon required in its twisted state and carefully untwist and flatten it to its full width before creating your bow.

PINHOLDER
The pinholder is a heavy metal disc approximately 2 cm (¾ in) thick which has an even covering of sharp metal pins, approximately 3 cm (1¼ in) long. Pinholders are available in a range of diameter sizes for different displays.

The pinholder is placed under the water and the bottom of the flower stems are pushed on to the pins. The weight of the stems is balanced by the weight of the pinholder. It is ideal for creating *Ikebana*-style displays or twiggy linear arrangements.

RAFFIA
A natural alternative to string and ribbon, raffia has several uses for the flower arranger. It can be used, a few strands at a time, to tie together a hand-arranged, spiralled bunch, or to attach bunches of dried or fresh

Start with the basic equipment and add items as your skill develops.

flowers to garlands and swags. In thicker swathes it can also be used to finish bouquets and arrangements by tying them off and being formed into decorative bows.

ROSE STRIPPER
This ingenious little device is a must when handling very thorny roses. Squeeze the metal claws together and pull the stripper along the stem, and the thorns and leaves will be removed. There is also a blade attachment to cut stem ends at an angle. Always wear thick gardening gloves.

SATIN RIBBON
Available in a large variety of widths and colours, satin ribbon is invaluable to the flower arranger when a celebratory final touch is required.

Satin ribbon is preferable to synthetic ribbon because it looks and feels so much softer. Its only drawback is that it frays when cut.

SECATEURS (GARDEN CLIPPERS)
These are necessary to cut the tougher, thicker stems and branches of foliage. Always handle scissors and secateurs with care and do not leave within the reach of young children.

TWINE
String or twine is essential when tying spiralled bunches, making garlands or attaching foliage to gates and posts.

WIRE MESH
Although plastic foam now offers much more flexibility for the flower arranger, wire mesh still has its place in the florist's armoury.

When creating large displays, wire mesh is essential to strengthen the plastic foam and prevent it from crumbling when large numbers of stems are pushed into it. The mesh should be cut in lengths from the roll, crumpled slightly, laid over the top and wrapped around the sides of the foam and wedged between it and the container, then secured in place with florist's adhesive tape.

DRIED FLOWER ARRANGEMENTS: EQUIPMENT

. . .

You will find it easier to create successful displays if you use the appropriate equipment. The following basic items are available from good florists' shops or suppliers:

CANDLEHOLDERS
These plastic fittings are available in a range of sizes. They have a star-shaped base which is easily pushed into dry foam to hold a candle.

CANES
These are used to create a square or triangular frame for a garland, or to fix terracotta pots.

CHICKEN WIRE
This is a useful base for a swag or to hold flowers in large containers.

COPPER OR STEEL RINGS
These comprise two thin wire rings, used as a strong base for garlands.

FLORIST'S CLEAR LACQUER
A fixative, specifically for dried materials. It holds loose material in place and also helps to keep it clean.

FLORIST'S TAPE (STEM-WRAP TAPE)
This useful tape is not adhesive, but the heat from your hands will secure it to itself as you wrap it around the stem of a plant. It is used to conceal florist's wires and also to seal stem ends. The tape is available in various colours, including green. It is made of plastic or crêpe paper, which will stretch to provide a thin covering.

FLORIST'S WIRE
Available in different lengths and gauges. Use wires as thick as you can comfortably work with, and buy long wire, which can be cut. The heavier the material, the thicker the wire.

GLUE GUN
A hot glue gun dramatically reduces the time needed to make a display. Better-quality guns are more expensive; a gun with a trigger feed for the glue is easiest to use. Take care not to burn yourself.

KNIVES
You will need two sharp kitchen knives, one short and one long, for cutting plastic foam.

MOSSING (FLORAL) PINS
These are used to hold material, especially moss, in place.

PLASTIC FOAM
Available in rectangular blocks, spheres and cones. Don't use foam that is intended for use with fresh flowers, as it tends to crumble.

Above: The shape and size of wicker baskets, terracotta pots and cane rings are an influential part of the final design.

PLIERS
These are used to secure and twist florist's wires and chicken wire.

RAFFIA
An attractive binding material, particularly if you want a rustic look. Keep the strands long for an attractive flowing and wispy effect.

SCISSORS
Many florists prefer to use sharp, strong scissors, for cutting stems and other materials.

SECATEURS
A strong pair of spring-loaded cutters will cope with tough material.

Above: Whenever possible, use the specified tools and materials – it always makes a display much easier to create.

Right: Dressings and ribbons can be found for all occasions and requirements.

SETTING CLAY
This is used to set trunks in pots for topiary displays. Leaving the clay bases to dry can take over 10 hours.

SILVER REEL (ROSE) WIRE
This comes in a range of gauges but it is generally a more delicate wire than florist's wire. Experiment with different thicknesses until you find one with which you like working.

STRING
Gardening string comes in various brown and green colours that blend well with dried materials.

CONTAINERS

· · ·

While an enormous range of suitable, practical, purpose-made containers is available to the flower arranger, with a little imagination alternatives will present themselves, often in the form of objects we might not have at first glance expected. An old jug or teapot, a pretty mug that has lost its handle, an unusual-looking tin, a bucket, a jam jar, all these offer the arranger interesting opportunities.

Remember, if the container is for fresh flowers, it must be watertight or properly lined. Consider the scale and proportion of the container both to the particular flowers you are going to use, and the type of arrangement.

Do not forget the container can be a hidden part of the design, simply there to hold the arrangement, or it can be an integral and important feature in the overall arrangement.

BAKING TINS (PANS)

Apart from the usual round, square or rectangular baking tins (pans), a number of novelty shapes are available. Star, heart, club, spade and diamond shaped baking tins (pans) are used to make cakes that are out of the ordinary and they can also be used very effectively to produce interesting flower arrangements.

These tins (pans) are particularly good for massed designs, either of fresh or dried flowers, but remember, the tin may need lining if it is being used for fresh flowers.

BASKETS

Baskets made from natural materials are an obvious choice for country-style, informal displays. However, there is a wide range of basket designs available to suit many different styles.

Large baskets are good for table or static displays while smaller baskets

Massed dried flowerheads in this baking tin (pan) produce a striking display.

with handles can be carried by bridesmaids or filled with flowers or plants and made into lovely gifts. Traditional wicker baskets can be obtained which incorporate herbs or lavender in their weave.

Wire or metal baskets offer an ornate alternative to wicker and twig, since the wire can be formed into intricate shapes and also can have a more modern look.

CAST-IRON URNS

More expensive than many other types of container, the investment in a cast-iron urn is repaid by the splendid classic setting it offers for the display of flowers. Whether the arrangement is large and flowing or contemporary and linear, the visual strength of a classical urn shape will provide the necessary underpinning.

Of course the physical weight of a cast-iron urn is a factor to consider; it is a plus in that it will remain stable with the largest of displays but a minus when it comes to moving it!

ENAMELLED CONTAINERS

The appeal of using an enamelled container probably lies in the bright colours available. Containers in strong primary colours work well with similarly brightly coloured flowers to produce vibrant displays.

GALVANIZED METAL BUCKET AND POT

The obvious practical advantage of galvanized metal containers is that they will not rust. The attractive silvered and polished texture is ideal for contemporary displays in both fresh and dried flowers.

Today lots of shapes and sizes of containers are available with a galvanized finish but even an old-fashioned bucket can be used to good effect in flower arranging.

GLASS VASES

A glass vase is often the first thing that springs to mind for flower arranging. And indeed, there is an enormous range of purpose-made vases available.

The proportions of this design give prominence to the classical urn.

A varied selection from the vast range of containers that can be used for flower arranging

Particularly interesting to the serious flower arranger will be simple clear glass vases which are made in all the sizes and geometric shapes you could ever need. Their value lies in their lack of embellishment which allows the arrangement to speak for itself. Remember the clear glass requires that the water be changed regularly and kept scrupulously clean, since below the water is also part of the display.

There are also many other forms of vase – frosted, coloured, textured, and cut glass – and all have their place in the flower arranger's armoury.

PITCHERS

Pitchers of all types are ideal flower receptacles. Ceramic, glass, enamelled or galvanized metal; short, tall, thin, fat – whatever their shape, size or colour, they offer the flower arranger a wide range of options.

Displays can range from the rustic and informal to the grand and extravagant, depending on your choice of pitcher and materials.

PRE-FORMED PLASTIC FOAM SHAPES

Clean to handle, convenient to use, pre-formed plastic foam comes in a wide range of shapes and sizes such as circles, crosses, rectangles and even "novelty" designs like stars, numerals, hearts and teddy bears. Each shape is a moisture-retaining foam with a watertight backing. Equivalent foam shapes are available for dried flowers.

Although often associated with funeral and sympathy designs, pre-formed plastic foam shapes also offer the flower arranger a variety of bases for many other types of display.

TERRACOTTA PLANT POTS

Traditional or modern, the terracotta pot can be utilized to hold an arrangement of flowers and not just plants. If the arrangement is built in plastic foam, line the pot with cellophane (plastic wrap) before

inserting the foam, to prevent leakage. Alternatively just pop a jam jar or bowl into the pot to hold the water.

The appearance of terracotta pots can be changed very effectively by techniques such as rubbing them with different coloured chalks, or treating them with gold leaf. They can also be aged by the application of organic materials such as sour milk which, if left, will enable a surface growth to develop.

WOODEN TRUGS AND BOXES

Old-fashioned wooden trugs and seedboxes can make charming and effective containers for floral displays. Their rustic appeal makes them particularly suitable for informal country-style designs where the container is an enhancing feature. Rubbing the surface of a wooden container with coloured chalk can create an entirely new look.

Of course you must remember to line the box with waterproof material if fresh flowers or plants are going to be used in the display.

TECHNIQUES

. . .

TAPING

Stems and wires are covered with florist's tape (stem-wrap tape) for three reasons: first, cut materials which have been wired can no longer take up water and covering with tape seals in the moisture that already exists in the plant; second, the tape conceals the wires, which are essentially utilitarian, and gives a more natural appearance to the false stem; third, wired dried materials are covered with florist's tape (stem-wrap tape) to ensure that the material does not slip out of the wired mount.

1 Hold the wired stem near its top with the end of a length of florist's tape (stem-wrap tape) between the thumb and index finger of one hand. With your free hand, hold the remainder of the length of tape at 45° to the wired stem, keeping it taut. Starting at the top of the stem, just above the wires, rotate the flower slowly to wrap the tape around both the stem and wires, working down. By keeping it taut, the tape will stretch into a thin layer around the stem and wires. Each layer should overlap and stick to the one before. If so desired, you may add flowerheads at different heights as you tape to create units. Finally, fasten off just above the end of the wires by squeezing the tape against itself to stick it securely.

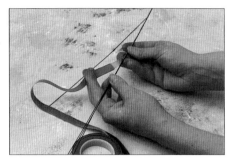

MAKING A STAY WIRE

1 Group together four .71 wires, each overlapping the next by about 3 cm (1¼ in). Start taping the wires together from one end using florist's tape (stem-wrap tape). As the tape reaches the end of the first wire add another .71 wire to the remaining three ends of wire and continue taping, and so on, adding wires and taping four together until you achieve the required length of stay wire.

SINGLE LEG MOUNT

This is for wiring flowers which have a strong natural stem or where a double weight of wire is not necessary to support the material.

1 Hold the flowers or foliage between the thumb and index finger of one hand while taking the weight of the material (i.e. the flowerheads) cross the top of your hand. Position a wire of the appropriate weight and length behind

the stem about one-third up from the bottom. Bend the wire ends together with one leg shorter than the other. Holding the short wire leg parallel with the stem, wrap the long wire leg firmly around both the stem and the other wire leg three or four times. Straighten the long wire leg to extend the stem. Cover the stem and wire with florist's tape (stem-wrap tape).

DOUBLE LEG MOUNT

This is formed in the same way as the single leg mount but extends the stem with two equal length wire legs.

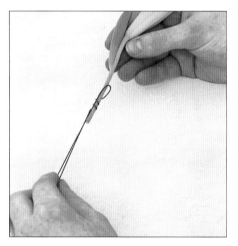

1 Hold the flower or foliage between the thumb and index finger of one hand while taking the weight of the plant material (i.e. the flowerheads) across the top of your hand. Position a wire of appropriate weight and length behind the stem about one-third of the way up from the bottom. One-third of the wire should be to one side of the stem with two-thirds to the other. Bend the wire parallel to the stem. One leg should now be about twice as long as the other.

Holding the shorter leg against the stem, wrap the longer leg around both stem and the other wire to secure. Straighten both legs which should now be of equal length.

PIPPING

Pipping is the process whereby small flowerheads are removed from a main stem to be wired individually. This process can be used for intricate work with small delicate plant materials.

1 Bend a thin silver wire into a hairpin about its centre and twist at the bend to form a small loop above the two projecting legs.

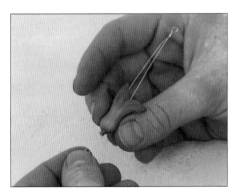

2 Push the legs into the flower centre, down through its throat, and out of its base to create a stem.

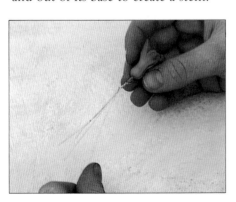

3 Using more silver wire, double leg mount this stem with any natural existing stem, and tape if required.

UNITS

A unit is the composite stem formed from two or more pieces of plant material. Units of small flowers can be used in corsages and hair-comb decorations, and units of larger flowers in wired wedding bouquets.

Units should be made up of one type of material only. For small units, first wire and tape the individual flowerheads, buds or leaves.

1 Start with the smallest of the plant material and attach a slightly larger head to it by taping the wires together. Position the larger head in line with the bottom of the first item. Increase the size of the items as you work downward.

For units of larger flowers you may have to join the wire stems by double leg mounting them with an appropriate weight of wire before taping.

EXTENDING THE LENGTH OF A STEM

Flowerheads with short stems, and flowers that are delicate may need the extra support of an extended stem. There are two methods of extending a stem.

1 Wire the flowerhead using the appropriate method and correct

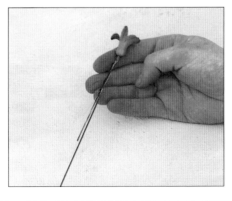

weight of wire. Then single leg mount the wired flowerhead using a .71 wire and tape the wires and any natural stem with florist's tape (stem-wrap tape).

Alternatively, push a .71 wire into the base of the flowerhead from the bottom, then at right angles to this push through a .38 silver wire from one side to the other.

Bend the .38 silver wire so that the two ends point downwards, parallel to the .71 wire. Wrap one leg of .38 wire firmly around its other leg and the .71 wire. Cover with florist's tape (stem-wrap tape).

WIRING AN OPEN FLOWERHEAD

This is a technique for the wiring of individual heads of lily, amaryllis and tulip and is also suitable for small, soft or hollow-stemmed flowers such as anemones and ranunculus.

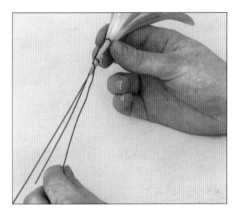

1 Cut the stem of the flower to around 4 cm (1½ in). Push one .71 wire up through the inside of the stem and into the base of the flowerhead. Double leg mount the stem and its internal wire with a .71 wire. Tape the stem and wire.

The internal wire will add strength to the flower's natural stem and the double leg mount will ensure that the weight of the flowerhead is given sufficient support.

WIRING A ROSE HEAD

Roses have relatively thick, woody stems so to make them suitable for use in intricate work, such as buttonholes, headdresses and corsages, the natural stem will need to be replaced with a wire stem.

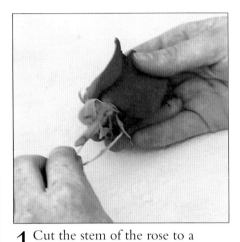

1 Cut the stem of the rose to a length of about 3 cm (1¼ in). Push one end of a .71 wire through the seed box of the rose at the side. Holding the head of the rose carefully in your left hand (opposite way if left-handed), wrap the wire several times firmly around and down the stem. Straighten the remaining wire to extend the natural stem. Cover the wire and stem with florist's tape (stem-wrap tape).

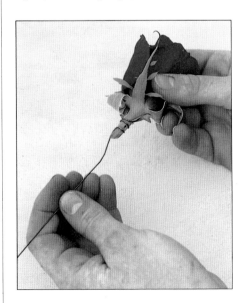

WIRING FRUIT AND VEGETABLES

Using fruit and vegetables in swags, wreaths and garlands, or securing them in plastic foam displays will require wiring them first. The method will depend on the item to be wired and how it is to be used.

Heavy fruits and vegetables, such as oranges, lemons or bulbs of garlic, will need a heavy .71 wire or even .90. The wire should be pushed through the item, just above its base from one side to the other. Push another wire through the item at right angles to the first and bend all four projecting wires to point downwards.

1 Depending on how the fruit or vegetables will be used, either cut the wires to a suitable length to be pushed into plastic foam, or twist the wires together to form a single stem.

2 Small delicate fruits and vegetables such as mushrooms or figs need careful handling as their flesh is easily damaged. They normally only need one wire. Push the wire through the

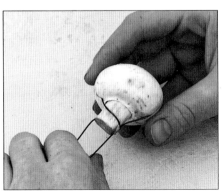

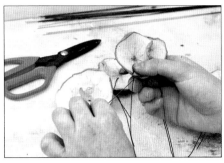

Preserved (dried) apple slices require careful handling when wiring.

base of the item from one side to the other and bend the two projecting wires downwards. Depending on how the material is to be used, either twist to form a single stem, or trim to push into plastic foam.

For the soft materials .71 is the heaviest weight of wire you will require. In some instances, fruit or vegetables can be attached or secured in an arrangement by pushing a long wire "hairpin" right through the item and into the plastic foam behind.

3 Fruit or vegetables that have a stem, such as bunches of grapes or artichokes, can be double leg mounted on their stems with appropriate weight wires.

Extend the length of a starfish by double leg mounting one of its legs.

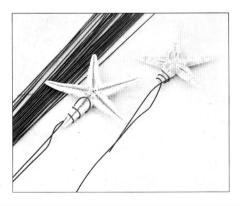

FRUIT AND VEGETABLES IN FLOWER DISPLAYS

The colours and textures of fruit and vegetables can provide harmony or contrast to enhance flower arrangements. The acid colours of citrus fruits, and autumn tints of apples and pears are all readily available to the flower arranger.

Some fruits such as pomegranates, passion fruits and blood oranges are particularly attractive when they have

The strong forms of fruit and vegetables lend themselves well to displays such as this wall swag (above) and unusual obelisk (right). Careful wiring ensures the materials stay in position.

been cut or torn open to reveal their flesh. However, remember that open fruits will deteriorate quickly so only use them for short-term displays at special events, parties or dinners.

Vegetables might seem a surprising choice for use in flower arrangements but the subtle colours and textures can be combined with blooms to beautiful effect. Purple artichokes, almost black aubergines (eggplants), pink and white garlic bulbs, and bright red radishes can give depth, substance and a focal point to a variety of differnt arrangements.

Dried citrus fruit slices look wonderful, and will retain a slight tangy perfume.

COVERING A WIRE HANDLE WITH RIBBON

To make carrying a wired bouquet more comfortable the wired stems can be made into a handle.

1 To ensure that the handle is the correct length, trim it to about 1.5 cm (½ in) longer than the diagonal measurement across your palm. Cover the wire handle with florist's stem-wrap tape. Hold the bouquet in your left hand (opposite way if left-handed) and, with your thumb, trap a long length of 2.5 cm (1 in) wide ribbon against the binding point of the bouquet, leaving 10 cm (4 in) of ribbon above your thumb.

Take the long end of the ribbon down the handle, under its end and approximately half way up the other side. Hold it in place there with the little finger of your left hand, making sure that your thumb remains firmly in place at the binding point.

2 Wind the ribbon back over itself, around and down the handle to its end. Next wind the ribbon back up the handle all the way to the binding point, covering the ribbon already in place and the tape on the handle.

3 Take the winding end of the ribbon, and the excess 10 cm (4 in) at the other end, and tie in a knot at the binding point. Finish in a bow and trim the ribbon ends.

LINING A CONTAINER

If a container is to be used for arranging fresh flowers then clearly it must be watertight. However, if you are arranging your flowers in plastic foam then you can use a container which is not watertight provided you line it with polythene or cellophane (plastic wrap).

1 Cut a piece of cellophane (plastic wrap) slightly larger than the container and push it into the container making sure that it gets into all the corners and has no holes or tears. Cut the soaked plastic foam with a knife to fit the container and wedge it in. Trim the lining around the edge of the container and secure the plastic foam in place with florist's adhesive tape.

Be sure not to allow any water to get between the lining and the container and do not trim the lining too short as the water may spill over the top and down on to the sides.

SPIRALLING STEMS

A hand-tied spiralled bouquet is an excellent way of presenting flowers as a gift because they are already arranged and the recipient only has to cut the string and place the flowers in a suitable vase.

1 Place all the materials close to hand so that you can pick up individual stems easily. Hold a strong stem of foliage or flowers in your left hand (opposite if left-handed) approximately two-thirds down from its top. Build the bouquet by adding one stem of your materials at a time, turning the bunch in your hand as you do so to produce a spiral of stems. If you add your materials in a pre-planned repeating sequence, it will ensure an even distribution of different varieties throughout the bouquet. By occasionally varying the position you hold the stems as you add them you can create a domed shape to the bunch.

2 When you have completed the bunch tie securely with twine, raffia or ribbon around the point where all the stems cross – the binding point.

3 Trim the stem ends so they are even, remembering that the stems below the binding point should comprise about one-third of the overall height of the finished bouquet.

STITCHING LEAVES

Stitching is a technique for wiring a leaf in such a way that it can be held in a "naturally" bent position.

1 Hold a leaf in your left hand with its back facing you (opposite way if you are left-handed) and stitch a thin wire horizontally through the central vein and back out again.

Bend the legs of the wire down along the stem forming a hairpin shape. Hold one leg of wire against the stem of the leaf and wrap the other leg of wire around both stem and wire several times. Then straighten the legs and tape if required.

Below: Very fine reel wire can also be used to secure flowers and foliage to wreaths and basket edgings.

AIR DRYING

Probably the simplest method of preserving plant material is to air dry it. Air drying is the generic term for a number of techniques but fundamentally it is the preservation of plant materials without the use of chemicals or desiccants.

•The ideal environment for air drying will be dark, warm, clean, dust-free, well ventilated and, most importantly, dry. Typically, attics, boiler rooms or large airing cupboards are the locations where these conditions are found.

HARVESTING MATERIALS

If you are preserving material you have grown yourself, be sure it is as dry as possible when you harvest it. Choose a dry day after the morning dew has disappeared and before the damp of evening begins to settle.

It is also important to harvest materials at the right point in their development, to ensure colours remain vibrant and petals do not drop. Experience will teach you about any variations from plant to plant, but in general the time to harvest is when the material is neither too young nor too mature – when the flowers have developed from bud to open bloom but are still young, fresh and firm. Seed pods and grasses must be just

Selecting the right drying method for a plant comes with experience.

fully developed – any more and the seeds may drop.

If you buy commercially grown materials to dry yourself, bear in mind the general principles of harvesting when you select them, and remember, drying must take place as soon as possible after harvesting or purchasing the plant materials.

AIR DRYING BY HANGING PLANT MATERIAL

In most instances the foliage on flowers does not dry as well as the blooms so, when your materials are fresh, remove the leaves from the lower half of the stems before drying.

As a rule plant materials are bunched together in groups of not more than 10 stems and each bunch should contain only one plant variety. Stems should be all around the same length with all their heads at the same level. Do not pack the heads too tightly together as this will inhibit the circulation of air around them and may distort their final dried shape.

Secure the stem ends together with twine, raffia or a rubber band. The stems will shrink as they dry so a rubber band is probably most practical because it will contract with them to maintain a firm hold.

Hang the bunches in a suitable environment in a safe position, high enough so that they will not be disturbed and with their heads down and stems vertical.

Drying rates vary from plant to plant and are subject to factors such as atmospheric conditions, bunch sizes and temperatures but it is essential that you make sure the materials are thoroughly dried before using them. This will be when the thickest part of the flowerhead has dried and when bending the stem causes it to snap. Any moisture retained in plant

The weight of the flowerheads help keep the stems straight.

materials will cause mould, resulting in drooping and shrivelling.

It should be noted that some materials which can be dried with this method should not be hung with their heads down. In particular physalis, with its pendulous orange Chinese lanterns, would look unnatural if dried upside-down. Instead, hook individual physalis stems over a horizontal length of twine in their upright growing attitude.

AIR DRYING PLANT MATERIAL ON A RACK

Some plants such as *Daucus cariba* (Queen Anne's lace) can be air dried, but their florets will curl up if they are hung upside-down.

Instead, make a rack from a piece of small mesh wire, place it in a suitable environment, and drop the stem down through the mesh so that it is held by its bloom. With the flower facing upwards, it will dry well.

*Hydrangea heads and gypsophila can both
be air dried with their stems in water.*

AIR DRYING PLANT MATERIALS WITH THEIR STEM ENDS IN WATER

This is the method of preservation for those types of flowers which have a tendency to wilt before the drying process is completed. It is sometimes called the "evaporation technique" and is particularly suitable for hydrangea, allium and heather.

Cut the bottoms of stems at an angle of 45 degrees and place them in a container with a depth of about 7.5 cm (3 in) of water and place the container in a suitable environment. This slows down the drying process to give the plant material time to dry fully in a natural position and without deterioration in the condition of the blooms.

AIR DRYING IN A "NATURAL" ATTITUDE

Some materials benefit from being dried in an upright position so that they retain a more natural shape.

Simply stand the material in the sort of container in which you might make an arrangement, place it in a suitable environment and it will dry in its natural shape. Grasses and stems of mimosa are suitable for this method.

However, with some material this method can produce extraordinary results. The normally straight stems of bear grass *(Xerophyllum tenax)* will,

when placed in a short container, form themselves into attractive ringlets as they dry. A simple alternative method for drying grasses is to lie them flat on paper in a suitable environment and they will retain a satisfactory shape.

DESICCANT DRYING

A particularly effective method of preservation is drying by the use of a desiccant such as sand, borax or, best of all, silica gel. The desiccant absorbs all the moisture from the plant material. This can be a time-consuming process but it is well worth the effort because the result is dried materials, with colour and form nearer their fresh condition than can be achieved by almost any other method of preservation.

This method is essential for the preservation of fleshy flowerheads that

cannot be successfully air dried. Flowers such as lilies, tulips, freesias, pansies and open garden roses all respond well to desiccant drying and provide the flower arranger with a wealth of preserved materials not generally commercially available.

For the flower arranger there is little point in using this method for flower materials that air dry well because on a non-commercial scale desiccant drying is only suitable for small amounts of material and silica gel is expensive.

Flowers to be preserved by this method must be in perfect, healthy condition and harvested preferably after a few hours in the sun, with as little surface moisture as possible.

It is important to choose a drying method which will allow the plant material to retain its original colour and form.

There are flowers and materials from every season suitable for drying.

WIRING FLOWERS FOR DESICCANT DRYING

Desiccant drying is normally only used for flowerheads as the process weakens stems to the extent that they become virtually unusable. Also, it should be remembered that the flowerheads themselves will become very fragile. Indeed, if you are going to make wire stems it should be done while the flowers are still fresh before beginning the desiccant process.

Flowers with hollow stems, like zinnias, are wired by inserting the wire through their natural stem and pushing it into the flowerhead. Be careful not to push it too far because the flowerhead will shrink as it dries and this might expose an unsightly wire. Heavy petalled flowers like dahlias have to be dried face up, so only provide them with short wired stems. These stems can be extended after the flowers have been dried. Flowers which have woody, tough or very thin stems may be wired through the seed box (calyx) at the base of the flowerhead from one side to the other. Bring the projecting wire ends down and form them into a mount.

During the drying process the flower and stem will shrink so a double or single leg mount will become loose and slide off unless its wire has been securely pushed into the stem while the flower was still fresh. Remember that you still need to make the gauge of wire used for a mount compatible with the weight of the flower when it is fresh.

DRYING WITH SILICA GEL

Nowadays silica gel is considered a superior material to borax or sand for desiccant drying. Sand and borax are heavy and great care must be taken to avoid damaging flowers dried in these materials. Silica gel on the other hand is lightweight and can be crushed very fine so it can be worked into complicated petal configurations without causing damage.

Flowers dry very quickly in silica gel, five to ten days being the usual time necessary for most plant material. Borax and sand are much slower and it can take up to five weeks to dry some materials! Use an airtight container when using silica gel as it absorbs moisture from the air, whereas sand and borax can be used in any container provided it has a lid. The method for sand and borax is generally the same as for silica gel.

Some silica gel crystals are blue and this changes to pink as they absorb moisture which will help you measure the progress of the drying process.

1 When you have prepared your silica gel crystals place a layer approximately 5 cm (2 in) deep in the bottom of your container. Place the flowerheads in the crystals face down or if the petals are complex face up. If their stems are wire mounted, bend them as necessary to fit the flowers into the container.

2 When all flowerheads are in position, spoon a second 5 cm (2 in) deep layer of silica gel over them to cover completely. Be sure to fill all parts of the flowerhead with crystals. If it has complex petals, lift them carefully with a toothpick and gently push the crystals into every crevice. Put the lid on the container and tape around to make airtight.

Since each flower type will probably require a different time to dry, check progress at regular intervals. Flowers left too long in a desiccant will eventually disintegrate. When you start using this method, there will, of course, be an element of trial and error before you are able to establish the time necessary for each flower type.

Some flowers with a deep cupped shape, such as tulips, should be dried individually in a plastic cup of crystals sealed with clear film to ensure they keep their shape.

After you remove the dried flowers from the silica gel, they will probably still have powder on them and this must be removed very carefully with a fine, soft paintbrush.

You can, of course, re-use the silica gel over and over again. All you need to do is spread it out on a tray and leave it in a warm oven until it is dry. This will be easy to recognize in the coloured silica because it will become blue again.

MICROWAVE METHOD

The silica gel process can be accelerated by using a microwave oven. Remember, however, that you must not put wired materials in a microwave oven. Any wiring will have to be done after drying which may be difficult given the fragility of the dried blooms.

Bury the material in silica gel in a container, but do not put a lid on it. Instead, place the uncovered container in the microwave oven with about half a cup of water next to it.

Set the microwave timer according to the type of flower you are drying. Delicate blooms may take less than two minutes while more fleshy flowers will take longer. You will need to experiment with your timing to get accurate settings. After the process is ended leave the silica to cool before removing the flowers.

STORAGE OF DESICCANT DRIED MATERIALS

To keep desiccant dried materials in good condition store them in an airtight container, packed loosely with layers of tissue paper inbetween.

Place a small pouch of silica gel in the container to absorb any moisture, taking care not to get the silica in direct contact with the flowers.

Of course, there are plenty of materials dried by Nature to try in a display.

PRESERVING WITH GLYCERINE

Foliage in particular does not respond well to air drying. Its green colours fade and the result is tired-looking, brittle material. Happily the use of glycerine works well for many varieties of foliage.

This method enables plant material to replace the moisture which has evaporated from its stems and leaves by absorption of a solution of glycerine and water.

Because this process relies on the ability of plant material to draw up the solution it is not suitable for autumn foliage which has, of course, already died. Indeed, it is important that materials to be treated with glycerine are harvested in the middle of their growing season, when the leaves are young but developed and are full of moisture. Foliage that is too young and is soft and pale green does not respond to glycerine.

The stem ends of material to be treated should be cut at an angle of 45 degrees and the lower leaves stripped. Peel the bark off the bottom 6 cm (2½ in) of the stem and split the end up to about 10 cm (4 in) to ensure efficient absorption of the solution.

Mix one part glycerine with two parts hot water and pour the solution into a substantial container to a depth of about 20 cm (8 in). The size of container will depend on the amount of material to be treated. Stand the stems of foliage in the solution for anything from two to six weeks, depending on the size and texture of the leaves, to achieve full absorption. Always keep an eye on the amount of solution in the container and top it up as necessary to maintain the level.

If you are treating individual leaves they can be completely submerged in the solution, but a thicker half-glycerine, half-water mixture should be used. It will take two to three weeks for leaves to be properly treated, after which time remove them from the solution and wipe off any excess.

Glycerine treatment works best for mature, sturdy plant material such as beech, hornbeam, magnolia and elaeagnus. Surprisingly it is also successful with less robust material like *Molucella laevis* (bells of Ireland) and trails of ivy.

As materials are preserved their leaves will change colour to a variety of shades of brown. When all the leaves have changed colour you will know the process is complete. The visual results on materials of treatment with glycerine may vary even for the same material but with increasing experience of the technique you will become better able to predict what you are likely to achieve. Berried foliage can also be preserved with glycerine but the berries will shrink slightly and change colour.

An advantage of glycerine-preserved foliage is that it remains malleable, and dusty leaves can be wiped with a damp cloth.

Preparing a Pot

A block of plastic foam should be carefully cut to fit the terracotta pot you intend to arrange your materials in. Many other types of china, porcelain and clay pots can be used. Even plain glass containers make good bases, although the preparation is a little different. When using clear glass, the foam needs to be cut smaller than the inside area of the container and the space between the foam and the sides filled with moss or pot-pourri to hide the foam. When using fine china or glass, take great care not to force the foam into place, in case the container breaks. Always work on a non-slip surface.

1 Hold the foam block next to the pot and trim it to roughly the same shape using a sharp kitchen knife. Be cautious and cut small pieces off, leaving the foam block a little larger than the inside of the pot.

2 Push the trimmed foam firmly into the pot so that it goes right to the bottom. If it is a little large, carefully trim some more.

3 Pack the spaces around the foam with hay or moss, pushing it down firmly. For a really permanent fit, put a little glue on to both the pot and the foam.

4 Trim the foam to the required height. If you need to trim it level with the top of the pot, use the rim of the pot as a guide for the knife.

Preparing a Basket

Cut a block of plastic foam to fit the shape of the basket. Make sure the foam is firmly fitted in the basket; if you have trimmed it too small, pack the area around it with hay or moss, so that there is no risk of the display falling out.

When choosing a basket, check that it stands evenly on a flat surface. If it does not, it is sometimes possible to trim a piece away; if not, the trimmed foam will often correct the shape, but will need to fit tightly.

If the weave of the basket is fairly open, pack the area around the foam with moss so that the foam cannot be seen.

1 Place the block of foam next to the basket and trim it to roughly the same shape using a sharp kitchen knife. If the basket is large, you may need more than one block of foam.

2 Push the trimmed foam into the basket. If it is a little over-sized, trim a little more foam but try to keep it on the large side, so that it is a tight fit. Depending on the shape and size of the basket, you may need to trim foam away around the top.

3 Push a wire through the side of the basket and across the top of the foam, twisting the ends back around the tightened wire. This will hold the foam in place, but may not be needed if the foam is a tight fit.

Filling a Container with Moss and Chicken Wire

Moss is an alternative to foam as a base. It is useful when the container is large and would require a lot of foam. However, a moss base isn't as good at holding bunches in place as foam, and can be tipped upside-down.

If the container is very large, there is no need to use moss at all; in this case the chicken wire will be needed to fill the basket so that it can support the stems of the materials.

To make a chicken wire ball for a topiary tree, try to make the shape as spherical as possible.

1 Cut the chicken wire into a square approximately twice the surface area of the open top of the container. Put an amount of moss to fill the container, plus a little more, in the centre of the wire. Fold the four corners in, creating a ball shape.

2 Push the ball into the basket, with the open, folded side underneath. Using wires, "sew" the chicken wire frame to the edge of the basket, about every 10 cm (4 in) around the rim.

Covering a Container with Moss

Old or poor-quality baskets or boxes, of all shapes and sizes, can be turned into useful display containers when covered in moss. To enable the moss to keep its green colour it should be kept well away from direct sunlight.

Before starting work on the outside of the basket, fill the inside with the foam, moss or mesh. This will ensure that the outer covering is disturbed as little as possible when it comes to making the display.

1 Attach silver reel (rose) wire to the container and cover part of it with a good handful of moss. Wrap the wire around the container, fastening the moss in place. Repeat the process until the whole container is covered, paying particular attention to the edges and corners.

2 Tie the wire to the top edge of the container and trim the moss evenly with scissors. Any small gaps can be filled by tucking moss under the wire or by gluing the moss in place using a glue gun. Trim any loose pieces.

Preparing a Copper or Steel Garland Ring

Copper or steel rings are a strong and inexpensive way of creating a good base for garlands. They are available in a large range of sizes and need to be covered in moss or hay.

1 Tie silver reel (rose) wire to one of the copper wires of the ring. Take a good handful of moss or hay and hold it on to both the top and the bottom of the ring, to form an even layer. Wrap the wire around the ring, fixing the moss in place. Repeat all the way round the ring.

Covering a Picture or Mirror Frame with a Chicken Wire Swag

A picture or mirror frame can be covered with moss as the base for a dried flower arrangement. The best base is a simple, heavy frame.

1 If the frame is a little flimsy, use wood screws and glue to strengthen it. Make four chicken wire and moss swags to fit the top, bottom and sides. Push one swag firmly around one side of the picture frame.

2 Make sure the swag is long enough, then use a staple gun to hold it in place. Make sure that the staples trap a piece of chicken wire and hold it firmly to the wooden frame each time you fire the gun. Repeat every 5–8 cm (2–3 in).

MAKING A TOPIARY BASE

Choose the container for your topiary carefully, since this will dictate the finished shape and size of the piece. The easiest method for fixing the materials to the trunk is a foam sphere. As a general rule, the ball of flowers or material should be a third larger in diameter than the diameter of the top of the container. The container, the trunk and the floral sphere should each be a third of the total height of the finished display.

Select tree trunks that are on the thick side; these give a better balance to the finished piece.

When using large or precious pots, first set the trunk into a plastic pot that you can put inside your good-quality pot without any fear of breakage. This also has the advantage that the display can easily be removed to another container.

Instead of using a plastic foam shape as the base for your topiary design, you can also make a base out of a chicken wire ball filled with moss. Attach the chicken wire ball firmly to the top of the trunk, using a staple gun.

Remember to turn the finished topiary pieces regularly to ensure that they fade evenly, and keep all dried materials out of direct sunlight.

1 Cover the base of your chosen container with a handful of setting clay, to make a layer about 2.5 cm (1 in) thick.

2 Push the bottom of the tree trunk into the clay. As long as it is in the centre, it doesn't have to be completely upright.

3 Cut some clay and roll into sausage shapes. Pack around the base of the trunk, pushing them down and filling the space between the sides of the container and the trunk. Repeat until at least half the depth of the pot is filled. Leave the clay to set hard – this may take between several hours for a small pot and up to two days for a large one.

4 Support the trunk with plastic foam, to fill the container, if you like. Push the foam sphere down on to the top of the trunk. Remove the sphere, blow away any loose foam particles from the top of the trunk and the hole in the foam. Place a spot of glue on the end of the trunk and push the sphere back into position. It is now ready for your design.

MAKING A HAY ROPE OR COLLAR

The method for making a hay rope and a hay collar is exactly the same, except that the collar needs to be thicker and the ends joined together to form a circle. Hay is inexpensive and versatile, so it is well worth mastering this basic technique, used for garlands and swags.

1 Take a good handful of hay and scrunch it up to form a sausage. Wind silver reel (rose) wire (or string or raffia) around this and tie in place. Twist the wire round the hay, leaving spaces of about 1 cm (½ in) between each twist. Keep adding more hay as you build up the length of rope. Make sure that the rope is firm and the wire is very tight. The hay should not give at all when you squeeze it.

2 Continue to add more hay, keeping the width of the rope even, until you reach the required length. If you are making a rope for a swag, it need only be about 5 mm (¼ in) in diameter. For a garland or a very large swag, the diameter needs to be about 2.5 cm (1 in). Whatever you are making, pack the hay as firmly as possible to make a good base for the decorative materials that you will be using. When the rope or collar is completed, trim any loose hay and fasten the end of the wire securely.

Below: A decorated collar on a basket makes an attractive storage container.

MAKING A CHICKEN WIRE SWAG

This method of creating a swag base makes a large surface to work with, useful if your materials are chunky or you need to cover a large area.

1 Carefully cut the required length and width of chicken wire, folding in the sharp edges.

2 Fill the centre of the wire mesh along its length with moss, as evenly as possible.

3 Fold the long edges into each other, creating a sausage shape, and join them together with short wires. You may need to remove or add moss, so that the shape is even.

4 Use one or two short wires to make a hanger. Push the wire(s) through the chicken wire and twist the ends together to create a loop.

MAKING A ROPE SWAG

This is the best base for a swag to which you are going to tie the decorative materials. The covering need not be too thick; the bulk for the swag will be provided by the stems of the materials. Don't be tempted to make the swag too short – a swag about 1 m (1 yd) long will look balanced in most projects.

1 Cut the rope to the required length, allowing enough for a loop at each end. Use a wire or glue to secure the loops.

2 Tie silver reel (rose) wire to the rope and wrap it around a good handful of moss, keeping the rope in the centre of the moss. Work along the whole length of the rope until it is completely covered with moss.

MAKING A BASKET BORDER WITH A ROPE SWAG

You can use a moss-covered rope swag to extend the edge of a basket, making it easier to fix dried materials in position.

1 Make a rope swag as above. Attach the rope to the edge of the basket by pushing wires through the basket under the rope. Twist the ends together on top, trim off the loose ends and push any sharp pieces back into the moss. Repeat every 5–8 cm (2–3 in) round the edge of the basket.

MAKING A HAY AND RAFFIA BASKET

1 Make a length of hay rope, about 2.5 cm (1 in) in diameter, tying with raffia as needed. Coil and glue the rope to form the base of the basket. Cut and glue the end when it has reached the required size.

2 Make a second hay rope and glue the end to the base. Coil and glue the rope into a cylinder, with the same diameter as the base. When the required height is reached, taper the end of the hay rope and glue.

WIRING FLOWERS

This is the most important skill to master when dealing with dried flowers. Practise on a handful of stems trimmed from a bunch of fresh flowers until you have a neat, tightly wired bunch.

1 Take 4–6 stems and cut them to the length you require. Hold them firmly together with one hand and pass the wire behind them, so that the wire and the stems are at right angles. The short end of the wire should be about 3 cm (1¼ in) above the stems.

2 Hold the wire and stems together between the thumb and forefinger of one hand. Bend the long end of the wire towards you, loop it around the stems and push it away from you.

3 Pull the short end of the wire up so that it lies lengthways along the stems. Now wrap the longer length of wire 3–4 times diagonally around the stems, to hold them together. The wire should be firm but not so tight that it breaks the flower stems.

WIRING A CANDLE

This method firmly fixes a candle into foam, and makes removing the spent candle very easy.

The combination of candles and dried material is, of course, potentially very dangerous. Make sure that you never leave a display with a lighted candle unattended.

1 Wrap florist's tape (stem-wrap tape) at least once around the base of the candle, so that it sticks firmly to the candle.

2 Place a mossing (floral) pin or a short bent wire under the loose end of the tape. Cover the top of the pin or wire with the tape so that it holds the pin or wire in place.

3 Repeat with at least three fixings for a small candle or six for a larger candle. Finish by pulling the tape around once more and trimming it neatly. Alternatively, you can also use a glue gun to fix the candle in the right position.

CENTRE-WIRING BUNCHES

By wiring a bunch of flowers in a central position you can achieve a fuller-looking bunch than one that has been wired at the base.

The advantage of this method is that you can put each bunch exactly where you want it, and need only commit it to the base when you are happy with that final position.

You can also tie on the bunches facing in different directions.

1 Trim the bunch to the required length. Put the stems together, each at a slight angle to the one before. Halfway along the total length, fold the wire around the bunch. Hold the bunch firmly in one hand, while the other hand folds the wire.

2 Cross the two ends over and firmly twist the wires together to produce a strong support. You can use a pair of pliers to twist the wires together, but take care to ensure that you don't break the stems under the pressure of the tight wire.

3 Use stronger wire to bunch together cinnamon sticks and other woody material, including twigs and even small branches. Twist the ends of the wire together with pliers, taking care not to damage the dried material. Once the material is in place use glue to fix it permanently. Cover unattractive fixings with a raffia or ribbon bow.

WIRING LEAVES

Leaves such as magnolia often arrive with little or no stem. This technique creates a stem to work with so that you can make bunches. Be careful not to trim away more of the leaf than is necessary; just enough to fix the wire.

1 Trim the bottom third of the leaf away on one side of the stalk and repeat on the other side, to leave a thick long stem. Bunch the leaves together and centre-wire. For a full look, alter the angle of each leaf.

WIRING FRUIT AND NUTS

Many fruits can be wired easily but nuts need to be drilled or make a hole very carefully with a bradawl (awl). It is advisable to hold the nut in a vice. You can also use a glue gun to fix fruit or nuts directly in place.

1 If necessary, make a hole through the base of the fruit or nut. Push a wire through so that an even amount of wire comes out either side.

2 Cross the two ends of the wire and twist them together to form a strong support.

STEAMING FLOWERS

This simple technique can greatly improve dried roses or peonies, which are imported in large boxes and often arrive at their destination looking rather squashed. Never try to open the very centre of the flower which is often discoloured.

1 Bring a kettle to the boil. Hold the rose by its stem, head downwards, in the steam for a few seconds, until the outside petals start to waver.

2 Remove the rose from the steam and gently push back the outer petals, one by one. If necessary, repeat the process.

CARE AND MAINTENANCE

How long a display of dried materials will last largely depends on the care that it receives. Avoid direct sunlight and keep your display in a dry and damp-free atmosphere and it should last at least one or two years.

After about a year, your display will need cleaning. Set an electric hairdryer on cold and move it backwards and forwards over the display. Use a small paintbrush to clean away dust also. Remove any bits that are old or broken. Spray florist's sealer on your display for a further lift. Frosted spray paints can also transform a display that is too old to revive.

MAKING A FABRIC BOW

For a more formal setting, a fabric bow looks smart. Crinkled paper can be used for a more quick and inexpensive method.

1 Fold a piece of fabric equally into three lengthways, making sure that the raw edge is not too close to one of the folded edges. Fold the length again, dividing it into three so that the middle section is approximately one-third larger than the outer two.

2 Grip the fabric in the middle, pressing it into a bow shape. Still holding the shape, wrap a thin wire around it and twist the ends together. Make sure that the creases on the front of the bow are even. Twist the wires tightly together with pliers and tuck the sharp ends into the bow.

3 Fold a much smaller piece of fabric into three lengthways. It should be wide enough to look well balanced as the centre of the bow. Wrap this around the bow, covering the wire. Trim the ends at the back then glue the two raw ends together.

PLANT PRESERVATION TECHNIQUES

. . .

The following is a list of plants and materials and the drying method suitable for each. The list is not exhaustive, so if you find a plant you wish to try drying, assess its characteristics, find a similar type and try the drying method for that.

COMMON NAME	LATIN NAME	PLANT SECTION	TECHNIQUE
African marigold	*Tagetes*	flower	air drying
anemone (windflower)	*Anemone*	flower	air drying / desiccant
asparagus	*Asparagus plumosus*	leaf	microwave
aspidistra	*Aspidistra*	leaf	glycerine
astilbe	*Astilbe*	flower	air drying
bay	*Laurus*	leaf	desiccant/glycerine
bear's breeches	*Acanthus*	flower spike / leaf	air drying / glycerine
beech	*Fagus*	leaf	glycerine
bellflower	*Campanula*	flower	air drying
bell heather	*Erica cinerea*	flower	air drying
bells of Ireland	*Moluccella laevis*	bract	air drying/glycerine
blackberry (bramble)	*Robus (Rosaceae)*	leaf / berry	glycerine
blanket flower	*Gaillardia*	seedhead	air drying
broom	*Cytisus*	flower spray	air drying/desiccant
bulrush	*Typha latifolia*	seedhead	air drying
buttercup	*Ranunculus*	flower	desiccant
camellia	*Camellia*	flower	desiccant
campion (catchfly)	*Silene*	flower	air drying
candytuft	*Iberis*	flower / seedhead	dessicant / air drying
caraway	*Carum carvi*	seedhead	air drying
carnation	*Dianthus*	flower	desiccant
celosia	*Celosia*	flower	air drying / air drying in water
chamomile	*Chamaemelum nobile Athemis*	flower	air drying / air drying in water
Chinese lantern	*Physalis*	stems and seedheads	air drying
chive	*Allium schoenoprasum*	flower	air drying / air drying in water
choisya	*Choisya*	leaf	glycerine
chrysanthemum	*Chrysanthemum*	flower	desiccant
clarkia	*Clarkia (syn Godetia)*	flower	air drying
clematis (old man's beard, travellers' joy)	*Clematis*	leaf / seedhead	air drying / air drying

COMMON NAME	LATIN NAME	PLANT SECTION	TECHNIQUE
cock's-foot grass	*Dactylis glomerata*	stems and seedheads	air drying
copper beech	*Fagus sylvatica*	leaf	air drying/glycerine
cornflower (bluebottle)	*Centaurea cyanus*	flower	air drying/ microwave/ air drying in water
corn cob	*Zea mays*	seedhead	air drying
cotinus	*Cotinus*	flower / leaf	air drying / glycerine
cow parsley	*Anthriscus sylvestris*	seedhead	air drying
daffodil	*Narcissus*	flower	desiccant
dahlia	*Dahlia*	flower	desiccant
daisy	*Bellis*	flower	desiccant
delphinium	*Delphinium*	flower spike	air drying/desiccant
dock	*Rumex*	seedhead	air drying
dryandra	*Dryandra*	flower	air drying
elaeagnus	*Elaeagnus*	leaf	glycerine/ microwave
eucalyptus	*Eucalyptus*	leaf	air drying/glycerine
fennel	*Foeniculum vulgare*	leaf / seedhead	air drying / microwave / air drying
ferns		leaf	glycerine
fescue grass	*Festuca*	stems and seedheads	air drying
feverfew	*Chrysanthemum parthenium*	flower	air drying/ air drying in water/ microwave
fig	*Ficus*	leaf	glycerine
forsythia	*Forsythia*	flower sprays	desiccant
foxglove	*Digitalis*	flower	desiccant
freesia	*Freesia*	flower	desiccant
gay feathers	*Liatris*	flower spikes	air drying
geranium (cranesbill)	*Geranium*	leaf and flower	desiccant
giant hogweed	*Heracleum mantegazzianum*	stem and seedhead	air drying
globe amaranth	*Gomphrena globosa*	flowers	air drying
globe thistle	*Echinops*	thistle heads	air drying
golden rod	*Solidago*	flower	air drying / microwave
grape hyacinth	*Muscari*	flower	desiccant
gypsophila	*Gypsophila*	flower	air drying/ air drying in water/ microwave
hare's-tail grass	*Lagarus ovatus*	stems and seedheads	air drying
heather	*Erica*	flower spikes	air drying in water/ glycerine
helichrysum	*Helichrysum*	flower	air drying
holly	*Ilex*	leaf	glycerine
hollyhock	*Alcea*	flower	desiccant
honesty	*Lunaria*	seedhead	air drying
hop	*Humulus*	leaf and bracts	air drying/glycerine
hosta (plantain lily)	*Hosta*	leaf	glycerine

COMMON NAME	LATIN NAME	PLANT SECTION	TECHNIQUE
hyacinth	Hyacinthus	flower	desiccant
hydrangea	Hydrangea	flower and bracts	air drying/ air drying in water/ microwave
ivy	Hedera	leaf	glycerine
Japanese aralia	Fatsia japonica	leaf	glycerine
Jerusalam sage	Phlomis fruticosa	flower, leaf and seedhead	air drying
kerria (Jew's mallow)	Kerria	flowers	air drying
knapweed	Centaurea	seedhead	air drying
lady's mantle	Alchemilla mollis	flower	air drying/ microwave
larkspur	Consolida	flower spike	air drying/desiccant
laurel	Laurus	leaf	glycerine
lavender	Lavandula	flower spikes	air drying/ air drying in water
lavender cotton	Santolina chamaecyparissus	leaf	air drying/ microwave
lilac	Syringa	small flower sprays	desiccant
lily	Lilium	flower	desiccant
lily-of-the-valley	Convallaria	flower	desiccant
linseed	Linum usitatissium	stems and seedheads	air drying
London pride	Saxifraga x urbium	flower	desiccant
Love-in-a-mist	Nigella damascena	flower and seedhead	air drying
love-lies-bleeding	Amaranthus caudatus	flower spike	air drying
lupin	Lupinus	flower seedhead	desiccant air drying
magnolia	Magnolia	flower	desiccant
maple	Acer	leaf	glycereine
marguerite	Chrysanthemum frutescens	flower	desiccant
marjoram	Origanum	flower	air drying microwave
Mexican giant hyssop	Agastache	flower	air drying
millet	Panicum miliaceum	seedhead	air drying
mimosa	Acacia	flower sprays	air drying/desiccant air drying in water
mullein	Verbascum	seedhead	air drying
narcissus	Narcissus	flower	glycerine
oats	Avena sativa	stems and seedheads	air drying
onion	Allium	flower	air drying in water/ air drying
orchid	Orchidacea	flower	desiccant
pampas grass	Cortaderia selloana	stems and seedheads	air drying
pansy	Viola wittrockiana	flower	desiccant
pearl everlasting	Anaphalis	flower	air drying/ air drying in water
peony	Paeonia	flower	air drying/desiccant
pine	Pinus	cones	air drying
pinks	Dianthus	flower	desiccant
polyanthus	Primula	flower	desiccant
poppy	Papaver	seedhead	air drying
pot marigold	Calendula officinalis	flower	air drying/desiccant
phalaris	Phalaris	stems and seedheads	air drying

COMMON NAME	LATIN NAME	PLANT SECTION	TECHNIQUE
primrose	Primula vulgaris	flower	desiccant
quaking grass	Briza	stems and seedheads	air drying upright or hanging
rhododendron	Rhododendron	leaf	glycerine microwave
rose	Rosa	bud, flower, leaf fully open flower hip	air drying desiccant glycerine
rosemary	Rosmarinus officinalis	leaf spike	glycerine/air drying microwave
rue	Ruta graveolens	seedhead	air drying
safflower	Carthamus tinctorius	flower	air drying
sage	Salvia officinalis	flower and leaf	air drying
sea holly	Eryngium	flower	air drying
sea lavender	Limonium	flower	air drying/ air drying in water
sedge	Carex	seedhead	air drying
sedum (stonecrop)	Sedum	flower	air drying/desiccant microwave
senecio	Senecio	leaf	air drying/ microwave
shoofly	Nicandra phyusalodes	seedpods	air drying
sorrel tree	Oxydendrum arboreum	seedhead	air drying
statice	Psylliostachys	flower	air drying
stock	Matthiola	flower	dessicant
strawflower	Helichrysum bracteatum	flower	air drying
sunflower	Helianthus	flower	air drying
sweet pea	Lathyrus odoratus	flower	desiccant
sweet William	Dianthus barbatus	flower	air dry quickly
tansy	Tanacetum vulgare	flower	air drying/ microwave
teasel	Dipsacus fullonum	seedhead	air drying
thistle	Carlina	seedhead	air drying
wheat (bearded)	Triticale	stems and seedheads	air drying
wheat (common)	Triticum aestiuum	stems and seedheads	air drying
tulip	Tulipa	flower	desiccant
vine	Vitus	leaf	desiccant
wallflower	Cheiranthus	flower	desiccant
winged spindle	Euonymus alatus	flower	air drying
xeranthemum (immortelle)	Xeranthemum	flower	air drying
yarrow	Achillea millefolium	flower	air drying
zinnia	Zinnia	flower	desiccant

NEW WAYS WITH FRESH FLOWERS

...

From an abundant armful of glorious old–
fashioned roses in full bloom in a jug, to the
subtle simplicity of woodland berries in a
tinted glass, every flower arrangement you
compose is an expression of your personality
and artistic style. The following pages will help
you to make the very most of fresh flowers, in
both classic and informal compositions.

INTRODUCTION

· · ·

Above: Candle Ring

*Below: Blue and Yellow
Arrangement in a Pitcher*

There is nothing else like the colour, texture and scent of a fresh flower display to enhance your home and to evoke different moods to match the seasons. This chapter covers a wide range of fresh flower arrangements, from very simple designs that require a minimum of time and effort, to more ambitious projects for elaborate, decorative displays.

One of the most stunning ways to display fresh flowers is to use one type of flower, to keep the arrangement simple and yet striking. A profusion of fragrant, fresh tulips or a basket of hydrangeas illustrate this idea perfectly, showing how effective a single type of flower can look when the eye is not distracted by competing colours and textures.

Fresh flower arrangements also provide an ideal opportunity for maximum impact, using the brightest, boldest of colours. A fruit and flower swag will brighten up any room, with its contrasting yellow lemons, green limes and black grapes, and an exotic table arrangement can be made with the liveliest red croton leaves combined with cockscomb, celosia, Scarborough lily flowers and glory lilies. Always be on the lookout for the brightest flowers, and never be afraid to experiment with different combinations – there are so many flower varieties to choose from that you will never be short of exciting new arrangements.

Above: Fresh Herbal Wreath

*Left: Old-fashioned
Garden Rose Arrangement*

Below: Napkin Tie

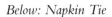

When choosing fresh flowers, don't forget that scent is just as important as colour. Entering a room or hallway and being inundated with the delightful perfume of a fresh flower arrangement is as welcoming as it is beautiful. This chapter includes many ideas designed specifically to produce a lingering scent, such as an arrangement of golden privet, tuberose, cream stocks, freesias and mimosa, a herbal nosegay made from chives, mint, rosemary, fennel and geranium, and an old-fashioned garden rose arrangement.

In addition to fresh flowers, experiment with fresh leaves and twigs; leaves can be used on their own – as in the all-foliage arrangement, for example – or combined with twigs to produce different textures as well as colours. Carefully chosen fresh foliage really adds to the impact of a well-designed flower display, so make sure you do think about this part of your arrangement.

Finally, it's important to choose a container that will look good with your fresh flower arrangement – but also remember that it needs to be watertight or properly lined, and its weight must be appropriate for the flowers it holds.

TULIP ARRANGEMENT

· · ·

MATERIALS

· · ·

50 'Angelique' tulips

· · ·

scissors

· · ·

watertight container, e.g. small bucket

· · ·

basket

The arrangement is technically relatively unstructured but, by repetition of the regular form of the tulip heads, the overall visual effect is that of a formal dome of flowers to be viewed in the round.

Sometimes the simple beauty of an arrangement which relies entirely on one type of flower in its own foliage can be breathtaking. This display of Angelique tulips in glorious profusion contains nothing to compete with their soft pastel pink colour and would make a dramatic room centrepiece.

1 Strip the lower leaves from the tulips to prevent them from rotting in the water. Fill the bucket with water and place in the basket.

2 Cut each tulip stem to the correct size and place the stems in the water. Arrange them to start building the display from its lowest circumference upwards.

3 Continue arranging the tulips towards the centre of the display until a full and even domed shape is achieved. The display should be able to be viewed from all sides.

BLUE AND WHITE TUSSIE MUSSIES

· · ·

Small, hand-tied spiralled posies make perfect gifts and, in the right vase, ideal centre decorations for small tables. Both of these displays have delicate flowers massed together. One features Japanese anemones, visually strengthened by blackberries on stems; the other delphiniums supported by rosehip stems.

MATERIALS

· · ·

TUSSIE 1 (on left)

· · ·

blackberries on stems

· · ·

white Japanese anemones

· · ·

1 stem draceana

· · ·

twine

· · ·

ribbon

· · ·

scissors

· · ·

TUSSIE 2 (on right)

· · ·

4-5 stems 'Blue Butterfly'
delphinium

· · ·

3 stems rosehips

· · ·

5 small Virginia creeper leaves

· · ·

twine

· · ·

ribbon

· · ·

scissors

1 Start with a central flower and add stems of foliage and flowers, turning the posy in your hand to build the design into a spiral.

2 Once all the ingredients have been used, and the bunch is completed, tie firmly at the binding point with twine. Repeat steps one and two for the second tussie mussie.

3 Trim the ends of the flower stems with scissors to achieve a neat edge. Finish both tussie mussies with a ribbon bow.

Whilst the flowers need to be tightly massed for the best effect, they have relatively large but fragile blooms, so take care not to crush their petals, and tie off firmly but gently.

HEAVILY SCENTED
ARRANGEMENT
· · ·

MATERIALS
· · ·
1 block plastic foam
· · ·
cellophane (plastic wrap)
· · ·
wooden trug
· · ·
scissors
· · ·
20 stems golden privet
· · ·
10 stems tuberose
· · ·
10 stems cream stocks
· · ·
20 stems freesias
· · ·
20 stems mimosa

Mimosa has a substantial main stem with slender offshoots. For greater flexibility, remove the offshoots and discard the heavier main stem.

The flowers used in this display are chosen for their distinctive and delicious scents, which combine to produce a heady perfume guaranteed to silence those who claim that commercially-grown blooms do not have the fragrance of their garden equivalents. It is an ideal arrangement for a hallway or living room where the scent will be most attractive.

The outline of the display is established in golden privet reinforced with waxy tuberose and soft-textured stocks. These provide a cream and yellow backdrop for the focal flowers, pale yellow, double-petalled freesias. The whole arrangement is visually co-ordinated by the introduction of the soft green, feathery foliage and powdery yellow flowers of mimosa.

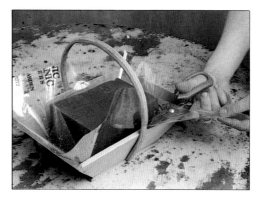

1 Firmly wedge a water-soaked block of plastic foam into a cellophane-lined (plastic wrap-lined) trug. Trim the excess cellophane from the edge of the trug. (If the finished arrangement is likely to be moved secure the plastic foam in the trug with florist's adhesive tape.)

2 First ensuring the leaves are stripped from the stem bottoms, insert the golden privet into the foam to build the outline of the arrangement. Because they make small neat holes, the slender stems of golden privet are ideal for arranging in plastic foam.

3 Reinforce the outline of the display with the tuberose and the stocks, arranging them in opposite diagonals.

4 Distribute the freesias throughout the display, using stems with buds to the outside and more open blooms to the centre. Break off the mimosa's offshoots so that a mixture of stem sizes can be arranged through the display which will visually pull everything together.

HYACINTH BULB VASES
. . .

MATERIALS
. . .
3 bulb vases
. . .
2 jam jars
. . .
4 thin sturdy twigs
. . .
raffia
. . .
scissors
. . .
5 hyacinth bulbs

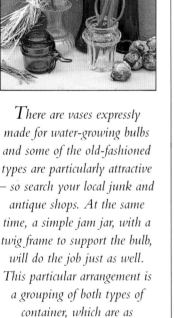

There are vases expressly made for water-growing bulbs and some of the old-fashioned types are particularly attractive – so search your local junk and antique shops. At the same time, a simple jam jar, with a twig frame to support the bulb, will do the job just as well. This particular arrangement is a grouping of both types of container, which are as important to the overall success of the display as the flowers themselves.

Bulbs can be grown in water as well as in soil. By employing this technique and with some long-term planning, the commonplace hyacinth has been given a new interest in this display.

1 If you are using bulb vases, simply fill each one with water and place the bulbs on the top with their bases sitting in the water. Top up the water occasionally, taking care not to disturb the roots. Then just wait until the hyacinth bulbs root, grow and flower!

2 The use of a jam jar requires making a square frame to sit on top of the jar. Use thin but sturdy twigs firmly tied together with raffia to form the frame. Trim the stem ends and the raffia when you have established that the frame fits the jar neatly, then position the bulb on the frame with its base in the water.

SPRING NAPKIN DECORATION
. . .

The sophisticated gold and white colour combination used in these elegant and delicate napkin decorations would be perfect for a formal dinner or an important occasion such as a wedding.

In addition to its exquisite scent, the tiny bells of lily-of-the-valley visually harmonize with the pure white of the cyclamen.

MATERIALS
. . .
napkins
. . .
small-leaved ivy
trails (sprigs)
. . .
scissors
. . .
1 pot lily-of-the-valley
. . .
1 pot tiny cyclamen (dwarf
Cyclamen persicum)
. . .
gold cord

The slender stems of both flowers enable each decoration to be made into a tied sheaf. The splayed stems echo the shape made by the flowers.

1 Fold the napkin into a rectangle, then roll into a cylindrical shape. Wrap an ivy trail (sprig) around the middle of the napkin. Tie the stem firmly in a knot.

2 Take 4–5 stems of lily-of-the-valley, 3 flowers of cyclamen on their stems and 3 cyclamen leaves. Using both flowers, create a small flat-backed sheaf in your hand by spiralling the stems. Place one leaf at the back of the lily-of-the-valley for support and use the other two around the cyclamen flowers to emphasize the focal point. Tie at the binding point with gold cord. Lay the flat back of the sheaf on top of the napkin and ivy, wrap the excess gold cord around the napkin, gently tying into a bow on top of the stems.

FRESH HERBAL WREATH

· · ·

MATERIALS

· · ·

*30 cm (12 in) plastic foam
wreath frame*

· · ·

scissors

· · ·

2 branches bay leaves

· · ·

2 bunches rosemary

· · ·

.71 wires

· · ·

6 large bulbs (heads) garlic

· · ·

6 or 7 beetroot (beets)

· · ·

*40 stems flowering
marjoram*

· · ·

40 stems flowering mint

*As well as being decorative, a
herb wreath can also be useful.
The herbs can be taken from it
and used in the kitchen
without causing too much
damage to the overall design.*

In many parts of Europe it is believed that a herb wreath hung in a kitchen, or by the entrance of a house, is a sign of welcome, wealth and good luck. This wreath will stay fresh for two or three weeks because the stems of the herbs are in water, but even if it dries out it will continue to look good for some time.

1 Soak the wreath frame thoroughly in cold water. Create the background by making a foliage outline using evenly distributed bay leaves and sprigs of rosemary. To ensure an even covering, position the leaves inside, on top and on the outside of the wreath frame.

2 Wire the garlic bulbs (heads) and beetroot (beets) by pushing two wires through their base so that they cross, then pull the projecting wires down and cut to the correct length for the depth of the foam. Decide where on the wreath they are to be positioned and push the wires firmly into the foam.

3 Infill the spaces in the wreath, concentrating the marjoram around the beetroot and the mint around the garlic.

SPRING BLOSSOM URN

· · ·

*The bright, fresh arrangement
joyously leaping out of a cold,
hard, metal urn, symbolizes
the winter soil erupting with
spring growth.*

The explosion of plant life in the spring is visually depicted in this arrangement of early flowers and foliage.

Heavily flowered heads of white lilac are the focal blossoms of the display set against the dark brown stems of pussy willow and cherry. The starkness of these stems is softened by the emerging pink blossom of the cherry and the furry silver pussy willow buds, both of which harmonize with the lilac.

1 Line the urn with cellophane (plastic wrap) and wedge in the water-soaked block of plastic foam. Trim away the excess cellophane.

2 Make hairpins from .71 wires and pin reindeer moss into the plastic foam around the rim of the urn. Make sure that the foam is entirely covered on all sides.

3 Arrange the pussy willow in the urn to establish the height and width of a symmetrical outline. Press the pussy willow stems firmly into the plastic foam to secure the arrangement.

4 Distribute the lilac throughout the pussy willow. Look carefully at the way lilac flowers hang from their stems and try to exploit their natural attitude in the arrangement. You will find there is no need to position the stems at extreme angles.

5 Position the pink cherry blossom throughout the display to reinforce the overall shape and provide a link between the slender stems of pussy willow and the large heads of the flowering lilac.

HYACINTH BULB BOWL
• • •

8 sprouting hyacinth bulbs
• • •
24 autumn leaves
• • •
raffia
• • •
scissors
• • •
glass bowl

This novel approach to the display of developing hyacinth bulbs takes them out of their pots and into organic containers which become feature elements in the design. This attractive display will last for many weeks.

The bulbs' roots, along with their soil, are simply wrapped in leaves and then grouped together sitting in water in a glass bowl. The bulbs take up the water and happily grow from these attractive green spikes through to full flowers.

1 Carefully remove the hyacinth bulbs from their pots, keeping the soil tightly packed around the roots. Wrap a leaf underneath the root ball and soil of each bulb, with two more leaves around the sides. Leave the majority of each bulb exposed as it would be in a pot.

2 Secure the leaves in position by tying around with raffia. Group the wrapped hyacinths in the glass bowl and fill to approximately 5 cm (2 in) deep with water. Remember to top up regularly. The bulbs will continue to grow and eventually bloom.

NAPKIN TIE

· · ·

This beautiful alternative to a napkin ring is easy to make and very effective in enhancing the look of your dinner table. Its appearance can be changed to suit many different occasions.

MATERIALS
· · ·
napkin
· · ·
scissors
· · ·
long, thin, flexible stem rosemary
· · ·
3 lemon geranium leaves
· · ·
2 or 3 heads flowering mint

1 Find a suitable length of rosemary, long and flexible enough to wrap around the rolled napkin once or twice. Tie the stem securely.

2 Arrange the lemon geranium leaves and mint flowerheads by gently pushing the stems through the knot of the binding rosemary stem.

The method is simply to use any reasonably sturdy trailing foliage to bind the napkin and then create a focal point by the addition of leaves, berries or flowerheads of your choice. If a firm fixing is required, wire the leaves and flowerheads before attaching to binding material.

TULIP POMANDER

. . .

MATERIALS

. . .

1 plastic foam ball

. . .

ribbon

. . .

scissors

. . .

*20 heads 'Appleblossom'
double tulips*

. . .

1 bunch myrtle

. . .

.71 wires

. . .

*a good handful
reindeer moss*

*The pomander illustrated does
not boast exotic aromas but it
does have a pleasing variety of
surface textures, ranging from
the spiky inner petals of double
tulips through the beady black
berries of myrtle to the softness
of grey moss, all set against
bands of smooth satin ribbon.*

I n Elizabethan times pomanders were filled with herbs or scented flowers and carried to perfume the air. Today the pomander is more likely to be a bridesmaid's accessory, a charming alternative to the conventional posy.

1 Soak the foam ball in water. Tie the ribbon around the ball, starting at the top and crossing at the bottom, and then tying at the top to divide the ball into four equal segments. Make sure there is enough excess ribbon to tie into a bow.

2 Cut the tulips to a stem length of about 2.5 cm (1 in) and push into the foam in vertical lines at the centre of each segment. Hold the tulip heads gently while positioning them on the foam ball to avoid the heads breaking off.

3 Cut sprigs of myrtle on short stems and push into the foam to form lines on either side of each line of tulips. The myrtle should appear quite compact.

4 Form hairpins from the .71 wires and use them to pin the reindeer moss to cover all remaining exposed areas of the foam ball.

AMARYLLIS LINE ARRANGEMENT

· · ·

The amaryllis has an extraordinary-looking stem which, though hollow, is large and fleshy and carries heavy blooms. Plastic foam will not support a flower of this size and weight unless used in large amounts, reinforced with wire mesh with the amaryllis stem firmly staked.

The pinholder will give the amaryllis the secure support it requires because the fleshy stems can be pushed firmly on to the pins. Furthermore, the weight of the pinholder is sufficient to counterbalance the weight of the blooms.

A line arrangement is just that: a display of flowers in a staggered vertical line. The large blooms of the amaryllis are particularly suitable and here they are reinforced by the spiky leaves of *Phormium cookiannum variagatum*.

1 Place the pinholder in the centre of the bowl and completely cover it with water. Arrange the amaryllis in a staggered vertical line by pushing the stems on to the pins. Position the more closed blooms on longer stems towards the rear, and more open blooms with shorter stems towards the front of the arrangement. (Any spare flowerheads on short stems should be recessed into the base of the display by securing them on pins.)

2 Arrange the leaves, with the largest at the back and shortest to the front, in a diagonal through the staggered vertical line of amaryllis.

3 To complete the display, place it in its final position and conceal the top of the pinholder by scattering glass marbles on top of it.

NOSEGAYS

· · ·

Popular in Elizabethan times for warding off unpleasant smells, today nosegays, or tussie mussies, still make charming decorations and lovely gifts. The instructions are for the posy on the right of the main picture.

1 Cut all the plant stems to a length suitable for the size of posy you are making and clean them of leaves and thorns. Starting by holding the central flowers in your hand, add stems of the chosen herb, turning the emerging bunch as you work. Make sure you complete a circle with one herb before you start another. Finally use a circle of lemon geranium leaves to edge the bunch.

2 When everything is in position, tie with twine and trim stem ends neatly. Finish each nosegay with raffia tied in a bow.

MATERIALS

· · ·

1 chive flower

· · ·

flowering mint

· · ·

rosemary

· · ·

fennel

· · ·

lemon geranium leaves

· · ·

twine

· · ·

scissors

· · ·

raffia

These tiny herbal posies are made up of tight concentric circles of herbs around a central flower, which will exude a marvellous mix of scents and can be used for culinary as well as decorative purposes. Alternatively they can be left to dry, to provide lasting pleasure.

FRUIT AND FLOWER SWAG

· · ·

MATERIALS

· · ·

.71 wires

· · ·

4 limes

· · ·

9 lemons

· · ·

4 bunches black grapes

· · ·

4 bunches sneezeweed
(Helenium)

· · ·

1 bundle tree ivy

· · ·

scissors

· · ·

straw plait (braid), about
60 cm (24 in) long

· · ·

raffia

· · ·

1 bunch ivy trails (sprigs)

The component parts have to be wired, but otherwise the swag is simple to construct. Do remember that although lemons and limes will survive in this situation, grapes and cut flowers will need regular mist spraying with water.

The colour and content of this decorative swag will brighten any room. Its visual freshness makes it especially suitable for a kitchen but, if it was made on a longer base, the decoration could be a mantelpiece garland or even extended to adorn the balustrade of a staircase.

1 First, all the fruit has to be wired. Pass a wire through from side to side just above the base of the limes. Leave equal lengths of wire projecting from either side, bend these down and twist together under the base. If the lemons are heavier than the limes, pass a second wire through at right angles to the first, providing four equal ends to be twisted together under their bases.

2 Group the grapes in small clusters and double leg mount with .71 wires. Then form 12 small bunches of sneezeweed mixed with tree ivy and double leg mount these on .71 wires.

3 Starting at its bottom end, bind three wired lemons to the plait (braid) with raffia. Then in turn bind a bunch of flowers and foliage, a lime, grapes and a second bunch of flowers and foliage.

4 Repeat binding materials to the plait in the above sequence until almost at the top. Secure by wrapping the remaining raffia tightly around the plait .

5 Make a bow from raffia and tie to the top of the swag. Trim off any stray wire ends. Entwine the ivy trails (sprigs) around the top of the swag and bow.

PINK PHLOX ARRANGEMENT IN A PITCHER

· · ·

MATERIALS

· · ·

scissors

· · ·

*15 stems pink phlox
'Bright Eyes'*

· · ·

pitcher

· · ·

*5 trails (sprigs) of Virginia
creeper in autumn tints*

*A simple-to-arrange pitcher of
flowers and foliage becomes an
explosion of colour and scent.*

The colour collision between a mass of pink phlox flowerheads and the vibrant autumn reds of Virginia creeper gives this arrangement its visual impact and is a simple, yet effective arrangement to create.

1 Cut the stems of phlox to a length proportionate to the container. Arrange the phlox evenly with taller stems towards the back of the pitcher.

2 Place the cut ends of Virginia creeper trails (sprigs) in the pitcher of water and weave them through the heads of phlox, spreading them out evenly.

CANDLE RING

· · ·

This pretty little candle ring is created on a very small diameter plastic foam ring. Filled with a heady combination of fennel, rosemary, lemon geranium, hyssop and violas, it would be perfect for an intimate dinner table.

MATERIALS

· · ·

15 cm (6 in) diameter plastic foam ring

· · ·

candlestick

· · ·

scissors

· · ·

small quantities of rosemary, lemon geranium leaves, fennel, hyssop and violas

The floral ring is simply placed over the candlestick to create this simple but effective decoration. Never leave a burning candle unattended and do not allow it to burn down to within less than 5 cm (2 in) of the foliage.

1 Soak the plastic foam ring in cold water and place it over the candlestick. Start the arrangement by making a basic outline in the plastic foam with stems of rosemary and geranium leaves, positioning them evenly around the ring. Try to arrange the leaves at different angles to produce a fuller effect.

2 Infill the gaps evenly with the fennel and hyssop, finally add a few violas for colour.

EXOTIC FLOWER ARRANGEMENT

• • •

MATERIALS

• • •

large fish bowl

• • •

scissors

• • •

*5 stems contorted
willow*

• • •

5 ginger flowers

• • •

10 lotus seed heads

• • •

7 celosia heads

• • •

2 pink pineapples

• • •

10 stems glory lily

• • •

5 fishtail palms

• • •

5 anthuriums

• • •

*7 Phormium tenax
'Bronze baby'*

• • •

*6 small bunches of bear grass
(Xerophyllum tenax)*

• • •

*6 passion flower trails
(sprays)*

*Most of the flowers and
foliage in this display can
subsequently be dried.*

The apparent delicacy of some of the flowers in this spectacular arrangement belies their robust nature. Commercially-produced, exotic cut flowers not only look fabulous but also have a long life span.

1 Three-quarter fill the fish bowl with cold water. Cut the contorted willow stems to about three times the height of the vase and arrange to form the framework of the display.

2 Add the ginger flowers and lotus seedheads so that the tallest is slightly shorter than the contorted willow and placed at the back, with stems of decreasing height positioned to the front and sides.

3 Distribute the celosia through the display in the same way as the ginger flowers and lotus heads. Recess the two pink pineapples in the centre of the arrangement, leaving one taller than the other.

4 Position the glory lilies through the arrangement concentrating on the front and sides where they will naturally overhang the container. Arrange the anthuriums, which are the focal flowers, with tallest to the back becoming shorter to the front.

5 Untypically the foliage is added last. Distribute the individual exotic leaves and bunches of bear grass throughout the arrangement. Push the cut ends of the passion flower trails (sprays) into the back of the fish bowl and drape them down and around over the front.

ORCHID POSY
• • •

MATERIALS
· · ·
*6 stems orange/brown spotted
spray orchid*
· · ·
*6 stems pink spotted spray
orchid*
· · ·
bear grass
· · ·
scissors
· · ·
twine

*This tied posy is spiralled in
the hand and contains just two
varieties of orchid with fronds
of bear grass. The strong stems
of orchids are ideal for the
spiralling technique and allow
the finished posy to stand on
its own and still keep its
shape. The elegance of the bear
grass helps the overall design
by softening the solid outlines
of the fleshy flowerheads.*

The orchid grows in a multiplicity of shapes and colours, from delicate spray forms to large fleshy varieties. All orchids look exotic and can easily upstage other more subtle blooms in an arrangement. It follows that the orchid is most effective when used on its own in a single variety, or perhaps with other compatible varieties and some carefully chosen foliage.

1 Starting with a central orchid stem held in your hand, add flower stems and foliage to form a spiral. Separate the bear grass into slim bunches for easy handling.

2 Keep turning the posy in your hand as you add the stems, not forgetting to include the bunches of bear grass, until the arrangement is complete. Trim the stems.

3 Using the twine, tie the finished bunch at the binding point - i.e. where all the stems cross. Finish the posy by tying bear grass around the binding point to conceal the twine.

EXOTIC BUD VASE
. . .

A selection of small colourful vases forms the basis of this attractive display of short-stemmed exotic flowers. Only one type of flower is used for each jar. Some have a single stem with a particular sculptural quality; others have flowers massed for colour and texture impact. It is a simple, effective display which relies as much on the choice of containers as the flowers used.

MATERIALS
. . .
1 anthurium
. . .
1 pink pineapple
. . .
contorted willow stems
. . .
3 exotic leaves
. . .
3 celosia heads
. . .
3 stems spray orchid
. . .
4 glory lily heads
. . .
*10 Scarborough lily
flowers*
. . .
*6 small different coloured
ceramic containers*
. . .
scissors

Sometimes we are left with flowers on stems which are too short for large arrangements. Perhaps they are flowers salvaged from fading displays which have been cut shorter to extend their lives or perhaps they are simply broken stems. Nevertheless, they can still be used to good effect.

1 Consider the shape, size, colour and texture of the materials and containers to decide which flowers are appropriate to which container. Also decide whether to use a single flowerhead, or a group display for each container.

2 Measure the flower stem lengths against their container. Anthurium is a single display, as is the pineapple but with willow and exotic leaves. The celosia heads, orchids, glory lily and Scarborough lily are all used to create a massed effect.

ALL-FOLIAGE ARRANGEMENT
• • •

MATERIALS
· · ·
2 blocks plastic foam
· · ·
*shallow bowl large enough for
the plastic foam blocks*
· · ·
florist's adhesive tape
· · ·
scissors
· · ·
.71 wires
· · ·
bun moss
· · ·
5 stems grevillea
· · ·
*10 stems shrimp plant
(Beloperone guttata)*
· · ·
*10 stems ming fern
(cultivar of Boston fern)*
· · ·
10 stems pittosporum
· · ·
5 stems cotoneaster

*Do not restrict yourself to
green foliage; remember the
bright yellow of elaeagnus, the
silver grey of senecio, not to
mention the extraordinary
autumn wealth of coloured
berries and leaves – all can be
used to achieve truly
wonderful results.*

If the garden is void of flowers, your budget is limited, or you simply fancy a change, then creating an arrangement entirely from different types of foliage can be both challenging and rewarding.

No matter what the season, finding three or four varieties of foliage is not difficult. Anything from the common privet to the most exotic shrubs can be used and to great effect.

1 Soak the plastic foam and secure it in the bowl with florist's adhesive tape.

2 Make hairpin shapes from .71 wire and pin clumps of bun moss around the rim of the bowl by pushing the wires through the moss into the plastic foam. This conceals the plastic foam where it meets the edge of the bowl.

3 Start arranging the grevillea from one side, to establish the maximum height, and work diagonally across with progressively shorter stems, finishing with foliage flowing over the front of the bowl. Arrange the shrimp plant in a similar way along the opposite diagonal, but make it shorter than the grevillea and emphasize this line by adding ming fern.

4 Strengthen the line of grevillea by interspersing it with the broader-leafed pittosporum. Finally, distribute the cotoneaster evenly throughout the whole arrangement.

GERBERA BOTTLE DISPLAY

· · ·

MATERIALS

· · ·

red food colouring

· · ·

yellow food colouring

· · ·

*pitcher, for mixing food
colourings*

· · ·

6 bottles or tall, slim vases

· · ·

12 gerberas in various colours

· · ·

scissors

*Gerberas have soft flexible
stems which tend to bend
naturally. To straighten them,
wrap together the top three
quarters of their stems in paper
to keep them erect. Then stand
them in deep cool water for
approximately two hours.*

The success of a display of flowers need not rely on its complexity; indeed it is held by many that simplicity is the essence of good design.

The flowers of the gerbera have an extraordinary visual innocence and a vast array of vibrant colours. This powerful graphic quality makes the gerbera perfect for simple, bold, modern designs which this arrangement demonstrates by isolating blooms in separate containers within an overall grouping. The impact is perpetuated in the water by the addition of food colouring.

1 Add the red and yellow food colourings separately to water and mix thoroughly together. Fill the various bottles or vases. For maximum impact, choose different shapes and sizes of bottles and vary the strength of food colouring to each vessel. The food colouring will not harm the flowers in any way.

2 Measure the gerbera stems to the desired height and cut them at an angle. Place them in bottles individually or in twos and threes, depending on the size of the bottle neck. Finally, arrange the bottles in an eye-catching group, using other colourful props if desired.

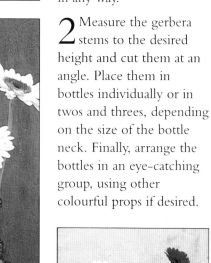

GROWING PLANTS TABLE DECORATION

· · ·

It is possible to avoid the time-consuming preparation which is a necessary part of flower arranging by using potted plants. A table decoration need not be the traditional arrangement of cut flowers. An interesting selection of contrasting small plants of different heights has been used in this display. Their status has been elevated by planting them in old terracotta pots of different sizes to give variation to the height of the decoration.

To tie the display together visually, the pots are grouped with interspersed coloured night-lights (tea-lights), each sitting on a leaf which is not only decorative, but will also catch the dripping wax.

MATERIALS
· · ·
2 violas
· · ·
2 ornamental cabbages
· · ·
1 African violet
· · ·
1 cyclamen
· · ·
6 small terracotta pots of different sizes
· · ·
bun moss
· · ·
night-lights (tea-lights)
· · ·
large leaves

1 Remove all the plants from their plastic containers, plant them in terracotta pots, and then water well. Cover the top of the soil in the pots with fresh, moist bun moss. Be sure to allow the pots to drain thoroughly. Arrange the pots at the centre of the table and intersperse with night-lights (tea-lights) placed on leaves, large enough to be visible and to catch the dripping wax.

The group can be as large or small as the table size dictates and the plants can be used around the house between dinner parties.
Never leave burning candles unattended and do not allow them to burn down to within 5cm (2in) of the display.

APRICOT ROSE AND PUMPKIN
. . .

The simple appeal of this design results from its use of just one type of flower and one type of foliage. The addition of tiny pumpkins gives body to the pretty combination of spray roses and flowering hypericum foliage. Note how the apricot colour is carried through the flowers, pumpkins and container in contrast to the red buds and yellow flowers of the foliage.

1 Soak the block of plastic foam and cut it so that it can be wedged in place in the container. Secure the foam with florist's adhesive tape.

2 Create the outline of the display using the hypericum and establish its overall height, width and length. The stems of commercially-produced hypericum tend to be long and straight with many offshoots of smaller stems. To create a more delicate foliage effect, and to get the most out of your material, use these smaller stems in the arrangement.

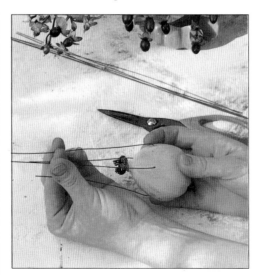

3 Wire each pumpkin by pushing one wire right through across the pumpkin base and out of the other side. Push another wire through to cross the first at right angles. Pull both wires down so that they project from the base. The pumpkins will be supported by pushing these wires into the plastic foam.

4 Position the pumpkins in the foliage, making sure that some are recessed more than others.

5 Infill the arrangement with the spray roses. Like the hypericum, spray roses tend to have lots of small offshoots from the main stem and these should be used to get the most out of your materials. To augment the overall shape of the display, use buds on longer stems at the outside edges with the most open blooms and heavily-flowered stems in the centre.

Substituting limes for the pumpkins will add a touch of vibrancy but for a more sophisticated look, use plums or black grapes.

EXOTIC NAPKIN DECORATION
• • •

• • •

napkin

• • •

*trails (sprays) passion
flower*

• • •

scissors

• • •

*2-3 virginia creeper
leaves*

• • •

1 glory lily head

• • •

1 celosia head

*Exotic flowers are surprisingly
robust, so you can prepare the
napkin decorations in advance
of your dinner party and they
will not droop.*

When Oriental food is on the menu, this easy-to-make napkin decoration will give the dining table the perfect finishing touch.

Passion flower trails (sprays) are bound around the napkin and tied off in a knot into which the flowerheads and leaves are pushed to hold them in place.

1 Fold the napkin into a rectangle and then loosely roll up. Wrap a passion flower trail (spray) around its middle, pulling quite tightly but taking care not to snap it, then tie off in a simple knot.

2 Using the virginia creeper leaves, start arranging the decoration on the napkin by carefully pushing the stems through the knot, then repeat the process with the flowerheads.

HERBAL TABLE DECORATION
· · ·

This table decoration is made up of five elements: four terracotta pots of various herbs, foliages contained within a plastic foam ring, night-lights (tea-lights) and white dill. This is an interesting alternative to the more conventional concept of an arrangement held in plastic foam, or wire mesh, in a single container.

MATERIALS
· · ·
6 night-lights (tea-lights)
· · ·
30 cm (12 in) diameter plastic
foam wreath frame
· · ·
2 blocks plastic foam
· · ·
4 terracotta pots
· · ·
cellophane (plastic wrap)
· · ·
scissors
· · ·
white dill
· · ·
rosemary
· · ·
mint
· · ·
marjoram
· · ·
guelder rose
(Viburnum opulus)
(European cranberry) berries

This display can be dismantled and the parts used separately to good effect in different situations. The individual terracotta pots of herbs can even be dried and their usefulness extended. Never leave burning candles unattended.

1 Press the night-lights (tea-lights) into the soaked plastic foam ring, at equal distances around its circumference. Soak the block of plastic foam and line the terracotta pots with cellophane to prevent leakage. Cut the plastic foam to size and fit it firmly into the pots.

2 Mass the white dill around the base ring between the night-lights (tea-lights). Then mass the individual pots with selected herbs and foliage. The effect is greater if each pot is filled with one type of herb only. Position the base ring and arrange the pots within it.

TABLE ARRANGEMENT WITH FRUIT AND FLOWERS

• • •

MATERIALS

• • •

basket

• • •

cellophane (plastic wrap)

• • •

2 blocks plastic foam

• • •

scissors

• • •

florist's adhesive tape

• • •

1 bundle tree ivy

• • •

3 bunches red grapes

• • •

.71 wires

• • •

6 black figs

• • •

15 stems antirrhinum

• • •

15 stems amaranthus (straight, not trailing)

• • •

15 stems astilbe

• • •

20 stems red roses

• • •

5 stems hydrangea

The addition of fruit brings a visual opulence to this arrangement of flowers. The sumptuous reds and purples of the figs and grapes used in this display harmonize beautifully with the rich deep hues of the flowers. The natural bloom on the fruit combines with the velvet softness of the roses to create a textural feast for the eye. The overall effect is one of ravishing lusciousness.

1 Line the basket with cellophane (plastic wrap) and tightly wedge in the blocks of water-soaked plastic foam. Trim the excess cellophane around the edge of the basket. If the arrangement is to be moved, tape the foam firmly in place.

2 To establish the overall shape of the arrangement, create a low dome of foliage with the tree ivy in proportion with the size and shape of the basket. Spread the tree ivy evenly throughout the plastic foam.

3 Wire the bunches of grapes by double leg mounting on .71 wires. Position the bunches recessed in the foliage in a roughly diagonal line across the display. Handle the grapes delicately.

4 Push a wire through each fig from side to side, leaving projecting ends to bend downwards. Group the figs in pairs and push the wires into the plastic foam around the centre of the arrangement.

5 Emphasize the domed shape of the display with the antirrhinums, amaranthus and the astilbe. Then add the roses, which are the focal flowers, evenly through the display. To complete the arrangement, recess the hydrangea heads into the plastic foam to give depth and texture. Water the foam daily to prolong the life of the display.

Although there are numerous ingredients in this display, the final effect is well worth the extra attention.

OLD-FASHIONED GARDEN ROSE ARRANGEMENT

· · ·

MATERIALS

· · ·

watertight container, to put inside plant pot

· · ·

low, weathered terracotta plant pot

· · ·

pitcher

· · ·

a variety garden roses, short- and long-stemmed

· · ·

scissors

The technique is to mass one type of flower in several varieties whose papery petals will achieve a textural mix of colour and scent.

The beautiful full-blown blooms of these antique-looking roses give an opulent and romantic feel to a very simple combination of flower and container. This arrangement deserves centre stage in any room setting.

1 Place the watertight container inside the terracotta plant pot and fill with water. Fill the pitcher as well. Select and prepare your blooms and remove the lower foliage and thorns.

2 Position the longer-stemmed blooms in the pitcher with the heads massed together. This ensures that the cut stems are supported and so can simply be placed directly into the water.

3 Mass shorter, more open flowerheads in the glass bowl inside the plant pot with the stems hidden and the heads showing just above the rim of the pot. The heads look best if kept either all on one level or in a slight dome shape. If fewer flowers are used, wire mesh or plastic foam may be needed to control the positions of individual blooms.

BLUE AND YELLOW
BUD VASES
· · ·

MATERIALS
· · ·
2 bud vases
· · ·
3 stems helenium
· · ·
scissors
· · ·
5 virginia creeper leaves
· · ·
3 stems delphinium
· · ·
2 stems campanula
· · ·
3 small vine leaves
· · ·
raffia

When deciding on a bud vase and its contents, consider both the size of the table and the proportion of flowers to the container used.
Generally bud vases are used on small dining tables and therefore must not be too large and obtrusive. Also a small container with tall flowers is unstable and likely to be knocked over. The water should be changed, or at least topped-up, daily.

The bud vase is possibly the most common form of table decoration, but that does not mean that it has to be commonplace. These delightful examples, using primary colours, demonstrate that with just a little imagination the simple bud vase can be exciting.

1 Fill the vases approximately three-quarters full with water. Measure the stems of your helenium next to your chosen vase in order to achieve the correct height, then cut the stems at an angle and place in the vase. Position virginia creeper leaves around the top of the vase to frame the helenium.

2 Use two or three flowered stems of delphinium and also use the delicate tendrils of buds which are perfect for small arrangements. Prune the relatively large leaves of the campanula before adding. Finally, position the vine leaves around the base of the flowers in the neck of the vase, and finish off each vase with a raffia tie.

SUMMER BASKET DISPLAY

. . .

Summer brings an abundance of varied and beautiful material for the flower arranger. The lovely scents, luscious blooms and vast range of colours available provide endless possibilities for creating wonderful displays.

This arrangement is a bountiful basket, overflowing with seasonal summer blooms which is designed for a large table or sideboard but could be scaled up or down to suit any situation.

MATERIALS

. . .

basket

. . .

cellophane (plastic wrap)

. . .

scissors

. . .

2 blocks plastic foam

. . .

florist's adhesive tape

. . .

*10 stems Viburnum
tinus*

. . .

*15 stems larkspur
in 3 colours*

. . .

*6 lily stems, such as
'Stargazer'*

. . .

5 large ivy leaves

. . .

10 stems white phlox

Keep the display well watered and it should go on flowering for at least a week. The lilies should open fully in plastic foam and new phlox buds will keep opening to replace the spent heads.

1 Line the basket with cellophane (plastic wrap) to prevent leakage, and cut to fit. Then secure the two soaked blocks of plastic foam in the lined basket with the florist's adhesive tape.

2 Arrange the viburnum stems in the plastic foam to establish the overall height, width and shape. Strengthen the outline using the larkspur, making sure you use all of the stems and not just the flower spikes.

3 Place the lilies in a diagonal line across the arrangement. Position the large ivy leaves around the lilies in the centre of the display. Arrange the phlox across the arrangement along the opposite diagonal to the lilies.

EXOTIC TABLE ARRANGEMENT
. . .

MATERIALS

· · ·

wire mesh

· · ·

bowl

· · ·

*10 croton (Codiaeum)
leaves*

· · ·

*10 red Scarborough lily
flowers*

· · ·

5 cockscomb

· · ·

7 celosia heads

· · ·

7 glory lilies

· · ·

.71 wires

· · ·

1 mango

*When planning a table
arrangement, choose the
container with care. If the
container is too large it may
obstruct your guests' view
across the dinner table.*

This feast of red flowers and coloured foliage with its touches of yellow and green is bursting with exotic vibrance. The tiny flame-like petals of the glory lily set against the velvet texture of the celosia create a rich display of light and shade, and the bright yellow ceramic container heightens the overall impact. Use it as a focal point for an extravagant party table.

1 Scrunch up the wire mesh and place it in the bottom of the bowl. Fill approximately two-thirds with water. Position the croton leaves by pushing the stems of leaves into the wire mesh for support, creating a framework within which to build the arrangement.

2 Distribute the Scarborough lily flowers throughout the arrangement by pushing the stems into the wire mesh.

3 Cut the cockscomb to between 15 and 20 cm (6 and 8 in) long and ensure that all foliage is removed as this will rot in the water. Distribute evenly throughout the arrangement pushing the stems into the wire mesh.

4 Cut the glory lily flowers to between 15 and 20 cm (6 and 8 in) and push into the arrangement and through the wire mesh. Ensure you have an even spread of flowerheads throughout the arrangement.

5 Push .71 wires in pairs into the bottom of the mango and cut to between 15 and 20 cm (6 and 8 in). Carefully position the mango off-centre and slightly recessed in the arrangement by pushing the wires through into the wire mesh. Gently part the flowerheads to position the mango to ensure no flowers are damaged in the process. Finally, ensure all stems are in water.

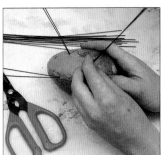

Take care when handling the mango to avoid bruising its delicate skin.

TULIP TOPIARY TREE
. . .

. . .

*1 block plastic foam for dried
flowers*

. . .

knife

. . .

basket

. . .

raffia

. . .

*5 30 cm (12 in) cinnamon
sticks*

. . .

scissors

. . .

glue gun and glue

. . .

.71 wires

. . .

reindeer moss

. . .

*1 plastic foam ball,
approximately 15 cm (6 in)
diameter*

. . .

open tulip heads

*T*o get the best result from the
flowerheads, they have been
spread open to reveal their
centres. This not only serves to
increase their visual impact but
also, of course, increases their
surface area which means fewer
blooms are needed.

The flowers used to make this stunning decorative tree are unlike conventional tulips which have only one layer of petals. These tulips have layer upon layer of different sized petals which together create a very dense, rounded head, reminiscent of a peony.

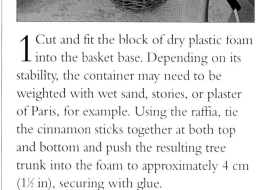

1 Cut and fit the block of dry plastic foam into the basket base. Depending on its stability, the container may need to be weighted with wet sand, stones, or plaster of Paris, for example. Using the raffia, tie the cinnamon sticks together at both top and bottom and push the resulting tree trunk into the foam to approximately 4 cm (1½ in), securing with glue.

2 Make hairpins out of the .71 wires and with these pin the reindeer moss into the plastic foam in the basket at the base of the tree, completely covering the dry plastic foam.

3 Soak the plastic foam ball in cold water. Carefully apply a small amount of hot glue to the top end of the cinnamon stick trunk and push the wet foam ball approximately 4 cm (1½ in) on to it.

4 Make sure that the flowerheads are as open as possible by holding the flower in your hand and gently spreading the petals back, even to the extent of folding those at the edge completely inside-out.

5 Cut the tulip heads with a stem length of approximately 4 cm (1½ in) and push them into the soaked foam ball, covering the surface evenly. Handle the flowerheads with care to avoid crushing.

LILY AND HYACINTH PLANTED BASKET

. . .

MATERIALS
. . .
large wire basket
. . .
bun or carpet moss
. . .
cellophane (plastic wrap)
. . .
scissors
. . .
3 flowering lily plants (3 stems per pot), such as 'Mona Lisa'
. . .
3 flowering hyacinth bulbs
. . .
8 red-barked dogwood (Cornus alba) branches (or similar)
. . .
raffia

When the budget is tight, an economic way of creating a large display with lots of impact is to use plants instead of cut flowers.

This arrangement in a basket combines two totally different plants, which will continue to flower for weeks. The lily buds will open in sequence and their scent, mixed with that of hyacinths, will fill the air with an intoxicating perfume.

The branches of red-barked dogwood are tied with raffia to form a decorative and supportive structure around the arrangement. A more formal look can be achieved by substituting bamboo canes, tied perhaps with strips of velvet in rich colours.

1 Line the whole basket with a layer of moss, then in turn line the moss with cellophane (plastic wrap) to contain the moisture. Cut to fit.

2 Using the soil from their pots, plant the three lilies into the lined basket, with the hyacinth bulbs between them. Cover the soil with moss.

3 Push four branches of dogwood through the moss and into the soil to form a square around the plants. Cross those horizontally with four more branches, tying them together with raffia to create a frame, then trim the raffia.

WHITE JAPANESE ANEMONE VASE

· · ·

This delightful arrangement combining forest fruits and rosehips with garden anemones, though simple in concept, becomes a sumptuous display when placed in this elegant vase.

MATERIALS

· · ·

vase

· · ·

scissors

· · ·

blackberries still on their stems

· · ·

rosehips on stems

· · ·

white Japanese anemones 'Honorine Jobert'

· · ·

vine leaves

The simplest things can be the most effective but when arranging flowers in water, without the help of plastic foam or wire mesh, it is important to consider very carefully the visual effect of the container on the flowers. The rosehips and blackberry stalks used here are very prickly; they need careful handling and the thorns need to be stripped. However, these stems form a strong framework to hold the delicate anemones in position. The addition of vine leaves around the neck of the vase provides a finishing touch for the arrangement.

1 Having filled the vase with water, use the blackberry stems to establish the outline shape. Add the stems of rosehips to reinforce both the structure and the visual balance of the display.

2 Add the anemones evenly throughout the arrangement. Take great care with anemones as they are extremely delicate.

3 Place the stems of the vine leaves in the water so that they form a collar around the base of the arrangement and are visible above the neck of the vase.

HYDRANGEA BASKET EDGING

· · ·

MATERIALS

· · ·

30 autumn leaves

· · ·

.71 wires

· · ·

scissors

· · ·

30 fresh late hydrangea heads

· · ·

basket

· · ·

.32 silver reel (rose) wire

Hydrangea heads cut late in their growing season have toughened and will not wilt out of water. These together with autumn leaves, selected so that they are pliable enough to wire, have been used in a floral decoration which can evolve from fresh to dry and remain attractive.

Take mature hydrangea heads and some autumn leaves, and with a little imagination an old wicker basket is transformed into a delightful container. Whether you fill it with fruit or seasonal pot pourri, this basket will make a decorative and long-lasting addition to your home.

1 Wire the leaves by stitching and double leg mounting on .71 wires.

2 Wire clusters of hydrangea by double leg mounting on .71 wires.

3 Secure the wired hydrangea clusters and leaves alternately around the basket edge by stitching through the gaps in the basket with .32 silver reel (rose) wire. Keep the clusters tightly together to ensure a full edging.

4 When the entire basket edge is covered, finish by stitching the .32 reel wire through several times. If the arrangement is placed in an airy position, the hydrangea heads will dry naturally and prolong the basket's use.

ORNAMENTAL CABBAGE TREE

· · ·

MATERIALS

· · ·

medium-sized terracotta pot

· · ·

cellophane (plastic wrap)

· · ·

sand

· · ·

*1 block plastic foam, for
dried flowers*

· · ·

knife

· · ·

scissors

· · ·

piece of tree root

· · ·

*2 large handfuls sphagnum
moss*

· · ·

twine

· · ·

.71 wires

· · ·

*10 miniature ornamental
cabbages*

*The tree "trunk" is simply a
piece of root, at the top of
which is fixed a moisture-
retaining ball of sphagnum
moss. The cabbage heads are
wired to the moss ball and, by
absorbing water from it and an
occasional mist spraying, will
survive for a week or more.*

Ornamental trees can be created from all sorts of materials for all sorts of decorative uses. This design might be thought unusual in that it uses cabbage heads to form a "topiary foliage" crown to the tree.

1 Line the medium-sized terracotta pot with cellophane (plastic wrap) and approximately half fill with wet sand for stability. Cut a piece of plastic foam and wedge it into the pot on top of the sand. Trim the cellophane if necessary.

2 Push the root into the plastic foam. Make sure you do this only once as repeated adjustments will loosen the grip of the foam and the "trunk" will not be stable. (Indeed, you could help make it more secure by placing some glue on the root base before pushing it into the foam.) Form a generous handful of sphagnum moss into a dense ball by criss-crossing it around with twine.

3 Push the moss ball on to the top of the root and secure it by threading wires horizontally through it, leaving the projecting ends to pull down and wrap around the "trunk".

4 Using .71 wires, double leg mount the miniature ornamental cabbage heads and individually stitch wire any loose cabbage leaves.

5 Push the wires projecting from the cabbage heads into the moss ball to cover it completely. Fill any gaps with the individual leaves.

6 Make hairpin shapes from .71 wires to fix sphagnum moss to the plastic foam at the base of the tree making sure it is completely covered.

SUNFLOWER PINHOLDER DISPLAY

• • •

MATERIALS

• • •

low ceramic dish

• • •

pinholder

• • •

scissors

• • •

3-5 stems contorted hazel twigs

• • •

9 stems sunflowers

• • •

5 large ivy leaves

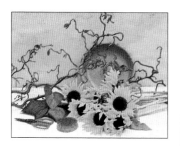

The pinholder enables the flower arranger to create beautiful and simple designs without the need for a large container.
The pinholder is weighted so that even the top-heavy sunflowers in this arrangement are totally stable once their stems are pushed onto the metal pins.

This pinholder display results in an informal and minimalist grouping whose glorious sunflowers, set against a backdrop of contorted hazel, shine out undiminished by the clutter of other flowers.

1 Fill the dish with sufficient water to cover the pinholder. Cut the stems of hazel and push them on to the pins to create a tall outline shape.

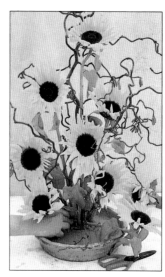

2 Position the sunflowers, pushing the cut stems on to the pins. Grade the flowers according to the size of their heads. The smallest heads should be on the tallest stems at the top of the arrangement, with the larger heads on shorter stems towards the focal point. Create a staggered line of blooms from top to bottom. Recess a couple of flowerheads and bring the line of flowers over the front of the container to one side, following the outline formed by the contorted hazel.

3 Position the ivy leaves around the focal flower at the centre and add others low down in the display. The leaves will help give visual depth and their dark, green colour will be a suitable background for the bright yellow of the flowers.

YELLOW CALLA LILY ARRANGEMENT

· · ·

This display highlights the striking beauty of the calla lily. It ingeniously exploits the visual power of the almost luminescent golden-yellow blooms of this flower by setting them against a carefully controlled background of blue and green accompanying material.

The chincherinchees have cool green stems and creamy white flowerheads with beady black centres which give interest as well as height to the arrangement.

The viburnum is used as a framework for the display and its metallic blue berries provide a visual bridge between the two flowers it accompanies.

MATERIALS
· · ·
shallow dish
· · ·
pinholder
· · ·
scissors
· · ·
*10 stems viburnum
berries*
· · ·
*11 stems Moroccan
chincherinchee
(Ornithogalum arabicum)*
· · ·
*5 stems yellow calla
lily*

1 Fill the shallow dish with sufficient water to cover the pinholder when placed within it. Arrange the viburnum by pushing the cut stem ends down onto the pins and use this foliage to create the outline shape of the display and establish its height and width.

2 Arrange the chincherinchees on the pins to run diagonally through the viburnum foliage outline, varying the stem heights.

The whole arrangement is mounted on a pinholder which becomes almost invisible, so avoiding the distraction of a container.

3 Arrange the calla lilies on the pins. Roughly follow an "S" shape, with the smallest bloom on the longest stem at the back, working forwards and down with larger blooms on shorter stems.

AUTUMN CROCUS TRUG

· · ·

MATERIALS

· · ·

trug

· · ·

cellophane (plastic wrap)

· · ·

6 flowering crocus bulbs

· · ·

bun moss

· · ·

autumn leaves

· · ·

raffia

· · ·

scissors

Although one expects to see crocuses in the spring, this beautiful autumn variety is a welcome sight as its flowers push up determinedly through the fallen leaves. Of course, they do not have to be confined to the garden.

Bring the outdoors inside by plant-ing up an old trug with flowering crocus bulbs in soil covered in a natural-looking carpet of moss and leaves. This simple display is as effective as the most sophisticated cut-flower arrangement.

1 Line the trug with cellophane (plastic wrap) and plant the bulbs in soil.

2 Ensure the bulbs are firmly planted and watered. Arrange the bun moss on top of the soil, then scatter the leaves over the moss to create an autumnal effect.

3 Tie raffia into bows, one on either side of the base of the trug handle.

AUTUMN CANDLE DISPLAY
· · ·

· · ·

1 block plastic foam

· · ·

1 metal candleholder

· · ·

6 crab apples

· · ·

1 small pumpkin

· · ·

*3 Chinese lantern
heads*

· · ·

.71 wires, .38 wires

· · ·

scissors

· · ·

hypericum buds

· · ·

2 stems spray roses

· · ·

1 beeswax candle

*Beeswax candles have an
attractive texture and natural
honey colouring which are the
perfect accompaniment for this
seasonal rustic display.*

The autumn fruits of Chinese lanterns, crab apples and baby pumpkins are put to good use in this charming and compact candle decoration. The natural rich colouring of the fruits and the deep red of the hypericum buds complement beautifully the soft apricot tones of the spray roses.

1 Soak the plastic foam in water and cut it into small pieces to fit into the candleholder drip tray. Firmly wedge into the drip tray to support the arrangement.

2 Wire the crab apples and pumpkin on .71 wires and Chinese lantern heads on .38 wires. All wires should be cut to approximately 4 cm (1½ in) in length.

3 By pushing wires into the foam, position the pumpkin, 2 groups of 3 crab apples and a group of 3 Chinese lantern heads, spacing them equally around the circumference of the drip tray.

4 Arrange the hypericum foliage between the fruits by pushing short stems into the plastic foam to create the outline shape of the display.

5 Cut flowerheads from the spray roses on stems long enough to push into the plastic foam amongst the foliage and fruits. Use rose buds towards the outside edge of the arrangement, and more open blooms towards the centre. Remember to ensure that there is enough space left to accommodate the beeswax candle.

Never leave burning candles unattended and do not allow them to burn down to within 5 cm (2 in) of the display height.

BLUE AND YELLOW ARRANGEMENT IN A PITCHER

• • •

MATERIALS

• • •

*10 stems 'Blue Butterfly'
delphinium*

• • •

*2 bunches sneezeweed
(Helenium)*

• • •

3 stems dracaena

• • •

raffia

• • •

scissors

• • •

pitcher

*The choice of container is
important since it becomes a
major element in the design.
The yellow pitcher gives the
display a country look, but of
course the same arrangement
would look more sophisticated
if the container was a
contemporary glass vase.*

The sunny yellow faces of sneezeweed become almost luminous when set against the electric blue colour of 'Blue Butterfly' delphinium, a brave colour combination guaranteed to brighten any situation. The easy-to-make, hand-tied spiral bunch is designed to look as though the flowers have just been cut and loosely arranged.

1 Lay out the materials for ease of working. Build the display by alternately adding stems of different material while continuously turning the growing bunch in your hand so that the stems form a spiral.

2 Continue the process until all materials are used and you have a full display of flowers. At the binding point, i.e. where all the stems cross, tie firmly with raffia. Trim the stem ends to the length dictated by the container.

LARGE DAHLIA ARRANGEMENT

• • •

Dahlias bloom vigorously all through the summer and until the first frosts of autumn, offering dazzling variations of colour and shape for the flower arranger. The complex and precise geometry of the dahlia flowerheads ensures that, even with the informality of the bright red rosehips and softness of the campanulas, the arrangement retains a structured feel.

MATERIALS

• • •

large, watertight pot

• • •

15 stems campanula

• • •

scissors

• • •

*10 stems long-stemmed
rosehips*

• • •

30 stems pompom dahlias

These beautiful golden dahlias have clean, long straight stems which makes them easy to arrange in a large display. They would also survive well in plastic foam.

1 Fill the pot three-quarters full with water. Create the basic domed outline and the structure using the leafy campanula.

2 Cut and strip the thorns from the stems of the rosehips and arrange in amongst the campanula, varying the heights as required to follow the domed outline.

3 Cut the pompom dahlias to the required heights and add to the arrangement, distributing them evenly throughout. The aim is to achieve a smooth domed effect.

MANTELPIECE ARRANGEMENT
. . .

MATERIALS
. . .
1 block plastic foam
. . .
plastic tray for plastic foam
. . .
florist's adhesive tape
. . .
scissors
. . .
5 stems birch twigs
. . .
6 stems butcher's broom
(Ruscus)
. . .
5 stems Eupohorbia
fulgens
. . .
7 stems straight amaranthus
. . .
5 stems spray chrysanthemums
. . .
5 stems alstroemeria
. . .
7 stems eustoma

On its own, or combined with a fireplace arrangement (pictured opposite and featured over the page), this mantelpiece arrangement creates a stunning focal point to a room.

The mantelpiece offers a prominent position for a floral display. The challenge is to create not just a visual balance, but a physical balance too. The mantel shelf is relatively narrow and flowers must be carefully positioned to avoid them toppling forwards. So, as you build, ensure stability by keeping the weight at the back and as near the bottom of the display as is practical.

The delicate stems of butcher's broom and euphorbia fulgens are lightweight in relation to their length and thus ideal for this type of arrangement. Their natural trailing habit means they can be positioned to give width along the shelf and length over its front edge and, together with birch twigs, they give the display its structure. The addition of a selection of strongly coloured flowers brings the arrangement vibrantly alive.

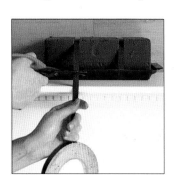  

1 Soak the block of plastic foam in cold water and securely tape into the plastic tray with florist's adhesive tape. Position the tray at the centre of the mantelpiece.

2 Arrange the birch twigs and butcher's broom in the plastic foam to establish height and width. Take advantage of the natural curving habit of the broom to trail over the container.

3 Add the euphorbia fulgens to emphasize the trailing nature of the display. Distribute the amaranthus throughout the display to reinforce the established shape.

4 The spray chrysanthemums are the focal flowers and should be roughly staggered to either side of the vertical axis at the centre of the display. The alstroemeria stems add strength and, by recessing one or two of them, depth to the arrangement.

5 A stem of good quality eustoma has two to three side stems. Split these off to make the most of the flowers. Use budded stems towards the outside of the display and more open blooms towards its centre, making sure some are recessed to give visual depth.

FIREPLACE ARRANGEMENT
• • •

MATERIALS
• • •
2 blocks plastic foam
• • •
1 plastic-lined basket
• • •
florist's adhesive tape
• • •
scissors
• • •
10 stems butcher's broom
(Ruscus)
• • •
6 stems birch twigs
• • •
10 stems Euphorbia
fulgens
• • •
5 stems orange lilies
• • •
5 stems red alstroemeria
• • •
5 stems spray
chrysanthemums
• • •
10 stems orange tulips
• • •
10 stems eustoma

A fireplace is the focal point of a room, but without a fire, an empty grate can be an eyesore. Turn this to your advantage by filling the hearth with an arrangement of flowers.

In the absence of real flames, this display substitutes the bright, fiery reds, oranges and yellows of euphorbia fulgens, alstroemeria, tulips, lilies and chrysanthemums. This colour palette is given depth and richness by the purple of eustoma. The languid forms of butcher's broom, with the stark outlines of birch twigs, define the architecture of the arrangement.

1 Soak the plastic foam in water and secure in the basket using florist's adhesive tape. Place the basket in the grate of the fireplace.

2 Arrange the butcher's broom and the birch twigs to create a foliage outline, taking advantage of the natural curves of the broom to achieve a flowing effect.

3 Use the euphorbia fulgens to reinforce the outline and define the height of the display. The lilies are the focal flowers and should be arranged to follow roughly a diagonal through the display. The alstroemeria should be positioned to follow the opposite diagonal. Decrease the length of the stems of both flowers from the rear to the front.

4 Arrange the spray chrysanthemums, approximately following, and thus reinforcing, the line of lilies. Again reduce the chrysanthemum stem height from rear to front. Finally, distribute the tulips and eustoma evenly through the arrangement using the most open of the eustoma blooms towards the centre.

ARUM LILY VASE

. . .

Pure in colour and form, elegant and stately, the arum lily has the presence to be displayed on its own, supported by the minimum of well-chosen foliage. Here it is arranged with the wonderfully curious contorted willow and the large, simple leaves of aucuba. Because they do not compete visually, the willow and the aucuba serve purely as a backdrop to the beauty of the arum.

MATERIALS

. . .

vase

. . .

scissors

. . .

*branches of contorted
willow*

. . .

6 arum lilies

. . .

*2 bushy branches aucuba
'Gold Dust'*

1 Fill the vase to approximately three-quarters with water. Arrange the contorted willow in the vase to establish the overall height of the arrangement. (When cutting a willow stem to the right length, cut the base at a 45° angle and scrape the bark off to approximately 5 cm (2 in) from the end, then split this section.)

The choice of container is of great importance, the visual requirement being for simple unfussy shapes, with glass and metal being particularly appropriate. The chosen vase should complement the sculptural impact of the arum.

2 Arrange the arum lilies at different heights throughout the willow to achieve a visual balance. The willow stems will help support the blooms.

3 Give visual substance to the display by adding stems of aucuba throughout to provide a dark backdrop to throw the arum blooms into sharp relief.

CANDELABRA TABLE DECORATION
· · ·

MATERIALS
· · ·

candelabra

· · ·

plastic foam ring,
30 cm (12 in) in diameter

· · ·

scissors

· · ·

20 short stems Viburnum
tinus, *in flower*

· · ·

20 short stems variegated
pieris

· · ·

15 heads Easter lily

· · ·

10 stems purple aster

· · ·

3 trails (sprigs) variegated ivy

*N*ever leave burning candles
unattended and do not allow
them to burn down to within
less than 5 cm (2 in) of the
display height.

The classic combination of flowers and candlelight is usually associated with romantic dinners for two. However, this candelabra table decoration is appropriate to a variety of special dining occasions. Stately candles floating on a sumptuous sea of white lilies and purple asters make a decoration suitable for even the most formal of events.

1 Soak the plastic foam ring in cold water and position the candelabra within the ring. As the arrangement will eventually involve ivy being attached to both the candelabra and ring, it is advisable to create this display *in situ*. Using approximately 10 cm (4 in) long stems of viburnum and variegated pieris, push into the foam to create an even foliage outline.

2 Cut the lily heads leaving about 7.5 cm (3 in) of stem to push into the foam. Group the heads in threes around the circumference of the foam ring. Generally the groups should have one open bloom placed towards the centre with two buds at the outside edge of the ring. But in so doing, remember buds will open in 24 hours to fill the areas.

3 Aster flowers usually have a sturdy main stem and several side stems with flowerheads which should be separated. Cut all the aster stems to approximately 10 cm (4 in) lengths, and distribute evenly through the arrangement, pushing firmly into the plastic foam.

4 Ivy will survive out of water for a time but to ensure it remains in good condition for the life of the decoration, push the cut end of the trail (sprig) into the soaked plastic foam before entwining it around the candelabra. For safety reasons, do not allow any ivy leaves to come up over the candleholder's wax guards.

ORANGE ARRANGEMENT
. . .

. . .

wire basket

. . .

reindeer moss

. . .

cellophane (plastic wrap)

. . .

1 block plastic foam

. . .

knife

. . .

florist's adhesive tape

. . .

scissors

. . .

10 stems salal tips

. . .

7 stems orange lily

. . .

10 stems orange tulip

. . .

20 stems marigold

The matt green of salal tips creates the perfect background for the spectacular zesty orange colour of the three different flowers used in this display. The arrangement is a dome of flowers supported in plastic foam in a wire basket.

1 Line the basket with a layer of reindeer moss, about 3 cm (1½ in) thick, and line the moss with cellophane (plastic wrap). Cut a block of water-soaked plastic foam to fit the basket and tape securely in place.

2 Push the salal tips into the plastic foam to create a dome-shaped foliage outline in proportion with the container. Salal tips have relatively large rounded leaves which generally should be used sparingly to avoid overwhelming the flowers. However, the strength of the colour and shape of the flowers in this particular arrangement works well with the bold salal leaves.

3 Cut the lily stems to a length to suit the foliage framework and push into the foam evenly throughout the arrangement to reinforce the overall shape.

4 Distribute the tulips evenly through the display, remembering they will continue to grow and their natural downward curve will tend to straighten.

5 Add the marigolds last, positioning them evenly throughout the display. Remember the marigold stems are soft, so take care when pushing them into the plastic foam.

There are two points worth remembering. First the tulips will continue to grow and straighten in the plastic foam, so make allowance for this in your dome shape; second, any buds on the lilies will open, so give them the space to do so.

DECORATED VASE WITH CALLA LILIES

· · ·

MATERIALS

· · ·

*a selection of lichen-covered
twigs*

· · ·

glass vase

· · ·

raffia

· · ·

scissors

· · ·

10 red antirrhinums

· · ·

15 calla lilies

· · ·

3 calla lily leaves

By making the twigs project above the top of the vase, they become an integral part of the arrangement and provide helpful support for the flowers. An alternative look could be created by gluing the heads of dried flowers, such as sunflowers, all over a plain glass vase.

A novel and simple way to transform a container is to decorate its outside with organic material. This example uses lichen-covered twigs and is particularly practical since after the arrangement in the vase has died the twigs will have dried out and, with careful handling, can be kept on the vase for the next display.

1 The twigs have to be fixed securely to the vase. To do this, make two lengths of bundles of raffia and lay on these sufficient twigs to go around the circumference of the vase. Place the vase on its side, on the twigs, and tie firmly with the lengths of raffia. Trim the twig stems level with the base of the vase.

2 Stand the vase upright and three-quarter fill with water. Begin with the red antirrhinums, placing them towards the back to establish the height and width of the arrangement's framework.

3 Distribute the calla lily blooms evenly throughout the arrangement, varying their heights to achieve a visual balance and a good profile. Add the calla lily leaves diagonally through the arrangement, reducing their height from the back to the front. This will visually emphasize the depth of the arrangement.

WINTER TWIGS ARRANGEMENT

. . .

Cut flowers can be expensive during the winter months but this does not mean flower arranging has to stop. This display is created from the types of winter growth found in domestic gardens. It is simple to arrange and offers a scale suitable to decorate a large space.

Delicate lichen softens the otherwise rough branches of larch while the beautiful and scented winter-flowering viburnum adds a touch of spring. Finally the deep red stems of red-barked dogwood provide a strength of colour which will persist throughout the life of the display and even beyond if dried.

MATERIALS

. . .

*5 stems lichen-covered larch
twigs*

. . .

scissors and secateurs

. . .

large ceramic pot

. . .

*5-10 stems red-barked
dogwood*

. . .

10 stems Viburnum x
bodnantense *'Dawn'*

1 Cut the larch twigs so that the majority are at the maximum height of the display, and arrange to the outline shape. The container should be about one-third of the overall display height.

2 Cut the red-barked dogwood and arrange amongst the larch twigs so that the stems at the rear of the display are at their maximum height, becoming shorter towards the front.

As a general rule when using twigs, remember to strip the stem ends of bark and lichen otherwise they will rot, accelerate the formation of bacteria, shorten the life of the display and very quickly cause the water to smell.

3 Add the flowering viburnum, again varying its length from tall at the rear to shorter at the front. To avoid rotting, be sure to strip off all bark and flowers from the stem ends in the water and split any thick woody stems to allow water in.

HERB OBELISK

· · ·

MATERIALS

· · ·

ruler

· · ·

pencil

· · ·

1 block plastic foam

· · ·

sharp knife

· · ·

suitable container

· · ·

7 radishes

· · ·

8 button mushrooms

· · ·

9 small, clean new potatoes

· · ·

.71 wires

· · ·

scissors

· · ·

dill

· · ·

curry plant

· · ·

marjoram

· · ·

mint

· · ·

bay leaves

The urn container gives the obelisk a grand look, but a less formal, more rustic feel can be achieved by using a terracotta plant pot or mossy basket.

A colourful pillar of herbs and vegetables which looks wonderful on its own and even more striking when used in pairs. It is particularly suitable for a buffet table decoration but can also be used simply as a decorative object in any appropriate setting.

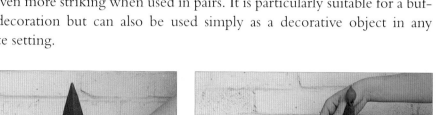

1 Using a ruler and pencil score the cutting lines on the block of plastic foam. Carve the block to the required shape using a sharp knife. Soak the carved plastic foam shape and secure firmly in your chosen container.

2 Wire all the vegetables by pushing a .71 wire through from one side to the other, leaving sufficient wire projecting on both sides to allow you to pull down and out of the base to approximately 4 cm (1½ in). Mushrooms are very fragile and particular care must be taken when wiring these. Having decided on the order you want to use the vegetables, work from the bottom of the obelisk upwards, pushing the wires into the plastic foam to position the vegetables in horizontal rings around the shape.

3 Fill in the gaps between rings of vegetables, using a different herb for each ring. Finally select a quantity of bay leaves of similar size and insert them into the plastic foam under the bottom layer of vegetables to create a formal border.

Right: Detail of the final arrangement

PARROT TULIP CANDLE DECORATION

· · ·

MATERIALS

· · ·

*plastic foam ring, 15 cm (6 in)
diameter, and holder*

· · ·

*candle, 7.5 x 22.5 cm
(3 x 9 in)*

· · ·

scissors

· · ·

*approximately 7-8 very open
'Parrot' tulip heads*

*Other flowers, such as roses
and buttercups can, when their
flowerheads are full, have their
useful lives extended by the use
of this technique.*
*Never leave a burning candle
unattended and do not allow it
to burn down to within less
than 5 cm (2 in) of the
display height.*

There is a tendency to think that a fully opened bloom is at the end of its useful life. However, these Parrot tulip heads have had their lives extended by the simple process of shortening their stems. The red and yellow of the spreading petals of these tulips create an impression of flames licking up the candle.

1 Soak the plastic foam ring in water and position the candle at its centre. Check that the candle is firmly in position.

2 Cut the tulips to a stem length of approximately 3 cm (1¼ in) and push them into the plastic foam. Repeat this around the entire ring making sure no foam is left exposed.

BERRIED CANDLE DECORATION

• • •

Acommercially-produced red candle in an earthenware pot can be made into a sumptuous table decoration by embellishing it with fruits and foliage from the garden and hedge. This is a technically simple, yet effective, decoration involving sitting the pot in a small wire basket through which the stems of fruit and foliage are artfully woven.

MATERIALS
• • •
candle in an earthenware pot
• • •
small square wire basket, to accommodate the pot
• • •
Virginia creeper leaves on stems
• • •
blackberry clusters on stems
• • •
scissors
• • •
rosehip clusters on stems
• • •
.32 silver reel (rose) wire

1 Place the candle pot in the wire basket. Weave Virginia creeper stems through the wire basket around its entire top edge. Then establish a thick garland of Virginia creeper leaves around the basket.

2 For safe handling strip the thorns from the blackberry stems and cut to approximately 6 cm (2 in) long. Push the stems into the Virginia creeper garland and through the wire basket.

The plant materials used are robust enough to survive in good condition for a day or two out of water but would benefit from mist spraying. Never leave burning candles unattended and do not allow them to burn down to within 5 cm (2 in) of the display.

3 Using the same procedure, add the rosehips but in separate small groups around the circumference of the basket. If the decoration is likely to be moved, it is safer to provide additional security for the stems by tying them to the basket with lengths of fine silver reel (rose) wire.

SECTION THREE

...

POTS OF INSPIRATION

...

Whatever the occasion or the season,
flowers always look good in a traditional
terracotta plant pot. Choose between abundant
country-style displays, reminiscent of summer
gardens, or more formal geometric shapes. Pots
are also ideal for standing candles in; place them
singly or group several candle pots together to
welcome your guests and create a
festive atmosphere.

INTRODUCTION
. . .

*Above: Rose-perfumed
Candle Pots*

Below: Winter Candle Pot

Pots are extremely versatile and can be highly decorative. You can fill a whole pot with bunches of colourful flowers, or with subtle autumnal arrangements of woodland materials. There are various ways of holding the materials in place, some very simple and others more professional. The following projects show examples of different florists' techniques, for example using plastic foam and wires, to create the desired effect.

Antique earthenware and terracotta pots have a warmth and texture which perfectly complement natural materials. If you cannot find any suitable old pots, choose good-quality hand-thrown modern pots and leave them outdoors to weather for a while. To match a dark wood table, you can stain the pot dark brown. Terracotta pots often have rough bases so you will probably need to glue felt on the bottom to protect a table surface.

For some displays, glazed china pots may be suitable and it is worth keeping your eye open for different containers. For variety, you may find that a particular arrangement looks very handsome and modern in a shiny galvanized container.

Moss is used in many of the pots, sometimes as a feature of the display but also to hide the fixings or the foam base. Use it generously in handfuls as it will shrink slightly as it dries. There are various kinds of moss, just as there are endless

Above: Simply Roses

Left: Floral Candle Pot

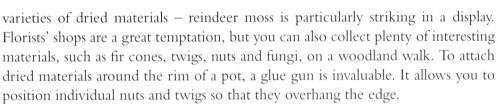

varieties of dried materials – reindeer moss is particularly striking in a display. Florists' shops are a great temptation, but you can also collect plenty of interesting materials, such as fir cones, twigs, nuts and fungi, on a woodland walk. To attach dried materials around the rim of a pot, a glue gun is invaluable. It allows you to position individual nuts and twigs so that they overhang the edge.

The following projects illustrate a range of decorative arrangements which complement pots. As well as informal mixed arrangements, there are also instructions for making elegant structures such as a pyramid of fir cones.

Alternatively, you can make a collar or border to fit round the edge of the pot, leaving the centre space empty for a candle. Decorate the border with fir cones and nuts, or dried flowers and herbs, to create a magical effect in the candlelight. These candle pots are perfect for dinner parties or special occasions. For safety's sake, be careful to keep the dried materials away from the base of the candle, and never leave the candle or candles burning unattended.

Below: Hot Chillies

Candle pots especially look wonderful if you spray the dried materials with clear florist's lacquer so they shine in the light. For an occasion such as Christmas, you can also frost the display lightly with gold, white or silver spray paint.

The displays on the following pages will also give you plenty of inspiration for your own ideas. There are pots here for every room in the house and garden, even a seashell pot for the bathroom.

BUNCHES OF ROSES

• • •

You can, of course, use a combination of any two colours from the many different roses available.

A single dried material often looks its best displayed on its own, without any other decoration. Here peachy-pink and yellow roses are very simply arranged in a terracotta pot. The same technique can be used with a selection of materials, such as lavender or oregano for a scented variation. Flower pot displays are some of the most basic designs, but they can be extremely attractive.

1 Trim the foam to fit snugly into the pot. Cut off any excess foam so that it aligns smoothly with the top of the pot. Press it down into the base of the pot so that it is just below the rim.

2 Steam the roses if they look a little old and dull. Lay out the roses in a pile on a clean surface and trim the rose stems to an even length.

3 Wire the roses into small bunches of 3–4 flowers (see Techniques). Leaving an empty outer ring of foam, press the roses firmly into the centre of the foam, positioning them quite closely together.

4 Fix handfuls of moss into the foam around the flowers, using mossing (floral) pins or wires bent into U-shapes. The moss should just cover the edge of the pot.

OLD-FASHIONED POSY POT

· · ·

Dried flowers often look their best when the blooms are massed together and the stalks are not too prominent. In this charming, traditional treatment, rosebuds and lavender are tucked into a tiny terracotta pot. A trailing raffia bow makes a perfect finishing touch to the arrangement.

MATERIALS

· · ·

knife

· · ·

1 block plastic foam for dried
flowers

· · ·

small terracotta pot

· · ·

dried rosebuds

· · ·

scissors

· · ·

dried lavender

· · ·

dyed raffia

· · ·

glue gun and glue sticks

Sweet-smelling lavender and roses have been a favourite combination for many centuries.

1 Trim the foam to fit snugly into the pot. Push the rosebuds into the foam around the edge of the pot.

2 Cut the lavender stalks to about 1 cm (½ in) and use them to fill the centre of the arrangement. Tie a raffia bow around the pot and secure at the back with glue.

SIMPLY ROSES

• • •

MATERIALS

• • •

knife

• • •

*1 block plastic foam for dried
flowers*

• • •

terracotta pot

• • •

about 30 dried roses

• • •

scissors

• • •

moss

• • •

*glue gun and glue sticks
or .91 wires*

*Pink and red roses are a
striking colour combination.*

For a large display, you do not need to wire roses into bunches. Instead, place them carefully in the foam one at a time, spacing them well to create a good balance. For a really stunning effect, use different combinations of size and colour, and try to retain as much of the green leaf as possible.

1 Cut the foam to fit the pot. Press it firmly down into the pot. Trim the top of the foam so that the foam and the top of the pot are level.

2 Steam the roses (see Techniques). Trim the stalks to different lengths, this way the flowerheads will not obscure or crowd each other.

3 Starting in the centre of the foam, press in the tallest rose. Work outwards, continuing to add the stems gradually, one by one.

4 Continue to press the roses into the pot. If you are using more than one size and colour, keep checking to ensure that you have a good balance over the whole display.

5 Attach moss around the base of the roses using a glue gun. Alternatively, you could bend short wires to form U-shaped staples and push them into the foam to trap the moss.

LAVENDER POT

· · ·

MATERIALS

· · ·

scissors

· · ·

20–25 stalks dried lavender

· · ·

small terracotta pot

· · ·

.91 wires

· · ·

knife

· · ·

1 block plastic foam for dried flowers

· · ·

glue gun, mossing (floral) pins or .91 wires

· · ·

moss

The beautiful colour of lavender will fade if it is exposed to too much light so place the pot away from direct sunlight.

Lavender is rich and dramatically coloured enough to warrant displaying all by itself. You can use any variety but the deeper the colour, the more impact it will make. If the lavender's powerful scent fades in time, you can easily bring it back by adding just a few drops of perfumed oil to the display. Add the oil to the moss at the base for the best results.

1 Trim the lavender stalks so that the heads will all come just above the rim of the pot and the bunch is even.

2 Wire together three small bunches each of about 6–8 lavender stalks (see Techniques).

3 Cut three small wedges of foam. Place one in the base of the pot then place the lavender bunches together in the centre. Press the other wedges down each side to hold the lavender in place. The foam should be about 1 cm (½ in) below the rim of the pot.

4 Glue the moss over the top of the foam, around the lavender. Alternatively, you can attach the moss in place with mossing (floral) pins or short wires bent into U-shapes.

RUSTIC POT

· · ·

MATERIALS

· · ·

knife

· · ·

1 block plastic foam for dried flowers

· · ·

terracotta pot

· · ·

silver reel (rose) wire

· · ·

hay

· · ·

scissors

· · ·

dried yellow roses

· · ·

dried poppy seed heads

· · ·

.91 wires

· · ·

raffia

For a more sophisticated look, replace the raffia with a paper or fabric bow.

This unusual pot has a pleasing dishevelled appearance, with a layer of hay attached to the outside. It is tied with a large, natural raffia bow that covers the wire nicely, and would look wonderful on a dresser or kitchen cabinet. Attach the hay with glue over the wire, if you wish.

1 Cut the foam to fit the pot and press firmly in. Tightly wrap silver reel (rose) wire two to three times around the pot near the top to secure the wire so that it does not slip when you add the hay.

2 Lay the pot on its side and wire on the hay in generous amounts, trapping it tightly. When the pot is covered, tie the end of the wire as tightly as possible. Trim the hay with scissors so that the base of the pot shows. Don't trim the top.

3 Wire the roses and poppies separately into small bunches, leaving long stems (see Techniques). Fill the centre of the pot with flowers and seed heads and finish with a raffia bow.

HAYFIELD POT
. . .

This country-style pot has a pleasingly dishevelled appearance, created by a tangled layer of hay attached to the outside. If you wish to be certain that the hay will not fall off, you can apply glue over the wire and into the hay.

MATERIALS
. . .
knife
. . .
1 block plastic foam for dried flowers
. . .
terracotta pot
. . .
silver reel (rose) wire
. . .
hay
. . .
scissors
. . .
dried red roses
. . .
dried poppy seed heads
. . .
raffia

Vibrant red roses could be combined with faded pink varieties for a romantic finish.

1 Trim the foam to fit snugly into the pot. Tightly wrap the silver reel (rose) wire several times around the pot near the top to secure. Lay the pot on its side and wire on the hay in generous handfuls, tightly trapping it under the wire.

2 When the pot is covered, tie the end of the wire as tightly as possible. Trim the hay from the base of the pot. Wire the roses and poppies separately into small bunches, leaving long stems so they show above the hay (see Techniques). Fill the centre of the pot with the flowers. Tie a raffia bow around the pot.

LAVENDER BLUE

· · ·

MATERIALS

· · ·

2 blocks plastic foam for dried flowers

· · ·

knife

· · ·

shallow terracotta pot

· · ·

.91 wires

· · ·

glue gun and glue sticks

· · ·

dried lavender

· · ·

scissors

The tiny blue-mauve lavender flowerheads look wonderful massed together with no other decoration.

What could be simpler than a terracotta pot tightly packed with sweet-smelling lavender? This arrangement is best viewed from above, so place it low down such as underneath a glass-topped coffee table. You can dry your own lavender from the garden or use a smaller pot if you want to keep costs down.

1 Place the two blocks of foam side by side and cut out a rounded shape that will fit into the pot. Wire together with pins made of bent wire. Apply glue to the underside of the foam. Lift the foam carefully and place glue-side down into the container, pressing firmly until secure. Wedge small pieces of discarded foam around the edge and fasten in position with wire pins.

2 Sort the lavender into small bunches. Level up the heads using the palm of one hand. Holding each bunch tightly, cut the stalks, leaving about 2.5 cm (1 in), and wire tightly (see Techniques).

3 Insert a bunch of wired lavender against the edge of the bowl. The heads should protrude about 1 cm (½ in) above the rim. Place each bunch tightly against the previous one, and at the same level.

4 Work around the pot until the whole surface is covered completely. Trim the lavender carefully with scissors to achieve a perfectly flat surface.

GRAND SUMMER POT
· · ·

This flamboyant display looks best when crammed full of summer flowers. Only two varieties are used here – deep yellow solidago and tiny pink miniature roses. Some of the roses were dried while still in bud, which adds a little green to the colour scheme. When planning the colour scheme, work out in advance where you are going to put the finished pot and choose your flowers and foliage so that they complement the surroundings.

MATERIALS
· · ·
knife
· · ·
2 blocks plastic foam for dried flowers
· · ·
large terracotta pot
· · ·
.91 wires
· · ·
dried flowers of your choice
· · ·
scissors

Follow the yellow and pink colour scheme shown here, or use your own choice of flowers.

1 Trim the foam so that it fits tightly into the pot. Cut a second piece of foam about half the height of the pot and a slightly smaller diameter. Fix to the lower piece of foam by placing on top and pushing U-shaped wires through.

2 Trim the flowers to about 10 cm (4 in) in length. Wire them in single varieties or as mixed bunches (see Techniques).

3 Push a bunch at a time into the foam, starting at the recessed rim and working across the top to the other side to create the large domed effect. If you are using bunches of one variety, place the filler-type materials into the foam first to establish the background colour. Keep large-headed flowers, such as roses and peonies, until the end. Turn your work regularly to check the balance.

HOT CHILLIES

· · ·

MATERIALS

· · ·

knife

· · ·

*1 block plastic foam for dried
flowers*

· · ·

galvanized container

· · ·

moss

· · ·

florist's tape (stem-wrap tape)

· · ·

mossing (floral) pins

· · ·

.91 wires

· · ·

creamy white candle

· · ·

dried red chillies

*Dried chillies look very
dramatic in any display,
especially here where they
are used on their own.*

Like spurting hot flames, dried chilli peppers make a fiery display which would be ideally suited to a modern interior. The galvanized container and creamy white candle contrast beautifully with the rich red chillies. For a more earthy, natural look you can use a traditional terracotta pot. Wash your hands when you have finished in case they have come in contact with any hot chilli seeds.

1 Cut the foam to fit comfortably inside the container. It should stand at least 2 cm (³/₄ in) above the rim. Wedge it inside with small offcuts of foam then fill the gaps with moss, packing it in tightly.

2 Wire the candle in the centre of the foam (see Techniques). Cover the foam around the candle with moss to create a mound, securing it with pins made from bent wires.

3 Wire the chillies firmly in groups of three (see Techniques).

4 Look carefully at the way the chillies bend before inserting them evenly around the base of the candle.

5 Complete the garland of chillies, readjusting the bunches if necessary.

SIMPLE CANDLE POT

· · ·

MATERIALS

· · ·

small terracotta pot

· · ·

sphagnum moss

· · ·

cream candle

The cream candle will give guests a warm welcome at Christmas, but you can also use red or green candles and decorate the lantern with a bunch of holly.

The most basic materials are used to great effect in this simple-to-make candle pot. Display it in an outside lantern where the flickering light will provide subtle, ambient lighting for hours. Candle pots also look particularly effective arranged in small groups. Remember never to leave burning candles unattended.

1 Fill the base of the pot with moss to about halfway up. Do not disentangle any twigs or natural debris from the moss – they will add to the overall effect.

2 Stand the candle in the middle of the pot then push more moss all around it. Press down firmly so that the moss holds the candle in place. Reduce the pressure near the rim of the pot so that the moss spills over the edge.

WOODLAND CANDLE POT
· · ·

Fir cones and small bundles of twigs make a simple and satisfying decoration for a candle pot. They can easily be collected on a winter's walk. For this display, open fir cones are used to give an attractive texture, but the variation shows how nice other materials look. Never leave a burning candle unattended.

MATERIALS
· · ·
moss
· · ·
terracotta pot
· · ·
hay
· · ·
*silver reel (rose) wire, string
or raffia*
· · ·
scissors
· · ·
glue gun and glue sticks
· · ·
small twigs
· · ·
.91 wires
· · ·
open fir cones
· · ·
candle

The natural colours of fir cones, twigs and terracotta blend beautifully together.

1 Push a good quantity of moss into the pot to form a platform for the candle. This will keep the flame away from the moss when it is lit. Make a hay collar to fit inside the rim of the pot (see Techniques). Glue in place then glue on moss, so that it extends a little over the rim of the pot.

2 Cut the twigs to a suitable length and wire into bundles (see Techniques). Glue the fir cones and twig bundles on to the moss, leaving enough room for the candle.

FLORAL CANDLE POT

· · ·

MATERIALS

· · ·

knife

· · ·

1 block plastic foam for dried flowers

· · ·

terracotta pot

· · ·

florist's tape (stem-wrap tape)

· · ·

mossing (floral) pins

· · ·

candle

· · ·

scissors

· · ·

dried flowers: solidago, Alchemilla mollis, lavender, miniature and standard pink roses, pink larkspur

· · ·

.91 wires

· · ·

green moss

The flowers used in this pot will complement the candlelight to make a very romantic display.

This pretty pot would look lovely on a summer garden table, especially if you use a scented candle to keep away insects. The dried flowers are carefully inserted in sequence to build up the attractive shape. The candle has been pinned and taped in position so that it can easily be replaced once used. Remember to never leave a lighted candle unattended, even outdoors.

1 Trim the foam to fit the pot. Wire the candle into the foam (see Techniques). Push the foam into the pot, so that it is 8 cm (3 in) above the rim. Trim all the materials to 10–13 cm (4–5 in), depending on the size of the pot, then bunch and wire them (see Techniques). Starting at rim level, push four bunches of solidago into the foam.

2 Continue to add some solidago in the spaces near the base of the candle. This will create an S-shaped arrangement of flowers when viewed from the side, running around the display.

3 Fill the spaces between the solidago with about eight small bunches of *Alchemilla mollis*. There should be very little space left. Add eight bunches of lavender, again in an S-shape. Fill any large spaces with solidago or *Alchemilla mollis*.

4 Add small bunches of miniature and standard roses at random to fill all the small gaps. If you use all the roses, add another material – in this display, larkspur was included.

5 Cover the base of the candle and the rim of the pot with green moss, using mossing (floral) pins to hold it in place.

ROSE-PERFUMED CANDLE POTS

· · ·

MATERIALS

· · ·

hay

· · ·

*silver reel (rose) wire, string
or raffia*

· · ·

scissors

· · ·

terracotta pot

· · ·

glue gun and glue sticks

· · ·

moss

· · ·

dried roses

· · ·

small-leaved green foliage

· · ·

rose-perfumed oil

· · ·

candle

*Small roses can be inserted
into any gaps in the design
left by larger rose heads.*

These two candle pots are variations of the same theme. One is a very simple combination of roses and foliage, while the other combines large as well as miniature roses, while using a larger candle. You could make a selection of small displays for dinner parties, using the larger pot as a centrepiece with vibrant green moss and small fruits arranged around the base. The wonderful long-lasting scent of the rose oil will be accentuated by the heat of the candle. Remember never to leave lighted candles unattended.

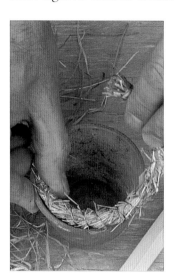

1 Make a small hay collar to fit inside the rim of the pot (see Techniques).

2 Glue the collar inside the rim of the pot, as close to the top as possible. Hold it firmly in place until the glue begins to harden.

3 Glue a layer of moss to the hay collar so that it also extends to cover the rim of the pot.

4 Cut the rose heads from their stems and glue them on to the moss, leaving enough room for the candle. Fill the gaps with foliage. If you are using miniature roses, add them after the foliage. Half-fill the pot with moss, pressing it down well to make a base for the candle. Sprinkle the moss with rose-perfumed oil. Finally, push the candle into the terracotta pot.

AUTUMN CANDLE POT

• • •

MATERIALS

• • •

knife

• • •

1 block plastic foam for dried flowers

• • •

terracotta pot

• • •

florist's tape (stem-wrap tape)

• • •

mossing (floral) pins

• • •

candle

• • •

scissors

• • •

.91 wires

• • •

dried materials, e.g. red amaranthus, fir cones, lavender, cinnamon sticks, twigs, chillies, oranges, mushrooms, magnolia leaves, holly oak leaves

• • •

raffia

• • •

moss

This rich design uses plenty of different materials, giving a feeling of autumn harvest and plenitude.

This rich display symbolizes the harvest of flowers and fruit at this time of year. For a more glossy look, spray it with clear florist's lacquer then lightly high-light with gold spray paint. You could also use a candle perfumed with spices to add to the effect. Remember never to leave a lighted candle unattended.

1 Trim the foam to fit snugly into the pot. Wire the candle in the centre of the foam (see Techniques). Fit the foam into the pot. Wire the dried materials individually or in bundles (see Techniques). Tie the lavender into bunches with raffia.

2 Insert the larger materials into the foam base, working on alternate sides of the display. Fill the spaces with the smaller materials. Finally add moss to hide the foam and candle base, using mossing (floral) pins.

WINTER CANDLE POT

• • •

This welcoming little candle pot is made by gluing nuts to a hay collar, which is completely disguised once the project is complete. Decorate the pot with nuts in different shapes and sizes – those shown here are walnuts, brazil nuts and hazelnuts (filberts). Remember never to leave a burning candle unattended.

MATERIALS

• • •

hay

• • •

silver reel (rose) wire, string or raffia

• • •

scissors

• • •

small terracotta pot

• • •

glue gun and glue sticks

• • •

moss

• • •

assorted nuts

• • •

candle

Nuts create a lovely festive effect, particularly when combined with the candle.

1 Make a small hay collar to fit the top of the pot (see Techniques). Glue it in place. Add some moss with glue.

2 Glue nuts on top to make an attractive arrangement, letting them hang over the edge of the pot. Insert the candle.

PINE CANDLE POT

• • •

MATERIALS

• • •

knife

• • •

*1 block plastic foam for dried
flowers*

• • •

terracotta pot

• • •

florist's tape (stem-wrap tape)

• • •

mossing (floral) pins

• • •

candle

• • •

hay

• • •

secateurs (garden clippers)

• • •

blue pine (spruce)

• • •

.91 wires

• • •

reindeer moss

• • •

small dried red roses

• • •

fir cones

• • •

*dried mushrooms and dried
kutchi fruit (alternatively, use
cinnamon sticks and slices of
dried orange)*

*Many other ingredients can be
combined with blue pine
(spruce), such as holly.*

Branches of blue pine (spruce), combined with red roses and fir cones, make a wonderfully rich centrepiece for the table. Use the blue pine (spruce) fresh so that you can enjoy its glorious scent. To match a dark wood table, paint the pot with dark stain and protect the table by fixing felt to the base of the pot. Remember never to leave a lighted candle unattended.

1 Cut the foam to fit the pot then wire the candle on top (see Techniques). Fix the foam into the pot, packing any spaces with hay. Group the blue pine (spruce) into pieces of various sizes. Trim the needles from the ends of the stems. Push the largest pieces into the base of the foam, so they lean down slightly.

2 Add slightly shorter pieces of blue pine (spruce) to make a layer above the first. Continue to build up a pyramid shape, keeping the blue pine (spruce) well away from the candle. Use wires to strengthen or lengthen the shorter pieces.

3 Fill any large spaces in the display with moss, attaching it with mossing (floral) pins. Put plenty of moss around the base of the candle to hide the tape.

4 Wire the roses into bunches then wire the fir cones and other materials (see Techniques). Add to spaces in the display to create a balanced arrangement.

SEASHELL POT

· · ·

MATERIALS

· · ·

reindeer moss

· · ·

small terracotta pot

· · ·

hay

· · ·

*silver reel (rose) wire, string
or raffia*

· · ·

scissors

· · ·

glue gun and glue sticks

· · ·

seashells

· · ·

candle

*The intricate shapes of
seashells make them ideal
decorative materials and an
unusual alternative to flowers
and leaves.*

Dried flower arrangements are often not suitable for the steamy atmosphere of a bathroom or shower room, but seashells will be entirely at home. They come in a wonderful range of colours and shapes and you can collect your own shells on a seaside walk. Seashells are also available from specialist suppliers. Remember never to leave burning candles unattended.

1 Take a good handful of reindeer moss and press it firmly into the pot until it is half full. Make a small hay collar to fit inside the top of the pot (see Techniques). Glue in place then use glue to cover both the hay collar and the rim of the pot with some moss.

2 Glue the largest shells on to the collar, leaving room for the candle. Fill in the gaps with smaller shells. Add a little moss where required. Insert the candle.

FIR CONE PYRAMID

. . .

This unusual pot is perfect for winter decorations. The natural colours of the fir cones, moss and terracotta work beautifully together. For a delicate frosted effect, lightly spray the tips of the fir cones with white paint.

MATERIALS

. . .

knife

. . .

1 block plastic foam for dried flowers

. . .

terracotta pot

. . .

glue gun and glue sticks

. . .

moss

. . .

fir cones

Fir cones are often mixed with other materials, but this design celebrates their unusual shape.

1 Cut the foam to fit tightly inside the pot. Make sure the top is flat as this will be the base for the pyramid of fir cones. Glue a layer of moss around the rim of the pot.

2 Glue a circle of fir cones on top, pointing outwards. Add a second circle, slightly overlapping the first. Continue to build up a pyramid shape until a full look is achieved.

DECORATED POT DISPLAY

· · ·

MATERIALS

· · ·

knife

· · ·

1 block plastic foam for dried flowers

· · ·

hand-painted terracotta plant pot

· · ·

florist's adhesive tape

· · ·

.71 wires

· · ·

reindeer moss

· · ·

scissors

· · ·

20 stems small globe thistles

· · ·

20 bleached cane spirals

· · ·

30 stems dried white roses

The display is basically massed dried flowers with the addition of curly cane spirals to add height and humour. It is quick-and-easy to make and would be a fun decoration for a child's bedroom.

This display is purely for fun. The container is a terracotta pot decorated with a painted head against a bright blue background. You can decorate a terracotta pot with your own design and create a complementary floral display for it.

As a general rule, if the container is in any way elaborate, then the floral display in it should be simple, but this display is deliberately flamboyant because it is designed to represent hair growing out of the painted head.

1 Cut the block of plastic foam so that it wedges into the decorated pot and extends approximately 4 cm (1¼ in) above the rim. Secure it in place with adhesive tape. Make hairpin shapes from the .71 wire. Tuck reindeer moss between the sides of the pot and the plastic foam and push the wire hairpins through the moss and into the foam to secure.

2 Cut the globe thistle stems to approximately 10 cm (4 in) in length and arrange them throughout the plastic foam to create an even domed shape.

3 Cut the cane spirals to a length of about 15 cm (6 in) and push their stems into the plastic foam, distributing them evenly throughout the globe thistles.

4 Cut the stems of the dried roses to approximately 10 cm (4 in) in length and arrange them evenly amongst the other materials in the display.

PEONY AND APPLE TABLE ARRANGEMENT

· · ·

MATERIALS

· · ·

1 block plastic foam for dried flowers

· · ·

knife

· · ·

terracotta bowl

· · ·

florist's adhesive tape

· · ·

scissors

· · ·

10 stems preserved (dried) eucalyptus

· · ·

18 slices preserved (dried) apple

· · ·

.71 wires

· · ·

2 large heads dried hydrangea

· · ·

10 pale pink dried peonies

· · ·

20 deep pink dried roses

· · ·

20 dried peony leaves

· · ·

10 stems ti tree

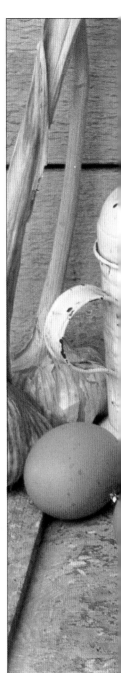

This delicate arrangement can be made for a specific occasion and kept to be used again and again, whenever a special decoration is called for.

The construction of the decoration is relatively simple, involving the minimum of wiring.

1 Cut the block of plastic foam so that it wedges into the bowl and hold it securely in place with the florist's adhesive tape. Cut the eucalyptus stems to about 13 cm (5 in), making sure that the cut ends are clean of leaves, and arrange them evenly around the plastic foam to create a domed foliage outline to the display.

2 Group the slices of preserved (dried) apple into threes and double leg mount them with .71 wires. Push the six groups of wired apple slices into the foam, distributing them evenly throughout the display. The apple slices should be a little shorter than the eucalyptus when in place.

3 Break each hydrangea head into three smaller florets and push them into the foam, distributing them evenly throughout the display, and recessing them slightly as you work.

4 Cut the stems of the peonies to approximately 12 cm (4¾ in) in length and arrange them evenly throughout the display. This time, the peonies should not be recessed.

This pretty arrangement is suitable for a small table.

5 Cut the dried rose stems to approximately 13 cm (4¾ in) in length and push them into the plastic foam throughout the other materials in the arrangement.

6 Arrange the dried peony leaves evenly amongst the flowers. Cut the ti tree into stems of approximately 13 cm (4¾ in) in length and distribute them throughout the display.

MASSED ARRANGEMENT IN BLUE AND YELLOW

· · ·

*This table decoration would
complement a modern kitchen
or dining-room.*

This contemporary arrangement uses simple massed materials in strong contrasting colours to achieve a strikingly bold display. The polished texture of the silver-grey galvanized bucket provides an ideal visual foundation on which to build the domed cushion of deep yellow achillea with contrasting spiky, blue globe thistles.

No special techniques are required to construct the display but you must ensure the materials are massed to achieve the surface density necessary.

1 Wedge the blocks of foam in place and tape. Cut the globe thistle stems to around 12 cm (4¼ in) and arrange in the foam. Use smaller heads around the outside and larger heads at the centre.

2 Cut the achillea stems to about 12 cm (4¾ in) and arrange them between the globe thistles, massing them carefully so that no gaps are visible.

TERRACOTTA PLANT-POT DISPLAY

• • •

This delightful selection of dried flower arrangements in terracotta pots shows the exciting colours and types of flowers now available. Massed flowers in bright colours are presented in a contemporary way but in old-fashioned terracotta thumb (rose) pots, the rustic charm of which has been enhanced by colouring their surfaces.

The display will have the greatest impact when used as a group but you could place them individually around the rooms of your house if you prefer.

MATERIALS

• • •

1 block plastic foam for dried flowers

• • •

knife

• • •

5 old-fashioned terracotta pots, coloured with chalk

• • •

scissors

• • •

16 pink dried roses

• • •

7 dried sunflower heads

• • •

1 bunch dried lavender

• • •

25 small cinnamon sticks

• • •

10 stems Craspedia globosa

• • •

9 stems blue globe thistle

1 Cut the plastic foam for each pot and wedge it in so that it is about 2 cm (¾ in) below the rim. Cut all the stems so that when they are pushed into the plastic foam only their heads are visible above the rim of the pot. Fill one pot with tightly massed rose heads. In the second pot, push the sunflower heads into the plastic foam. Again, make sure that only the heads are visible above the rim of the pot. The aim is to achieve a massed domed effect in each pot.

Even the least experienced flower arranger will have no difficulty in creating these charming arrangements.

2 Fill the third pot with lavender stems, cut so that the bottoms of the flower spikes are level with the rim of the pot. Break the cinnamon sticks to create jagged ends, making them about 10 cm (4 in) long. Push them into the foam of the fourth pot, with the tops slightly varying in height. Cut the *Craspedia* and the globe thistle stems so their heads will appear just above the rim of the pot. Fill the fifth pot by creating a regular pattern of blue globe thistle in a yellow carpet of *Craspedia*.

AUTUMNAL ORANGE DISPLAY
. . .

MATERIALS
. . .

3 blocks plastic foam for dried flowers

. . .

terracotta pot, 30 cm (12 in) high

. . .

florist's adhesive tape

. . .

10 stems glycerine-preserved adiantum

. . .

.71 wires

. . .

9 dried split oranges

. . .

scissors

. . .

10 stems dried carthamus

. . .

10 stems orange-dyed globe thistles

. . .

10 stems dried bottlebrush

This is designed as a feature display which would be particularly effective positioned where it could be viewed in the round.

Warm autumn colours dominate this display both in the floral arrangement and in its container. The lovely bulbous terracotta pot is a feature of the display and the arrangement is domed to reflect the roundness of the container. Indeed, in order to focus attention on the pot, the container unusually takes up half the height of the finished display.

The autumnal red and burnt-orange colours of globe thistle, bottlebrush, oranges and adiantum contrast with the green of the carthemus, the orange tufts of which act as a colour link. Texturally varied, the display incorporates tufted flowers, spiky flowers, feathery foliage and recessed leathery skinned fruits.

The arrangement involves simple wiring of the oranges but is otherwise straightforward and just requires a good eye and a little patience in arranging the materials individually in order to achieve the right shape.

1 Pack the blocks of plastic foam into the terracotta pot and secure in place with florist's adhesive tape. The surface of the foam should be about 4 cm (1¼ in) above the rim of the pot.

2 Create a low domed foliage outline using the adiantum stems at their length of about 25 cm (10 in). Wire the dried oranges with .71 wire.

3 Bend down the wires projecting from the bases of the oranges and twist together. Arrange the oranges throughout the adiantum by pushing their wire stems into the foam.

4 Cut the carthamus stems to approximately 25 cm (10 in) and push them into the plastic foam throughout the display to reinforce the height, width and overall shape.

5 Cut the globe thistle stems to a length of approximately 25 cm (10 in) and push them into the foam evenly throughout the display. These are the focal flowers.

6 Finally, cut the stems of bottlebrush to a length of 25 cm (10 in) and push them into the plastic foam to distribute them evenly throughout the display.

LAVENDER-FILLED BUCKET

· · ·

MATERIALS

· · ·

craft knife

· · ·

1 block plastic foam for dried flowers

· · ·

galvanized bucket, 10 cm (4 in) diameter

· · ·

400 dried lavender stems

· · ·

scissors

Make sure you pack the lavender stems tightly together. The metal "bow" adds an unusual finishing touch.

Lavender is a very beautiful plant, with silvery grey foliage and flowers in shades from pale pink to indigo. Simply stacked in bunches, it makes a wonderful display. Grow as much as you can and beg extra from your neighbours' gardens – you will need approximately 400 stalks to fill this 10 cm (4 in) diameter bucket. Finish with a metal mesh "bow", cut with tin snips. The decorative mulch round the edge is pea shingle.

1 Cut the block of plastic foam to fit inside the bucket, filling it to just below the rim.

2 Make up bunches of approximately 25 lavender stems. Turn each bunch upside down and tap it gently on the work surface to level off the flowerheads.

3 Gauge the finished height of the display by holding each bunch against the bucket. Cut the stems to the required length. Push each bunch firmly into the foam, packing the bunches closely together.

PEONY AND SHELL DISPLAY

• • •

This display cleverly mixes sea shells with flowers in a lovely pink, mauve and green arrangement. The result is a beautiful compact dome. The main feature of the display is the beautifully patterned rose-pink conical sea shells which are echoed by the colour and texture of the cracked glazed ceramic container.

MATERIALS

• • •

knife

• • •

1 block plastic foam for dried flowers

• • •

ceramic bowl

• • •

florist's adhesive tape

• • •

scissors

• • •

12 stems dried pale pink peonies

• • •

3 dried heads hydrangea

• • •

7 pink conical shells

This arrangement would be perfect for a bathroom, as long as it is not allowed to become too damp.

1 Cut the plastic foam so that it fits snugly into the container and secure it in place with the florist's adhesive tape. Strip the leaves from the peony stems and cut the stems to about 9 cm (3½ in) long. Push the stems into the foam to create a regular dome shape. Arrange the peony leaves liberally throughout the display.

2 Break each hydrangea head into three clusters and push them into the foam, distributing them among the peony heads. Distribute the sea shells throughout the display by pushing their wider bottom ends between the flowers so that they are held in place by the mass of blooms (secure with glue if necessary).

BASKETS OF ABUNDANCE

• • •

The natural texture of baskets makes them
ideally compatible with all kinds of materials –
summer or winter, colourful or muted. Fill
a whole basket with an exuberant display and
place it on the floor, in a fireplace or on a table.
Alternatively, decorate the edge of the basket
and fill it with fresh fruit or pot-pourri –
a perfect gift or a symbol of hospitality.

INTRODUCTION

· · ·

Above: Round Tiered Basket

Below: A variation on the Grand Garden Basket

Baskets come in a huge range of shapes and sizes, and part of the fun is to choose the right basket for your display. Some baskets may not be sturdy enough, depending on the weight of the materials you are using. Sturdy willow baskets are still made today and even an old, battered one with worn edges can be rejuvenated with a decorative border. The edges or handle (or even the whole basket) can be covered with moss, which is used to hide a multitude of other sins such as fixing wires and foam. Hunt out old baskets in junk shops and garden sheds – their distressed appearance can actually be an asset in some displays where a rustic look is called for, and they are sure to have character.

For an informal massed basket of flowers, one of the tricks of the florist's trade is to insert the bunches of flowers in S-shapes rather than straight lines so that the colours merge together naturally and there are no hard lines. Large flowerheads such as roses and peonies are usually added separately at the end so that there is no risk of them being damaged while you work on the rest of the display. If your dried roses are rather squashed or you would like them to be more open, you can gently steam them before using.

The essence of basket displays is for them to look abundant and generous, so use plenty of material and aim to fill the basket almost to overflowing. Handfuls of

Above: Basket of Bulbs

Left: Flat-backed Tiered Basket

moss spilling over the edge will help to add to the luxurious effect. Experiment with unusual materials from the huge range available in florists' shops if you want to create an exotic display. If you are able to dry your own flowers and herbs from your garden this will, of course, be a considerable saving and also be very satisfying. Lavender is one of the most popular plants to grow and dry; if you have an abundance of flowerheads, lavender is wonderful used on its own to make a scented laundry basket. The tiny mauve-blue flowers also look very pretty in an old-fashioned arrangement with pale pink or red roses.

A large basket display is ideal for placing in an empty fireplace during the summer months, and if you use a chicken wire base it is very simple to replace individual stalks if any of the materials are damaged. You will need to regularly dust the display to keep it looking fresh.

As well as a host of inspirational ideas for all shapes and sizes of basket, this chapter also covers tiered displays in various forms, showing how it is possible to

Below: Pot-pourri Basket

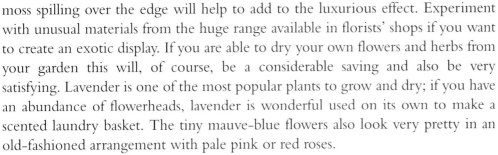

adapt a traditional design in several ways to look different. A rectangular basket is the base for a large, flat-backed display in which the dried materials stand in formal rows one behind the other; this display would look good placed on the floor against a wall. The other tiered displays are both round, and are quite different in scale and character. Tiered displays may look impressive but they are one of the easiest flower designs to achieve and are therefore particularly recommended for a beginner.

COUNTRY BASKET

· · ·

*D*ried summer flowers and
herbs make a traditionally
beautiful display for any room.

This display will make the most of your wiring skills. Using
lots of material in a fairly small space means that the wiring
must be as neat as possible, so that all the stems fit into the foam
base. The centre of the basket is filled with dried flowers, and the
long trailing *Amaranthus caudatus* is placed around the edge.

1 Trim the foam to
fit snugly into the
basket, leaving 2.5 cm
(1 in) between the top
of the basket and the
foam. Pack moss between
the edge of the basket
and the foam.

2 Trim the flowers
and herbs to about
20 cm (8 in) long.
Wire each variety into
small bunches (see
Techniques). Starting
with the least fragile
flowers, push the stems
into the foam. Add one
variety at a time, using
the oregano as the
main filler.

3 Begin to build up the display, saving
the larkspur, *Amaranthus caudatus* and
roses until last. Create a well-filled display,
with little space between the bunches.

4 Push the *Amaranthus caudatus* into the
foam around the edge of the basket so
that it hangs down to touch the work
surface. Add the larkspur to the display.

5 Add the roses evenly around the basket. Finally, use the green moss and mossing (floral) pins to fill the edge of the basket quite generously.

The draping effect created by the Amaranthus is exquisite.

CORNER DISPLAY

· · ·

MATERIALS

· · ·

wire cutters

· · ·

chicken wire

· · ·

large basket, with or without handle

· · ·

dried green amaranthus

· · ·

dried pink larkspur

· · ·

dried pale yellow and dark red roses

· · ·

dried lavender

Amaranthus is an ideal filler for many basket displays as its long stalks accentuate a feeling of height.

This is an extremely simple arrangement to make, and has the advantage that you can remake it as many times as necessary to create the right look, without damaging the dried materials. This particular display has been made to look the same from all angles; turn it occasionally, so that it fades evenly. If it is used as a fireplace filler, you will need to clean it more regularly than other displays.

1 Cut a piece of chicken wire about twice the surface area of the basket and fill the whole of the inside. Push a few stems of amaranthus into the basket, through to the bottom.

2 Arrange the individual stems of larkspur in the spaces between the amaranthus. Stand back from the display from time to time to check that the balance is correct.

3 Add the roses and lavender, putting some rose heads low down at the front of the basket for added interest. Adjust the display if necessary by moving the flowers.

BASKET OF BULBS

• • •

MATERIALS

• • •

.91 wires

• • •

small twigs

• • •

glue gun and glue sticks

• • •

*large round basket, with a
broad rim*

• • •

dried pomegranates

• • •

dried lotus pods

• • •

dried Protea compacta

• • •

fir cones

• • •

reindeer moss

Plant early spring bulbs in small terracotta pots then bring them indoors to be displayed in a large basket with a decorated rim. Cover the earth in the pots with fresh moss so that the pots blend with the rich mixture of dried materials in the basket border. If you cannot obtain a basket with a broad rim, you can simply make a hay collar to support the decoration.

You can find all kinds of dried natural materials in woodland areas suitable for decorating baskets.

1 Wire the twigs into small bunches (see Techniques). Glue the wires to the rim of the basket at regular intervals to make an attractive border.

2 Divide the other dried materials into five equal groups. Space the pomegranates evenly around the rim and glue in place. Add the other materials to create a pleasing design, finishing with the reindeer moss to fill in small gaps.

MOSS-EDGED
BAY LEAF BASKET
• • •

MATERIALS
• • •
moss
• • •
old basket, with handle
• • •
silver reel (rose) wire
• • •
wire cutters
• • •
.91 wires
• • •
pliers
• • •
bay leaves
• • •
gold spray paint

*The simplest of materials –
bay leaves, moss and gold
spray paint – make an
attractive display.*

This simple method for covering the handle and edge of a basket with moss is perfect for rejuvenating an old basket which has seen better days. Here the moss makes a secure base for a very simple but effective display of glossy green bay leaves, some sprayed with gold paint.

1 Wrap plenty of moss around the handle of the basket, twisting silver reel (rose) wire around to hold it in place. Start at the base of the handle at one side, working up and down to the other side.

2 Make a sausage-shaped length of moss, of even thickness, to fit around the top of the basket. Bind it together with the reel (rose) wire, leaving about 2.5 cm (1 in) between each twist of wire.

3 Attach the moss to the basket with wires. Twist the ends of each wire together and tuck into the moss out of sight. Spray any faded bay leaves with gold paint and fill the basket with them.

TWIGGY BASKET

• • •

In this striking arrangement the starkness of the winter twigs is offset by the rich red roses around the base, which add drama to the display. It looks particularly effective placed on a windowsill, so that the light can silhouette the intricate shapes. To adapt the display for Christmas, spray the twigs gold.

MATERIALS

• • •

knife

• • •

1 block plastic foam for dried flowers

• • •

basket

• • •

long twigs

• • •

green moss

• • •

mossing (floral) pins

• • •

scissors

• • •

dried red roses

Dark twigs and red roses make a stunning and very simple winter arrangement.

1 Cut the foam to fit the basket and press it in firmly. Push the twigs one at a time into the centre of the foam. Pack them together quite densely, placing the tallest twigs in the centre. Add clumps of moss around the twigs to cover the foam, secured with mossing (floral) pins.

2 Trim the rose stems to about 8 cm (3 in). Push them through the moss into the foam, to form an even circle around the base of the twigs.

169

MATERIALS

. . .

knife

. . .

1 block plastic foam for dried flowers

. . .

basket

. . .

scissors

. . .

twigs

. . .

.91 wires

. . .

dried red roses

. . .

preserved (dried) leaves

. . .

moss

. . .

mossing (floral) pins (optional)

. . .

raffia

. . .

glue gun and glue sticks

Instead of holly oak leaves, try using preserved (dried) copper beech leaves, here dyed green, to provide a neutral background for some roses.

HOLLY OAK AND ROSE BASKET

. . .

Preserved (dried) leaves make unusual yet very attractive displays, and their bold abstract shapes lend themselves to sculptural arrangements. The leaves also act well as a counterbalance against the colours and softer forms of other materials. Here holly oak leaves are used, but beech, maple, ferns and many other leaves would be equally effective, depending on what's available.

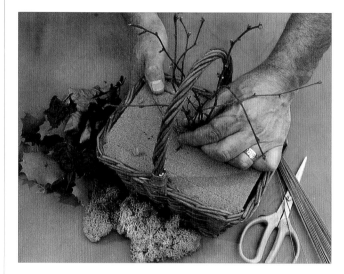

1 Cut the foam so that it fits tightly into the basket and press it firmly in. Add extra pieces of foam around the sides to make it sturdy, if you need to. Make sure that the surface of the foam is just below or level with the top of the basket, so that it will not be seen. Start the arrangement at the centre. Trim the twigs to similar sized lengths and then wire them in bunches (see Techniques) and push into the foam. Make sure that they are evenly positioned.

2 Trim the roses and the stems of the preserved (dried) leaves to the required length, remembering to allow extra to push into the foam. Steam the roses if necessary (see Techniques). Push them carefully into the foam, either wired into small bunches or one stem at a time. Start in the centre of the basket and work outwards. Turn the design frequently to check for any gaps and to make sure that the arrangement is well balanced.

3 When you reach the edge of the basket, lean the flowers out slightly. Add moss to fill any small gaps around the edge of the display, holding it in place with wires bent into U-shaped staples or mossing (floral) pins. Cut twelve strands of raffia and tie in a bow. Glue to the centre of the basket.

The display will look stunning in a rustic setting.

CLASSIC COUNTRY BASKET

· · ·

MATERIALS

· · ·

knife

· · ·

1 block plastic foam for dried
flowers

· · ·

round or oval basket

· · ·

hay or moss

· · ·

scissors

· · ·

dried larkspur

· · ·

dried red amaranthus

· · ·

dried oregano

· · ·

dried blue Eryngium
alpinum

· · ·

dried red roses

· · ·

dried peonies

· · ·

.91 wires

· · ·

mossing (floral) pins

This lovely basket is filled
with a mass of traditional
flowers and herbs.

In this traditional basket, the aim is to create a well-filled display, with very little or no space between the bunches of dried material. Each variety is inserted in an S-shape so that the colours and forms appear to flow together, with no harsh lines between them. Add the larger, more dramatic roses and peonies last.

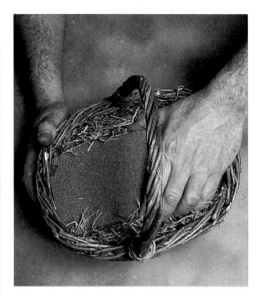

1 Trim the foam to fit snugly into the basket, leaving at least 2.5 cm (1 in) between the top of the basket and the foam. Fill any spaces with hay or moss.

2 Trim the materials to approximately 25 cm (10 in) long. Starting with the least fragile flowers, wire them into bunches (see Techniques). Push them into the foam, creating an S-shape with each variety across the basket.

3 Build up the display, saving the roses and peonies until last. Finally, insert the roses and peonies, distributing them evenly across the basket.

4 Add moss around the edge of the basket, to hide the foam and as many stems as possible. Hold the moss in place with mossing (floral) pins. Let the moss hang over the side, to give a soft look to the edge of the basket.

GRAND GARDEN BASKET

· · ·

MATERIALS

· · ·

knife

· · ·

*1–2 blocks plastic foam for
dried flowers*

· · ·

round or oval basket

· · ·

.91 wires

· · ·

*dried materials, e.g.
Alchemilla mollis,
hydrangeas, lavender,
marjoram, nigella, peonies,
pink roses*

· · ·

scissors

*The colours of the flowers will
last longer if they are kept out
of direct sunlight.*

This is intended to be a bold, extravagant display, so use the best materials you can find to create an abundant mixture. Flowers including peonies, roses, lavender and hydrangeas have been used in this sumptuous basket.

1 Cut the foam to fit snugly into the basket and press in firmly. Make sure the top of the foam is level, trimming the foam if needed. Place a second piece of foam, about two-thirds the size of the base piece, on top of the first. Fix firmly in place with U-shaped staples made by bending wires in half.

2 Separate each variety of dried material. Trim the stems so that they are all about 10 cm (4 in). Wire the smaller flowers into bunches about 5–8 cm (2–3 in) wide (see Techniques). Insert the bunches in an S-shape, working from one side to the other as you build up the layers.

3 Fill in the background colour first. Save the larger peonies, roses and hydrangeas until last or you may damage them as you work. The aim is to create a well-filled dome. Allow the flowers to hang well over the edge of the basket by working horizontally into the foam around the sides, as well as vertically.

SIMPLE SUMMER DISPLAY

· · ·

This beautiful display of pale pink roses and peonies, solidago and wheat is in fact a very simple project to make. Because it uses no foam or wires it is ideal for a beginner. The dark wooden logs positioned in the back of the basket give an extra, rustic texture to the design.

MATERIALS

· · ·

wire cutters

· · ·

chicken wire

· · ·

large basket, with handle

· · ·

dark wooden logs

· · ·

*dried pale pink and
yellow roses*

· · ·

dried pale pink peonies

· · ·

dried solidago

· · ·

dried wheat

· · ·

scissors

· · ·

raffia

Large-headed flowers such as roses and peonies make it easy to fill space.

2 Position the logs upright, at the back of the basket. Push the dried material stems through the chicken wire to the bottom of the basket, trimming them to the required length. Place the basket on the floor and stand back frequently to check that the balance is correct and that the amount of filling is right.

1 Cut a piece of chicken wire approximately twice the surface area of the basket. Scrunch it up and place it inside the basket, completely filling it up.

3 Cut several long strands of raffia and tie to the base of the handle in a huge, simple bow. Allow the strands to flow loosely over the side of the basket.

RICH AND EXOTIC

· · ·

MATERIALS

· · ·

wire cutters

· · ·

chicken wire

· · ·

moss

· · ·

small round basket

· · ·

scissors

· · ·

.91 wires

· · ·

dried fruits and fungi

· · ·

small dried oranges

· · ·

dried red chillies

· · ·

clear florist's lacquer

The rich colours and textures of dried fruits and chillies make a stunning basket.

This basket is very simple to make but relies for its impact on interesting and unusual materials. It is a good excuse to experiment with some of the exotic dried fruits and fungi that you see in florists' shops. The display is sprayed with clear florist's lacquer to give a glossy finish; for a special Christmas centrepiece you could also lightly frost it with gold spray paint.

1 Using wire cutters, cut a square of chicken wire. Fill the chicken wire with moss and pull together to form into a ball. Push the ball into the basket to make a mound of moss.

2 Trim and wire the dried materials (see Techniques). Set aside the oranges and chillies. Push the other wires into the moss, starting round the edge of the basket where the materials should hang over slightly. Fill any small gaps with moss.

3 Add the strongly coloured oranges and chillies at the end, positioning them carefully to balance the design. Spray the finished display with clear florist's lacquer to bring out the rich colours and make it last much longer.

WOODLAND BASKET

· · ·

For this forest-filled basket, try to incorporate items that you have gleaned yourself from a country walk – leaves, seed pods, acorns, nuts, moss, lichens – for a truly natural display. Do not worry if the material is a little damp, as the display will soon dry out. For a long-lasting piece of work, spray the finished arrangement with clear florist's lacquer.

MATERIALS

· · ·

hay

· · ·

silver reel (rose) wire, string or raffia

· · ·

scissors

· · ·

basket

· · ·

.91 wires

· · ·

pliers

· · ·

equal quantities of mixed nuts, e.g. walnuts, brazil nuts, hazelnuts (filberts)

· · ·

fir cones

· · ·

glue gun and glue sticks

· · ·

small twigs

· · ·

moss

Use nuts of all shapes and sizes to create an authentically natural basket with an uneven and haphazard effect.

1 Make a hay collar to fit inside the top edge of the basket (see Techniques). Fix it in place with wires, twisting the ends tightly together and tucking them into the collar. Begin to glue the nuts and fir cones to the hay collar in small groups.

2 When you have added most of the larger nuts and the fir cones, wire small bunches of twigs together (see Techniques). Glue in place then cover with small nuts. Fill in any gaps with some moss.

DECORATIVE BASKET BORDER
. . .

MATERIALS
. . .
sphagnum moss
. . .
knife
. . .
rope
. . .
wide, shallow basket
. . .
.91 wires
. . .
scissors
. . .
dried lavender
. . .
silver reel (rose) wire
. . .
reindeer moss
. . .
mossing (floral) pins
. . .
dried red roses
. . .
glue gun and glue sticks

In many displays only the lavender flowers are visible, but in this pretty basket the stalks are also part of the design.

In this lovely basket criss-cross bunches of dried lavender, red roses and reindeer moss decorate the rope swag border, leaving the centre of the basket as a useful container for fresh fruit. Make sure the roses are glued on to the rope swag, not to the reindeer moss, otherwise they may fall off.

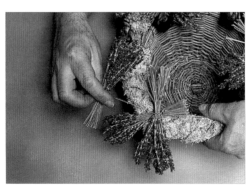

1 Using sphagnum moss, make a rope swag to fit round the top of the basket (see Techniques). Attach it to the basket with wires. Trim the lavender and centre-wire into small bunches using silver reel (rose) wire (see Techniques). Push the wire of one bunch lengthways into the moss, then add two more bunches so they cross at the same point. Repeat at equal intervals all around the border.

2 Add the reindeer moss, attaching it firmly with mossing (floral) pins. Cover most of the border but leave a few spaces for the roses. Steam the roses if necessary (see Techniques). Cut the rose heads from their stems and glue them directly on to the spaces on the rope swag.

POT-POURRI BASKET

· · ·

This country garden display will continue to remind you of summertime throughout the year. Fill the pretty basket with rose-scented pot-pourri, which will blend beautifully with the evocative scent of the dried roses and oregano that are included in the richly textured border.

MATERIALS

· · ·

hay

· · ·

silver reel (rose) wire, string or raffia

· · ·

scissors

· · ·

small basket

· · ·

.91 wires

· · ·

pliers

· · ·

dried Alchemilla mollis

· · ·

dried oregano

· · ·

dried nigella

· · ·

dried pink larkspur

· · ·

dried pale pink roses

· · ·

glue gun and glue sticks

· · ·

green moss

· · ·

rose-scented pot-pourri

The combination of green moss and pink flowers is quite exquisite.

1 Make a hay collar to fit the inside edge of the basket (see Techniques). Attach it with wires through the basket just under the collar then twist the ends together. Repeat at regular intervals around the basket. The collar should be the same level as the top of the basket. Trim the ends of wire and bend them into the hay.

2 Trim all of the stems to 8 cm (3 in). Wire the *Alchemilla* and oregano separately in bunches (see Techniques).

3 Glue all the materials to the collar. Separate the large single flowers from the small bunches of *Alchemilla* and oregano to create a pleasing design. Fill any gaps with small flowers and moss. Finally, fill the basket with pot-pourri.

LAVENDER BASKET

· · ·

MATERIALS

· · ·

silver reel (rose) wire

· · ·

scissors

· · ·

dried lavender

· · ·

wide, flat basket, with handle

· · ·

glue gun and glue sticks

· · ·

blue paper ribbon

· · ·

blue twine

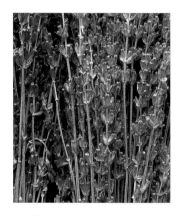

Because of its fresh scent, lavender is the perfect decoration for a basket that holds laundry or towels.

A traditional willow basket decorated with bunches of dried lavender makes an exquisitely pretty and scented storage place for linen. It could also be kept on the kitchen dresser, filled with freshly laundered tea towels (dish towels) ready on hand when you need them, or used to decorate a guest room. This display is very appealing because the final result is practical as well as pretty.

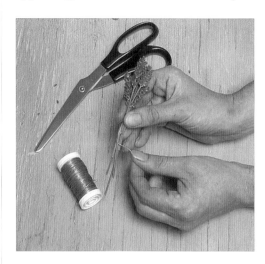

1 Using silver reel (rose) wire, wire small bundles of about six lavender heads (see Techniques). You will need enough to cover the rim of the basket generously. Arrange the lavender heads so they are staggered, to give fuller cover. Trim the stalks short.

2 Wire the remaining lavender into twelve large bunches of about twelve lavender heads, for the handle. Leave the stalks long.

3 Wire three of the large bunches of lavender together as shown to make a fanned criss-cross shape. Repeat the process with the rest of the large lavender bunches.

4 Glue the small bunches to the rim of the basket, starting at one end and working towards the handle. Overlap the bunches to cover the width of the rim.

5 Add individual heads of lavender to cover any spaces, ugly wires or stalks that are still showing through. Pay particular attention to the area near the handle.

6 Wind paper ribbon around the handle. Wire the longer lavender bunches to the handle. Leave the stalks long but trim them to neaten. Cut the stalks on the inside of the handle shorter to fit. Bind the wired joints with twine.

Criss-cross bunches of long lavender stalks make a bold, unusual decoration for a linen basket.

AUTUMN FRUIT BASKET

. . .

MATERIALS

. . .

copper or steel garland ring

. . .

sphagnum moss

. . .

silver reel (rose) wire

. . .

round shallow basket

. . .

.91 wires

. . .

scissors

. . .

dried eucalyptus

. . .

dried red roses

. . .

dried marjoram

. . .

glue gun and glue sticks

. . .

dried pomegranates

. . .

dried hydrangeas

. . .

dried tolbos

. . .

green moss

. . .

mossing (floral) pins

Roses, pomegranates, hydrangeas and eucalyptus are just some of the materials used in this beautiful basket.

This stunning basket uses a rich collection of different materials to produce an eye-catching display. Left empty it is very decorative, and for a quick dinner table centrepiece you can fill it with sweets or fresh fruit. You could also fill the centre with two or three candle pots but, as always, make sure they are well away from the dried materials and do not leave them burning unattended.

1 Flatten the garland ring and cover it with sphagnum moss, using silver reel (rose) wire. Wire the ring to the top of the basket. Trim and wire the eucalyptus into bunches (see Techniques) and place with stems pointing inwards. Push the ends of the wire into the moss.

2 Continue to add the other materials at even intervals. Trim and wire the roses and marjoram. Add them to the ring, criss-crossing them over the eucalyptus and each other. Make sure the bunches completely cover the inside and outer edge of the ring.

3 Glue the pomegranates in place. Bunch together some hydrangeas with a wire and fix them to the base. Cut off the stems of the tolbos close to the heads and glue in twos and threes to give more impact. Fill any small spaces with green moss, using mossing (floral) pins.

BASKET OF CHOCOLATES
· · ·

This delightful little basket is decorated with an exuberant border which includes poppy seed heads, gold-sprayed nigella, red roses, red amaranthus and bundles of cinnamon sticks. Fill the basket to overflowing with chocolates and mints wrapped in shiny coloured papers. It will make a lovely gift or an ideal decoration for the home with treats for family and guests.

MATERIALS
· · ·

hay

· · ·

silver reel (rose) wire, string or raffia

· · ·

scissors

· · ·

small basket

· · ·

.91 wires

· · ·

pliers

· · ·

dried nigella

· · ·

gold spray paint

· · ·

dried red amaranthus

· · ·

dried poppy seed heads

· · ·

cinnamon sticks

· · ·

raffia

· · ·

glue gun and glue sticks

· · ·

dried red roses

Poppy seed heads are an easy material to work with because they are so sturdy. In this arrangement they bring a touch of natural colour to an otherwise vibrant display.

1 Make a hay collar to fit neatly around the inside edge of the basket (see Techniques). Attach it firmly in place with wires, twisting the ends of each wire together and bending the ends back in the hay to hide them.

2 Spray the nigella with gold paint and leave to dry. Wire the amaranthus in small bunches (see Techniques). Bind small bundles of cinnamon sticks with wire, twisting the ends together. Tie strands of raffia around the wire.

3 Begin to glue the materials to the collar, leaving the roses until the end. Leave the stems fairly long so that the heads lean out and down slightly.

CANDLE BASKET

· · ·

MATERIALS

· · ·

sphagnum moss

· · ·

knife

· · ·

rope

· · ·

silver reel (rose) wire

· · ·

small round basket

· · ·

.91 wires

· · ·

scissors

· · ·

*dried Achillea ptarmica,
lavender, marjoram*

· · ·

dried poppy seed heads

· · ·

glue gun and glue sticks

· · ·

dried mintola balls

· · ·

green moss

· · ·

mossing (floral) pins

· · ·

*1 block plastic foam for dried
flowers*

· · ·

large-diameter candle

*White candles always
look attractive, but you can
of course choose any colour to
complement the other materials.*

In this colourful arrangement of mixed materials, the candle simply sits on top of a piece of foam, with no fixing at all. A large-diameter candle like this will stand quite securely and safely provided that the basket is on a firm surface, but it should not be left unattended when it is burning.

1 Using sphagnum moss, make a rope swag to fit around the top of the basket (see Techniques). Attach it with wires. Trim the achillea, lavender and marjoram stalks to 15 cm (6 in) then wire each variety into small bunches (see Techniques). Insert the bunches one variety at a time in small groups, criss-crossing the stalks so that some flowers face outwards and some inwards.

2 Trim the poppy stalks directly under the seed heads. Using a glue gun, attach the poppy heads and the mintola balls in small groups around the ring. Use the poppy heads to cover any wires that may be showing.

3 Fill any small gaps with green moss, using mossing (floral) pins, covering any wire fixings or outer edges. Add the moss in generous handfuls to make an even shape. Cut the foam to fit into the basket and place the candle on top.

FOREST CANDLE BASKET

· · ·

This dramatic structure is made from a basket base, with terracotta pots attached around the outside with a tight binding of raffia. It is important that the pots are tied firmly in place as they will contain burning candles. If you are not able to obtain a basket with a broad top, make a hay collar and glue it securely on to a round basket. The display is created with autumn fir cones, nuts, twigs and moss. Do not leave the lit candles unattended.

MATERIALS

· · ·

5 small terracotta pots

· · ·

thick wires

· · ·

large round basket, with a broad rim

· · ·

pliers

· · ·

.91 wires

· · ·

twigs

· · ·

glue gun and glue sticks

· · ·

fir cones

· · ·

nuts, e.g. walnuts, hazelnuts (filberts), brazil nuts

· · ·

5 candles

· · ·

moss

· · ·

raffia

This is a great way of converting spare old flowerpots into a wonderful display.

1 To tie the terracotta pots to the basket, pass the wire through the hole in the base of the pot then through the top and bottom of the basket, twisting the two ends together. Make sure that they are evenly placed. Begin to add the decorative material to the basket. Firstly, wire the twigs in small bunches (see Techniques) and glue the wires to the basket.

2 Divide the other materials into five equal amounts. Working in sections, glue the fir cones to the basket. Repeat with the nuts, placing the different varieties to create a balanced design.

3 To hold the candles firmly in the pots, push moss down firmly all around them. Continue the display, turning the basket as you work. Fill any small gaps with moss. Circle the display with raffia and tie in a bow.

FLAT-BACKED TIERED BASKET

· · ·

MATERIALS

· · ·

knife

· · ·

1 block plastic foam for dried flowers

· · ·

large rectangular basket

· · ·

scissors

· · ·

.91 wires

· · ·

dried wheat

· · ·

dried lavender

· · ·

dried roses

· · ·

fresh moss

· · ·

mossing (floral) pins (optional)

The tall wheat is perfect at the back of this basket. Because it will shield the flowers from the sun, the basket can be placed on a windowsill.

This formal design is one of the easiest for beginners to perfect. As long as you make sure that each layer is the correct height, you can create a dramatic display. Loose, flowing materials work well within the confines of a disciplined structure. Place it against a wall or to fill a fireplace during the summer months.

1 Cut the foam to fit the basket and press firmly in. Trim and wire the wheat into bunches of 8–10 stems (see Techniques). Starting in the centre of the foam, pack the stems closely together. Check that the height balances with the basket size.

2 Trim and wire the lavender into small bunches of 5–6 stems. Push them into the foam directly in front of the wheat, packing them close together. The lavender flowers should come just below the heads of wheat. Make sure the flowers are all facing the same way.

3 Add the roses individually, positioning them in front of the lavender. Keep as much foliage as possible to fill out the tier and give it shape. Place the roses at slightly varying heights so that each flowerhead is visible and evenly placed.

4 Cover the foam with generous handfuls of moss. Fix it in place with wires bent into U-shapes or mossing (floral) pins. Fresh moss shrinks when it dries, so allow it to overhang the sides of the basket.

SMALL TIERED BASKET

· · ·

MATERIALS

· · ·

*2 small natural willow or
wicker garlands*

· · ·

.91 wires

· · ·

knife

· · ·

*1 block plastic foam for dried
flowers*

· · ·

moss

· · ·

scissors

· · ·

dried lavender

· · ·

dried red roses

*Using two garlands as a base
helps to make this an unusual
structured display.*

This pretty tiered display is made with two favourite dried materials – red roses and lavender. The bottom tier is, in fact, the trimmed stalks from the lavender, their sculptural lines adding an extra dimension to the design. You can use a shallow basket instead of the two garlands.

1 Join the two garlands securely together with wires. Cut a piece of the foam to fit snugly into the centre of the garlands and push in firmly.

2 Attach hanks of moss to the edge of the foam, using wires bent into U-shaped staples. Allow the moss to hang over the edge of the top garland.

3 Trim about 12 cm (5 in) off all the lavender stalks. Wire the trimmed stalks at one end into even-sized bunches of about ten stalks (see Techniques). Insert the stalk bunches into the foam, just inside the moss.

4 Trim the remaining lavender so the flowerheads are level and will stand just above the stalks. Wire them into even-sized bunches and insert in a circle just inside the trimmed stalks, leaving room for the roses. Trim the roses the same way, wire them into bunches of 2–3 flowers and insert in the centre, facing outwards at an attractive angle.

ROUND TIERED BASKET

· · ·

MATERIALS

· · ·

knife

· · ·

*1 block plastic foam for dried
flowers*

· · ·

round basket

· · ·

scissors

· · ·

dried deep blue larkspur

· · ·

.91 wires

· · ·

dried yellow roses

· · ·

dried hydrangea heads

· · ·

moss

· · ·

mossing (floral) pins (optional)

*The vibrant blue and bright
yellow of the larkspur and
the roses make for a very
cheerful display.*

This colourful basket is an informal round version of the traditional flat-backed tiered basket. The effect is simple to achieve as all you have to do is to keep each layer the same height. Insert the tallest flowers first then stand back to check that the height balances well with the size of the basket.

1 Cut the foam to fit the basket and press firmly in. Trim all the larkspur to the same length and wire into bunches of 8–10 stems (see Techniques). Insert the larkspur in the centre of the foam, packing the bunches closely together.

2 Trim and wire the roses, leaving as much green foliage as possible. Insert them individually in a circle around the larkspur, placing the rose heads at slightly varying angles to add interest, and so that each one is visible.

3 Trim the hydrangea heads, wire and insert around the bottom of the display. Cover the foam with moss, allowing it to trail over the edge of the basket, attaching it with mossing (floral) pins or wires bent into U-shapes.

SUMMER TIERED BASKET

· · ·

Flowering mint is an unusual material in a tiered basket, combined here with more traditional roses and lavender. Its delicious strong scent will last well, as will that of the lavender, reminding you of summer.

MATERIALS

· · ·

knife

· · ·

1 block plastic foam for dried flowers

· · ·

large basket

· · ·

scissors

· · ·

dried lavender

· · ·

.91 wires

· · ·

dried mint flowers

· · ·

dried deep pink roses

· · ·

fresh sphagnum moss

· · ·

mossing (floral) pins

When lavender is combined with mint a wonderful strong scent is created, while the roses help to accentuate the colour contrast in the design.

1 Cut the foam block to fit the basket and press firmly in. Trim all the lavender to the same length and wire into small bunches (see Techniques). Insert into the foam at the back of the basket, leaving space at either end for the other materials.

2 Trim the mint flowers so that they are shorter than the lavender. Insert them in front of the lavender and at the sides, allowing the row of flowerheads to create an informal, natural effect. Make sure that there is space for the row of roses.

3 Trim the roses so that they are shorter than the mint. Position them naturally in front of the mint and around the sides.

4 Cover the foam with handfuls of moss, attaching it with mossing (floral) pins.

SUMMER TABLE DISPLAY

· · ·

This delicate and pretty little display is designed as a centrepiece for a table laden with summer foods – and whether your dinner party is inside or outside, this display is perfect.

The materials in the arrangement, peach-pink spray roses and pale green honesty and phalaris, combine to create a soufflé of summer colours. Enhance its seasonal feel by sprinkling it with summer scented oil.

1 Cut the plastic foam to fit the basket, so that it projects 2 cm (¾ in) above its rim, and tape it into place using florist's adhesive tape.

2 Take a stem of honesty and cut off the small offshoots of dried seed heads. Use these seed heads on stems cut to about 8 cm (3¼ in), to create a foliage outline.

3 Cut the dried spray roses to a stem length of approximately 8 cm (3¼ in) and arrange them evenly and densely in the plastic foam throughout the honesty.

All the materials have relatively fragile stems which require careful handling, especially when pushing them into the plastic foam.

4 Cut the phalaris stems to a length of about 8 cm (3¼ in) and distribute them evenly throughout the honesty and spray roses.

5 Once all the materials have been used up, tie the ribbon around the basket, finishing it in a bow at the front.

EDGING BASKET
IN BLUE

· · ·

MATERIALS

· · ·

scissors

· · ·

33 stems globe thistle

· · ·

.71 wires

· · ·

24 stems sea holly

· · ·

.38 silver wire

· · ·

1 bunch floss flower

· · ·

1 bunch marjoram

· · ·

60 stems lavender

· · ·

florist's tape (stem-wrap tape)

· · ·

.32 silver reel (rose) wire

· · ·

*wire-mesh and rectangular
cane basket*

*Dried flowers transform the
basket into an attractive object
you would happily put on
display in your house.*

Tired household containers can be decorated to give them a new lease of life. This might simply be a fresh coat of paint or, as in the case of this wire mesh and cane basket, a dried-flower edging around its rim.

The display uses the blues and mauves of marjoram, floss flower, lavender, globe thistle and sea holly to create a decoration with memorable colour and texture.

1 Cut the globe thistle stems to 2.5 cm (1 in) long and double leg mount each with .71 wire. Cut the sea holly stems to 2.5 cm (1 in) and double leg mount each with .38 silver wire. Split the floss flower and the marjoram into 20 small clusters of each on stems 5 cm (2 in) long and double leg mount them individually with .38 silver wire. Cut the lavender stems to about 5 cm (2 in) long, group in threes and double leg mount each group with .38 silver wire. Cover all the wired elements with florist's tape (stem-wrap tape).

2 Lay a wired stem of sea holly on the edge of the basket and attach it by binding it in place with a length of .32 silver reel (rose) wire. Slightly overlap the sea holly with a cluster of floss flower, binding in place with .32 silver reel (rose) wire. Overlap the floss flower with a globe thistle head, the globe thistle with the marjoram and the marjoram with the lavender, binding all of them firmly to the basket with the same continuous length of reel wire. Repeat the sequence of materials all around the edge of the basket. When the entire edge of the basket is covered, stitch the reel wire through the basket several times to secure.

BATHROOM DISPLAY

• • •

MATERIALS

• • •

2 blocks plastic foam for dried flowers

• • •

knife

• • •

pale-coloured wooden trug

• • •

florist's adhesive tape

• • •

scissors

• • •

50 stems natural phalaris

• • •

40 stems shell-pink roses

• • •

20 stems cream-coloured helichrysums

• • •

150 stems dried lavender

• • •

15 small dried starfish

• • •

.71 wires

Though a steamy environment will cause dried flowers to deteriorate, if you accept the shorter life span, such arrangements are an opportunity to add an attractive decorative feature to a bathroom. The starfish in this arrangement evoke images of the sea, whilst the soft pastel colours – shell-pink, apricot, blue, pale green and cream – give it a soft summer look.

Oval shaped, in a rectangular wooden trug, the display is a traditional full arrangement which can be viewed in the round and used anywhere in the house where its pastel shades would look appropriate. The scale and colour of the arrangement is designed to show off the faded blue container.

1 Cut the block of plastic foam to fit the wooden trug and secure it in place with adhesive tape. Cut the individual stems of phalaris to a length of approximately 10 cm (4 in) and push them into the plastic foam to establish the height, width and overall shape of the arrangement.

2 Cut the stems of the dried roses to a length of approximately 10 cm (4 in) and push them into the plastic foam, distributing them evenly throughout.

3 Cut the stems of the helichrysum to a length of about 10 cm (4 in) and push them into the foam amongst the roses and phalaris, recessing some. Cut the dried lavender to 11 cm (4½ in) and, by pushing into the foam, arrange it throughout the display in groups of five stems.

4 Wire all the starfish individually by double leg mounting one of the arms with a .71 wire. Cut the wire legs of the starfish to a length of about 10 cm (4 in) and push the wires into the foam, distributing them evenly throughout the display.

This display involves some wiring but the even distribution of materials helps make it simple to build.

PINK BASKET DISPLAY

• • •

T he natural deep pink hues of these roses, helichrysum and amaranthus have survived the preservation process and here work together to produce a richly-coloured dense textural display of dried flowers.

The arrangement, mounted in an oval basket, is a low dome and thus would be good as a table arrangement, but its lavish formal appearance would make it appropriate to any reception room in the house.

MATERIALS

• • •

knife

• • •

1 block plastic foam for dried flowers

• • •

oval basket, about 20 cm (8 in) long

• • •

florist's adhesive tape

• • •

scissors

• • •

20 stems dried red amaranthus (straight)

• • •

20 stems dried deep pink roses

• • •

20 stems deep pink helichrysum

1 Cut the block of plastic foam to fit snugly into the basket and fix it securely in place with adhesive tape.

2 Cut the amaranthus to an overall length of 14 cm (5¾ in) and push them into the plastic foam to create a dome-shaped outline.

3 Cut the stems of dried roses to a length of 12 cm (4¾ in) and push them into the foam, distributing them evenly throughout the amaranthus.

4 Cut 10 of the helichrysum stems to approximately 12 cm (4¾ in) in length and push them into the foam evenly throughout the display. Cut the other 10 stems to approximately 10 cm (4 in) in length and push them into the foam evenly throughout the display, so that they are recessed to give visual depth to the arrangement.

The materials in the display have nicely contrasting textures: papery helichrysum, roses and velvet-spiked amaranthus.

AUTUMN HARVEST

· · ·

· · ·

rustic wire mesh basket

· · ·

carpet moss

· · ·

3 blocks plastic foam for dried flowers

· · ·

.90 wire

· · ·

wire cutters

· · ·

lichen

· · ·

slices dried orange

· · ·

dried sunflowers

· · ·

dried pomegranates

· · ·

dried physalis (Chinese lantern)

· · ·

scissors

· · ·

.71 wire

· · ·

dried roses

· · ·

dried hydrangea

· · ·

sea moss

The rich colours of autumn are artistically combined in this rustic basket arrangement. Reminiscent of an artist's palette, the materials are closely arranged in blocks of colour. By keeping the stems slightly longer in the centre, the arrangement has a soft, cushion shape.

1 Cover the base of the wire mesh basket with a layer of carpet moss. Place the three blocks of plastic foam inside the basket. Tip the basket on to its side, fold a long length of .90 wire in half and pass it through the wire mesh and into the foam, until it comes through at the top. Repeat this process several times until the foam is secure.

2 Bend the ends of the wires over to form a loop and push them firmly back into the plastic foam. Fill the gaps between the sides of the basket and the foam with alternate clumps of carpet moss, lichen, orange slices and sunflower heads.

3 Prepare and position the pomegranates. They need to be wired up securely. Insert two lengths of .90 wire through the middle of a fruit to form a cross. Then push the four wire ends down towards the stalk and twist them round one another to create a single, solid stalk (see Techniques). Insert the pomegranates into the arrangement in three groups of three – two groupings at opposite, diagonal corners and one in the centre.

4 Snip the physalis heads off the branches and wire them together in clusters of three, using .71 wire. Insert two clusters close together in the basket to give a solid grouping of the fruit beside the pomegranates. Continue to build up the display by introducing large, solid clusters of wired roses and other materials tightly beside one another (see Techniques). Position the hydrangea to conceal the wiring on the other materials and to cover the foam.

This rustic basket would add a lovely warm, golden colour to a kitchen table.

5 To achieve a rounded, cushion shape, leave the stems of the materials you are inserting into the centre of the arrangement slightly longer that those at the edge, and insert the materials at the edge at almost right angles to the basket. Check that the overall shape looks rounded as you go.

6 Wire up the sea moss in small clumps using short lengths of .71 wire and use these to fill the gaps between the main materials. Turn the basket around as you work and check for any obvious gaps. Fill any gaps you find with moss or other materials.

FOUR SEASONS IN A BASKET

· · ·

MATERIALS

· · ·

knife

· · ·

2 blocks plastic foam for dried flowers

· · ·

round shallow basket

· · ·

florist's adhesive tape

· · ·

scissors

· · ·

60 stems dried natural phalaris

· · ·

17 stems cream helichrysum

· · ·

40 dried deep pink roses

· · ·

160 stems dried lavender

· · ·

25 stems carthamus

· · ·

5 stems preserved (dried) brown adiantum

· · ·

10 cinnamon sticks

· · ·

5 dried oranges with splits

· · ·

.71 wires

*I*nvolving only a small amount of wiring, the display is not difficult to make but is an excellent exercise in massing dried flowers, and would make a powerful centrepiece for a circular table.

This contemporary massed display in a circular basket is divided into quarters, each representing – by its material content and colours – one of the four seasons. It is important to keep the materials tightly assembled for maximum effect.

1 Cut the plastic foam to fit and wedge it in the basket. Divide the surface of the foam into quarters by making a cross with adhesive tape. Cut the stems of phalaris and helichrysum to a length of about 6 cm (2½ in). Group the phalaris stems in fives and arrange them evenly throughout one quarter of the basket. Distribute the helichrysum among the phalaris with all the heads at the same level.

2 Insert the roses and lavender in another quarter, cutting the stems of the roses to 6 cm (2½ in) and the lavender to an overall length of 7 cm (2¾ in).

3 Cut the stems of carthamus to 6 cm (2½ in). Break fronds of adiantum from the main stems and cut them to 7 cm (2¾ in). Push the carthamus stems and adiantum into a third quarter of the basket.

4 Cut the sticks of cinnamon to 6 cm (2½ in). Single leg mount the dried oranges (see Techniques) and cut the protruding wires to a length of 4 cm (1½ in). Push the wires of the oranges into the foam to arrange them evenly throughout the fourth quarter of the basket. Push the cinnamon sticks into the foam, massing them tightly between the dried oranges.

FRUIT AND FUNGI BASKET RIM DECORATION

• • •

Creating a dried flower embellishment for the rim of an old and damaged wicker basket gives it a new lease of life by transforming it into a resplendent container for the display of fruit. The decoration is full of the bold textures and rich colours of sunflowers, oranges, lemons, apples and fungi.

MATERIALS

• • •

45 slices dried orange

• • •

45 slices dried lemon

• • •

45 slices preserved (dried) apple

• • •

.71 wires

• • •

18 sunflower heads

• • •

16 small pieces dried fungus

• • •

florist's tape (stem-wrap tape)

• • •

scissors

• • •

old wicker basket, without a handle

• • •

.32 silver reel (rose) wire

1 Group the orange slices in threes and double leg mount each group with .71 wires. Repeat with the lemon and apple slices. Cut the sunflower stems to about 2.5 cm (1 in) and individually double leg mount them on .71 wires. Double leg mount the pieces of fungi with .71 wire. Finally tape over all the wires with florist's tape (stem–wrap tape).

2 Starting at one corner of the basket, bind a group of orange slices to its rim by stitching .32 silver reel (rose) wire through the wicker and around the stem. With the same wire, stitch on the apple slices, the sunflower heads, the lemon slices and the fungi. Repeat this sequence until the rim is covered. Stitch the wire around the last stem and the basket.

The principles of this design can be used to decorate a wicker container of any type.

BOXES AND BUNDLES

· · ·

Terracotta pots and baskets are only two of the many kinds of container that you can use for a floral display. Experiment with unusual boxes, or make your own base from a simple piece of cardboard. You can even dispense with a container altogether, and gather your materials into a hay-covered bundle or a hand-tied posy.

INTRODUCTION

· · ·

Above: Rose Bundle

Below: Quartered Box

After a while, you may find that working with conventional pots and baskets becomes a little predictable and that you want to try something different to expand your repertoire. This is an ideal chance to experiment, and to improvise by finding new bases for your displays.

A valued receptacle such as a glass bowl or antique pine tub may inspire a display specifically designed for that container. At the other end of the spectrum, recycled metal is now very fashionable in interior design and even a large tin looks effective when it is filled with a vivid display of flowers.

Other containers are not so attractive to look at and need to be disguised with paint or fabric. A basic wooden crate or humble cardboard box makes an excellent base for all kinds of displays, although you may need to reinforce the corners of a cardboard box so that it doesn't lose its shape under the weight of the dried materials. One of the simplest and most successful designs is a quartered box: this is a cardboard box sectioned with string or cord into four equal spaces, each of which is filled with a different-coloured material.

Another attractive option is to fill the top of a cardboard box with a still life composed of unrelated objects such as shells, fungi, sticks and flowers. You can also add a candle, depending on where you wish to place the finished display. This theme can be successfully repeated many times, using quite different objects. Yet another idea is to wrap an oval-shaped gift box with large preserved (dried) leaves,

Above: Rope-tied Bunch

Left: Tiered Box

allowing the leaves to extend above the edge of the box and make an attractive border for the contents. And if you don't have a suitable box for a particular project, you can cut a piece of cardboard and wrap it around the base of plastic foam, disguising it with fabric or leaves.

To make a bundle arrangement of dried material, you need something like a small piece of foam covered with brown paper or fabric to structure the display. For a country look, attach hay to the outside so that the flowerheads appear above a rather unruly collar of hay. These displays often include dried grasses and ears of wheat, combined with colourful flowers.

Hand-tied bunches of dried flowers are completely self-supporting, with no base at all. Creating one is not as easy as it looks however; it takes a little practice to learn how to spiral the stems as you add them to the bunch, and to achieve the slightly domed shape.

Perfumed bunches of material are made quite differently. Flowers and herbs are arranged on top of long cinnamon sticks so that the flowerheads are at either end

Below: Spring Perfumed Bunch

of the sticks, then simply tied around the centre. These lovely designs use very little material and are quick and easy to make. To increase the perfume you can add a few drops of perfumed oil to the centre, avoiding the flowerheads themselves, which may go soft.

Many of these informal displays look best tied very simply with a large raffia bow, but for a more sophisticated look you can use an elaborate paper ribbon or fabric bow.

SIMPLE FLORAL BOX

· · ·

MATERIALS

· · ·

knife

· · ·

*1 block plastic foam for dried
flowers*

· · ·

small wooden crate

· · ·

green moss

· · ·

scissors or secateurs

· · ·

dried Protea compacta

· · ·

fresh bay leaves

· · ·

mossing (floral) pins

· · ·

rope

*Protea and bay leaves make
an unusual combination which
is very effective.*

This quick display can be made in a variety of boxes; even
a cardboard box can look good if it is covered with spray
paint or fabric. For a rustic feel, use a small wooden crate. Bay
leaves are best used fresh from the bush as there is less risk of
the leaves falling off the stems. When they are completely dry,
their appearance will be improved with clear florist's lacquer.

1 Trim the block of
foam so that it is a
little smaller than the
crate. Place the foam in
the crate and pack any
spaces with moss so
that the foam fits
firmly. Tease some of
the moss through the
gaps in the crate so that
it hangs out.

2 Trim the stems of
the protea to the
required height,
allowing at least an
extra 3 cm (1¼ in) of
the stem to penetrate
the foam. Starting
slightly off-centre,
insert a row of protea
into the foam.

3 Add a second row of the protea stems
to one side of the first, so that the
two rows completely fill the centre of
the display.

4 Trim the stems of the bay leaves and
push them into the foam, so that the
tops of the bay leaves are just below the
bottom of the protea heads.

5 Add a collar of bay leaves all around the edge, completely covering the foam base. Add more moss, fixing it in place with mossing (floral) pins. Wrap the rope loosely around the crate a couple of times and tie in a knot or bow.

Place this arrangement in a prominent position so that the striking protea can be seen and admired.

QUARTERED BOX

· · ·

MATERIALS

· · ·

knife

· · ·

*1 block plastic foam for dried
flowers*

· · ·

*rectangular cardboard box, with
lid*

· · ·

string or cord

· · ·

scissors

· · ·

dried lavender

· · ·

.91 wires

· · ·

dried pink roses

· · ·

dried poppy seed heads

· · ·

cinnamon sticks

· · ·

tillandsia moss

*Cinnamon sticks are a good
material for displays, adding
both texture and scent.*

Here, a cardboard shoe box is divided equally into four sections, which are filled with separate materials. The lid of the box helps to support the weight of the display so that the shape does not distort.

1 Trim the foam block to fit into the box then place the box in its lid. Tie a piece of string or cord around the centre of the box in both directions, to divide it into four sections.

2 Prepare the dried materials. Cut the flower stems to similar lengths. Wire the lavender in small bunches (see Techniques). Handle the cinnamon sticks with care.

3 Insert a separate material into each section, so that they lean outwards slightly. Cover the foam with moss then add a few wispy strands to soften the formal effect.

ANTIQUE PINE BOX

· · ·

Complement the beautiful golden colour of antique pine with a lively display of multicoloured flowers. The dried materials are very simply packed into the container, without any foam or wiring. If you cannot find a suitable pine box, you can wax or stain modern pine to the same rich colour.

MATERIALS

· · ·

wire cutters

· · ·

chicken wire

· · ·

pine box or plant container

· · ·

dried flowers, e.g. pink larkspur, echinops, miniature orange-pink roses

· · ·

scissors

· · ·

moss

Hang a selection of your favourite flowers until dried, and use them to fill a container of your choice.

1 Cut a piece of chicken wire to fit the box. Scrunch it up slightly and place inside the box.

2 Separate the flowers into groups. Trim the stems as necessary.

3 Push individual stems through the wire to the bottom of the box, so that the different varieties are mixed together. Aim to create a rich, natural display. When the display is complete, add plenty of moss around the edges.

ROSE BOWL

· · ·

MATERIALS

· · ·

*2 blocks plastic foam for dried
flowers*

· · ·

container

· · ·

pen

· · ·

knife

· · ·

.91 wires

· · ·

lichen

· · ·

scissors

· · ·

dried white roses

*This display looks most
effective when the rose heads
are packed in tightly with no
visible gaps – but not so tight
that they become misshapen.*

A bowl of closely packed white roses makes a classic table centrepiece. The idea is updated here by placing the rose flowerheads in a diamond-shaped glass container to create a contemporary look.

1 Place the foam blocks side by side then place the container centrally over them. With a pen, mark the edges of the container. Measure in the thickness of the bowl edges to make a second set of lines.

2 Remove the container and cut directly through the foam with the knife. Place the foam inside the container.

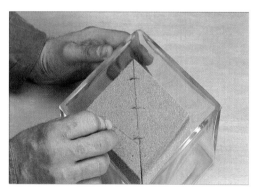

3 To further secure the foam base, use wire pins made of short lengths of wire to hold the two halves of the foam together. The base should fit snugly into the container.

4 Fill the gap between the foam and the container with lichen. Ensure that the lichen is packed tightly, as this not only looks attractive but will act as a further anchor for the foam.

5 Prepare the roses by cutting them to the same length, leaving the stems at least 5 cm (2 in) in length. Begin to insert them into the foam, starting at the outer edge and working inwards.

6 Continue this process until the foam is completely covered, leaving no gaps between the rose heads. Ensure that all the heads are level, giving the display a flat, symmetrical look.

Try to find an interesting-shaped container for this stunning rose display.

LEAF-WRAPPED BOX

• • •

MATERIALS

• • •

glue gun and glue sticks

• • •

large preserved (dried) leaves

• • •

cardboard box

• • •

knife

• • •

1 block plastic foam for dried flowers

• • •

candle

• • •

scissors

• • •

dried miniature pink roses

• • •

moss

• • •

mossing (floral) pins

• • •

raffia

A raffia bow gives a lovely informal touch.

This is a way of making use of gift boxes that are just too good to throw away. The candle is an option; a bigger box may need more than one candle to give the finished display a balanced look. Instead of raffia, you could use a wide ribbon tied in a bow for a softer look. Never leave a burning candle unattended.

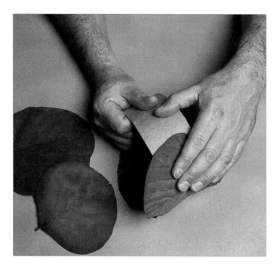

1 Spread a little glue on the back of each leaf and press it firmly on to the side of the box. If the leaves are not large enough to cover the depth of the box, start the first row at the top then overlap the bottom row with next. The top row of leaves should extend above the lip of the box.

2 Trim the foam block to fit the box. Apply glue to the inside base of the box and push the foam block firmly in. Try to create a good, tight fit, to help ensure that the box keeps its shape.

3 When the glue has set, push the candle into the foam in the centre of the box. Remove the candle and put a little glue into the hole then firmly replace the candle. This will ensure that the candle is safe.

4 Trim the roses so that the finished
length will allow about 3 cm (1¼ in)
to be pushed into the foam, with about
5 cm (2 in) above the leaves. Insert them
around the outside edge of the box.
Leave a space around the candle so that
there is no risk of the flowers burning.
Fill spaces with moss, attached with
mossing (floral) pins. Trim the moss
around the candle. Tie raffia around the
outside of the box, finishing in a bow.

*Choose a long candle to create
an attractive tall display and so
that you do not have to change
it too frequently.*

WOODLAND TREASURE BOX

· · ·

MATERIALS

· · ·

knife

· · ·

*1 block plastic foam for dried
flowers*

· · ·

small wooden crate or box

· · ·

green moss

· · ·

mossing (floral) pins

· · ·

glue gun and glue sticks

· · ·

small terracotta pots

· · ·

*small selection of different
mosses, fungi, fir cones, nuts
and woody items, e.g.
magnolia seed heads*

· · ·

candle

*Fir cones, nuts and other
decorative woody items can be
collected on a woodland walk.*

Transform a plain wooden box with a collection of mosses, fungi, fir cones, nuts and other woodland finds together with a candle pot. As there are no fixings except for the candle pot, it is easy to rearrange the ingredients so that the collection looks different all the time. You can even change the materials to suit a particular season. Never leave a burning candle unattended.

1 Trim the foam so that it fits into about a third of the box. If the box is open-sided, cover the sides of the foam with green moss. Fix it in place with mossing (floral) pins.

2 Using a glue gun, carefully apply glue either to the foam base or to the bottom of the box.

3 Push the foam firmly on to the bottom of the box and into one corner. Tease out a little moss through the gaps in the sides of the box. Hold the foam down until the glue has hardened to make a solid base for the candle pot.

4 Cover the remaining sides of the foam with moss, leaving a space on top large enough for the candle pot.

5 Glue the candle pot firmly on to the top of the foam. Cover any small spaces with moss.

6 Line the rest of the box with more moss, saving any unusual moss to trim the arrangement near the top. Fill the box with extra pots, fir cones, nuts, fungi, etc. Glue a candle inside the candle pot.

This interesting display is a still life of different woodland materials.

BOXED TABLE CENTREPIECE

· · ·

MATERIALS

· · ·

knife

· · ·

*1 block plastic foam for dried
flowers*

· · ·

cardboard box

· · ·

glue gun and glue sticks

· · ·

large preserved (dried) leaves

· · ·

raffia

· · ·

scissors

· · ·

reindeer moss

· · ·

candle

· · ·

nuts and dried fruit

· · ·

.91 wires

· · ·

dried red chillies

*Nuts and dried fruit in a
table centrepiece continue the
"food" theme.*

This idea completely transforms a plain cardboard box into an unusual table centrepiece. The centre could be filled with sugared almonds or crystallized fruit surrounding the candle. Never leave a burning candle unattended.

1 Trim the foam block to the shape of the box. Apply some glue to the base of the box and push the foam firmly into it. Try to create a good, tight fit, to ensure that the box keeps its shape.

2 Spread a little glue on the back of each leaf and press it firmly on to the side of the box. Position the leaves so that they extend well above the lip of the box. Make sure that they are evenly placed.

3 Wrap several strands of raffia around the leaf-covered box and tie in a bow.

4 Trim all the leaves that extend over the base of the box so that it will stand flat. Take care not to split the leaves.

5 Arrange some reindeer moss inside the edge of the box, leaving the centre empty for the candle.

6 Take the candle and push it into the foam, in the centre of the box. Remove the candle and put a little glue into the hole then replace the candle.

7 Arrange the nuts and dried fruit in the box. Make sure that a varied selection is visible, keeping the best items, such as dried oranges, until last.

8 Bunch and centre-wire the chillies (see Techniques). Tie them with raffia to cover the wire then gently push the ends of the wire through the fruit into the foam.

Autumn colours make a lovely table decoration, and the candle adds a magical touch.

STILL-LIFE BOX

· · ·

MATERIALS

· · ·

scissors

· · ·

hessian (burlap)

· · ·

rectangular cardboard box

· · ·

glue gun and glue sticks

· · ·

knife

· · ·

1–2 blocks plastic foam for dried flowers

· · ·

secateurs

· · ·

willow sticks

· · ·

string

· · ·

shells

· · ·

dried fungi

· · ·

other dried materials, e.g. echinops, seed pods, garlic cloves

· · ·

reindeer moss

· · ·

candle (optional)

Blue echinops always adds an attractive and warm glow to any display.

Cover a box with hessian (burlap) to make a neutral base then fill it with a carefully arranged collection of shells, fungi and dried materials. Remember you should never leave a burning candle unattended.

1 Cut a piece of hessian (burlap) to cover the outside of the box and extend about 5 cm (2 in) inside it. Glue it to the box, mitring the corners neatly. The raw edge inside will be hidden by the display.

2 Trim the foam blocks to fit into the box, slightly lower than the top edge. Cut the willow sticks to length and tie together in two bundles with string. Glue all the materials on to the foam, building up an attractive arrangement. Leave space for a candle if desired. Fill any gaps with reindeer moss, gluing it in place.

CINNAMON-WRAPPED TIERS

• • •

Cinnamon sticks are used here instead of leaves to cover the base of a tiered display. The tartan trim gives the impression of holding the cinnamon sticks in place but in fact is purely for decoration.

MATERIALS

• • •

craft knife

• • •

cardboard

• • •

1 block plastic foam for dried flowers

• • •

mossing (floral) pins

• • •

scissors

• • •

dried dark red roses

• • •

.91 wires

• • •

dried lavender

• • •

dried pink larkspur

• • •

glue gun and glue sticks

• • •

cinnamon sticks

• • •

tartan fabric

The delicate materials in this display will keep their colours for a long time, but they should be kept away from direct sunlight.

1 Cut a piece of cardboard to fit the bottom and about 5 cm (2 in) up the sides of the foam block. Fix it in place with mossing (floral) pins.

2 Trim the rose stems to the longest length required for the display. Push them into the foam in two rows, leaving space at either end and the front.

3 Wire the lavender into small bunches (see Techniques). Push into the foam along the front and sides of the roses so that the tops of the lavender are level with the bottoms of the roses. Repeat with the larkspur, so that their tops are level with the bottoms of the lavender.

4 Glue cinnamon sticks of equal length carefully around the front and sides of the cardboard collar, placing them close together like a fence.

5 Fold a strip of tartan fabric and glue around the base of the display. Make a fabric bow and glue in the centre of the display (see Techniques).

TIERED BOX

· · ·

· · ·

craft knife

· · ·

cardboard

· · ·

*1 block plastic foam for dried
flowers*

· · ·

glue gun and glue sticks

· · ·

fabric

· · ·

mossing (floral) pins

· · ·

scissors

· · ·

dried peonies

· · ·

.91 wires

· · ·

dried lavender

· · ·

dried Alchemilla mollis

· · ·

*preserved (dried) leaves, e.g.
cobra leaves*

· · ·

raffia

· · ·

green moss

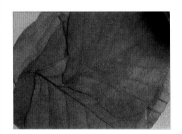

*The leaves cover the foam
block and make an innovative
container for an arrangement.*

This display has a flat back, so it can stand against a wall or in a small fireplace. If you want it to be viewed from all sides, the process is almost exactly the same but the first two rows of flowers need to start in the centre, and not at one edge. Then add the other flowers, working all the way around. For a larger display, simply glue several blocks of foam together.

1 Cut a piece of cardboard to fit around the bottom of the foam block and glue it in place. Lay the foam block on the fabric and cut a piece large enough to cover the bottom and up the sides by about 5 cm (2 in). Hold the sides of the fabric in place with mossing (floral) pins, making sure that the base is crease-free.

2 Trim the peony stems to the desired length. Starting at the back of the display, push two rows into the foam block, leaving space at either end for the other materials. Make sure that at least 3 cm (1¼ in) of the stems penetrate the foam. Do not put material right at the edge of the foam as it will weaken the foam and break away.

3 Wire the lavender into medium-sized bunches (see Techniques). Push them into the foam block, along the front and sides of the peonies so that the tops of the lavender are level with the bottoms of the peonies. Repeat the same process for the alchemilla, so that their tops are level with the bottoms of the lavender bunches.

4 Fix the leaves along the front and the sides of the display, above the fabric, with mossing (floral) pins. Wrap at least one of the leaves around each back corner of the display.

5 Tie several strands of raffia around the arrangement, to cover the pins, and tie into a bow. Tuck green moss in the back of the display to cover any foam that may still be visible.

HARVEST DISPLAY
· · ·

MATERIALS
· · ·
knife
· · ·
*4 blocks plastic foam for dried
flowers*
· · ·
large tin
· · ·
dried wheat
· · ·
dried lavender
· · ·
dried poppy seed heads
· · ·
reindeer moss

*The lavender stalks look
very impressive when
massed together in a
simple arrangement.*

The soft blue shades of lavender have been teamed with golden wheat and poppy seed heads in a tin container whose gentle grey tones offset the blues, greens and golds perfectly. Here, a traditional tiered display has been given an effective modern treatment, using simple dried materials.

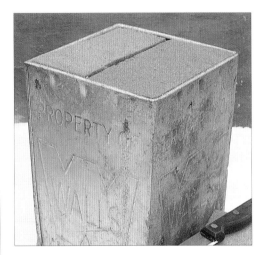

1 Trim the foam blocks and fit them into the container. If you are using a tall container, stand two foam blocks upright in the bottom to support two on top. It is important that the bricks on top fit the container tightly.

2 Insert the wheat, a few stalks at a time, into the centre of the foam. Discard any broken or imperfect stems.

3 Working in rows, insert the lavender stalks one by one around the wheat. Graduate the height of the lavender so that the front rows are slightly lower than the back ones.

4 Trim the stalks of the poppy seed heads to about 5 cm (2 in). Insert a row all around the rim of the container. Place another row behind them so that it rests on top of the first. Tuck the reindeer moss carefully under the front row, lifting the seed heads a little if necessary.

OLIVE-OIL CAN ROSE ARRANGEMENT

. . .

MATERIALS

. . .

1 block plastic foam for dried flowers

. . .

knife

. . .

small rectangular olive oil can

. . .

scissors

. . .

40 stems dried 'Jacaranda' roses

. . .

raffia

If you come across an eye-catching container, however unlikely, remember it may be just right for a floral display. And if you are using dried flowers it does not even need to be watertight.

An old olive oil can may not be the first thing to spring to mind when consid-ering a container for your dried flower arrangement, but the bright reds, yellows and greens of this tin make it an attractive option.

Since this container is so striking, the arrangement is kept simple with only one type of flower and one colour used. This creates an effective contemporary display.

1 Cut the plastic foam to fit snugly in the olive oil can, filling it to 2 cm (¾ in) down from its rim.

2 Cut the dried roses so that they protrude about 10 cm (4 in) above the rim of the tin. Starting at the left-hand side of the tin, arrange a line of five tightly packed roses in the plastic foam from its front to its back. Continue arranging lines of five roses parallel to the first and closely packed to each other across the width of the tin.

3 Continue adding lines of roses until the roses are used up. Then take a small bundle of raffia about 3 cm (1¼ in) thick and twist it to make it compact. Loosely wrap the raffia round the stems of the roses just above the top of the tin and finish in a tied knot.

WALL HANGING SHEAF
• • •

The rustic charm of this delightful hand-tied sheaf is difficult to resist especially since it is so easy to make once you have mastered the ever-useful stem-spiralling technique.

The focal flowers are large, round, orange globe thistle heads, the hard, spiky geometry of which is set against the creamy-white papery flowers of the helichrysum and country green of linseed and amaranthus. The green carthamus, with its curious orange tufts, acts as a visual bridge between the other materials.

1 Set out the materials so that they are easily accessible. Divide each of the bunches of linseed and helichrysum into 10 smaller bunches. Break off the side shoots from the main stems of the carthamus and the globe thistle to increase the number of individual stems available. Take the longest stem of amaranthus in your hand and, to either side of it, add a stem of carthamus and a bunch of linseed making sure all the material is slightly shorter than the amaranthus. The stems of the materials should be spiralled as they are added. Add materials to the bunch to maintain a visual balance between the bold forms of the globe thistle and helichrysum and the more delicate linseed and carthamus.

MATERIALS
• • •
1 bunch dried linseed
• • •
1 bunch white helichrysum
• • •
10 stems dried carthamus
• • •
8 stems large dried orange globe thistle
• • •
10 stems dried green amaranthus (straight)
• • •
twine
• • •
scissors
• • •
green paper ribbon

The sheaf shape makes a feature of the stems as well as the blooms. Finished with a green ribbon, this decoration would look lovely hung in a country-style kitchen.

2 When all the materials have been incorporated, tie with twine at the binding point. Trim the ends of the stems.

3 Make a paper ribbon bow and attach it to the sheaf at the binding point with its tails pointing towards the flowerheads.

COUNTRY BUNDLE
· · ·

The combination of raffia and grasses accentuates the informal, country feel of a display.

This wonderful design requires more skill than you might expect to achieve its deliberately informal appearance, which creates a wonderful countryside look. If you plan to trim the hay at the bottom, choose fabric that will match your decor, otherwise any fabric can be used.

1 Cut the foam block in half. Take one piece and make sure it is square. Use the foam as a template to draw a square on the cardboard then cut it out with a craft knife. Glue it to the bottom of the block. Using the foam base as a guide, cut the fabric into a square about 5 cm (2 in) larger than the cardboard.

2 Fold the fabric up around the foam base. Use mossing (floral) pins to hold it in place, turning the corners and smoothing it so that there are no wrinkles.

3 Wrap silver reel (rose) wire 3–4 times round the fabric-covered foam and add the hay to form a collar around the sides as you tightly wrap the wire. Cover the sides completely then secure the end of the wire by tying it to a mossing (floral) pin pushed into the base. Trim the hay at the base so that it is even and remove any straggly strands. If you want some of the fabric base to show, trim the hay about halfway up the sides of the block.

4 Trim the stems of the dried materials. They need to be long enough for about 5 cm (2 in) to be pushed into the foam, while allowing the flowerheads to show above the hay. Wire the flowers into small bunches of mixed or single varieties (see Techniques). Fill the space inside the hay collar, leaving no gaps. Make the centre a little higher and lean the bunches nearest the edge slightly outwards. Tie a raffia bow around the base.

EXOTIC BUNDLE

· · ·

MATERIALS

· · ·

knife

· · ·

1 block plastic foam for dried flowers

· · ·

pencil

· · ·

fairly thick cardboard

· · ·

craft knife

· · ·

fabric

· · ·

mossing (floral) pins

· · ·

silver reel (rose) wire

· · ·

hay

· · ·

scissors

· · ·

dried materials, e.g. Achillea ptarmica, *catkins,* Nigella orientalis, *nicandra, oregano, poppy seed heads, red roses*

· · ·

.91 wires

· · ·

raffia

The natural colours of this display contrast strongly with the vivid red of the roses.

G ive extra interest to an informal arrangement by including some surprising materials. In this display catkins and seed pods dominate the flowers, and the red roses add a very dramatic note.

1 Cut the foam block in half. Take one piece and trim into a square. Using the foam as a template, draw a square on the cardboard and cut out with a craft knife. Cut a square of fabric 5 cm (2 in) larger than the cardboard. Sandwich the cardboard on top of the fabric and under the foam. Fold the fabric up over the foam, fixing with mossing (floral) pins.

2 Wrap the silver reel (rose) wire 3–4 times around the foam. Add handfuls of hay, trapping it under the wire and keeping the wire as tight as possible.

3 Secure the end of the wire by tying it to a mossing (floral) pin pushed into the base. Trim the stems of all the materials, allowing about 5 cm (2 in) to be pushed into the foam while allowing the heads to show above the hay. Wire into small bunches (see Techniques). Fill the space inside the hay collar, leaving no gaps and creating a slightly domed shape. Add the material at varying heights to give the display a natural feel.

4 Position the roses last. Tie a raffia bow around the base.

TIED FLOWERS

• • •

This fresh arrangement is cleverly designed to look as if you have gathered a handful of flowers straight from the countryside. In fact, you need to take plenty of time to compose the shape and choose the right balance of materials. Long grasses look particularly good.

MATERIALS

• • •

dried flowers and grasses, e.g. carthamus, echinops, blue larkspur, honesty, nigella, wheat

• • •

scissors

• • •

silver reel (rose) wire

• • •

raffia

This particular selection of dried materials is rich in different textures and colours.

1 Prepare the materials. Separate all the flowers and foliage into separate piles. Trim any waste material from the stems. Select 2–3 stems of each variety to make a small bunch, holding them tightly in one hand. Initially, keep all the flowerheads level.

2 Continue to add stems, but change the angle a little each time. As you build up the shape, lower the height of the flowerheads slightly so that they almost create a dome. When the bundle looks complete, wind silver reel (rose) wire firmly around the stems about 5–6 times. Trim the stems so that the bundle stands on its own. Add a large raffia bow to conceal the wire.

ROSE BUNDLE

· · ·

MATERIALS

· · ·

1 plastic foam round for dried flowers

· · ·

brown paper

· · ·

glue gun and glue sticks

· · ·

craft knife

· · ·

.91 wires

· · ·

pliers

· · ·

scissors

· · ·

12 dried orange or yellow roses

· · ·

moss

· · ·

large preserved (dried) leaves, e.g. cobra leaves

· · ·

mossing (floral) pins

· · ·

raffia

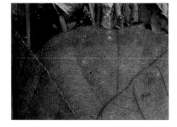

Preserved (dried) leaves make an attractive wrapping for a dozen roses.

This little display is very easy to make, using a ready-made plastic foam circle covered with brown paper. Raffia gives the bundle a country feel; for a smarter look, tie the roses with a ribbon or paper bow.

1 Place the foam round in the centre of the brown paper and glue it in position. Using a craft knife, cut from the edge of the foam to the outer edge of the paper, working all the way around at roughly 1 cm (½ in) intervals.

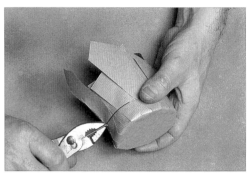

2 Fold the paper strips up to wrap the foam. Wrap a wire around the paper and the foam, making sure all the paper strips are straight and neat at the base, and twist the two ends of the wire tightly together with pliers.

3 Trim the paper in line with the top of the foam. Trim the rose stems, retaining as many leaves as possible. Starting in the centre, push them carefully, one at a time, into the foam.

4 Cover the foam with roses and use moss in the gaps. About twelve roses should be enough. If more rose leaves are required, wire some together in bunches and add to the foam (see Techniques).

5 Wrap 3–4 leaves around the base, fixing each one in place with a mossing (floral) pin. Make sure you place each pin at the same height as the last.

6 Wrap a wire around the leaves at the same level as the mossing (floral) pins and twist the ends together to make a tight fixing.

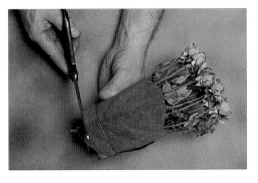

Orange and yellow roses keep their colour for a very long time, which makes them perfectly suited to the role of brightening a dark corner.

7 Trim the leaves at the base of the display so that it will stand evenly.

8 Tie raffia around the base to cover all the fixings, finishing with a bow. Fill any spaces with extra moss.

SUMMER FLOWER BUNDLE

• • •

MATERIALS

· · ·

1 plastic foam round for dried flowers

· · ·

brown paper

· · ·

glue gun and glue sticks

· · ·

craft knife

· · ·

.91 wires

· · ·

pliers

· · ·

scissors

· · ·

dried pink larkspur

· · ·

dried pink roses

· · ·

moss

· · ·

large preserved (dried) leaves

· · ·

mossing (floral) pins

· · ·

raffia

Larkspur looks very summery against the dark leaves, and combines beautifully with pink roses.

This pretty arrangement would be a welcome gift for someone unwell at home or in hospital, with the advantage that it would take up very little precious bedside space. A dinner table with an individual small flower bundle for each place setting would also look very welcoming.

1 Place the foam round in the centre of the brown paper and glue it in place. Using a craft knife, make cuts from the edge of the foam to the outer edge of the paper, working all the way around at roughly 1 cm (½ in) intervals.

2 Fold up the paper strips to wrap the foam. Twist a wire around the paper and the foam. Make sure all the paper strips are straight and neat at the base then twist the ends of the wire together. Trim the paper in line with the foam.

3 Trim the larkspur and rose stems, retaining as many of the leaves as possible. Starting in the centre, push them one at a time into the foam.

4 Cover the foam with flowers using moss to fill the gaps. If you want more leaves, add some wired bunches of rose leaves (see Techniques).

5 Wrap 3 or 4 leaves around the base, fixing each one in place with a mossing (floral) pin. Make sure each pin is placed at the same height as the last.

6 Using pliers, neatly wrap a wire around the leaves at the same level as the pins. Twist the ends together to make a tight fixing.

7 Trim the leaves at the base of the display with scissors, so that the display will stand evenly without wobbling.

8 Tie raffia around the base, covering all the fixings. Finish with a bow or a simple knot. If the roses had a limited number of leaves, fill the spaces around the stems with extra moss.

This arrangement is bright and compact, making it a perfect gift as well as an attractive decoration.

235

SPRING PERFUMED BUNCH

· · ·

MATERIALS

· · ·

dried Alchemilla mollis

· · ·

dried white larkspur

· · ·

dried lavender

· · ·

dried pale yellow roses

· · ·

dried oregano

· · ·

long cinnamon sticks

· · ·

.91 wires

· · ·

scissors

· · ·

raffia

· · ·

moss

· · ·

perfumed oil

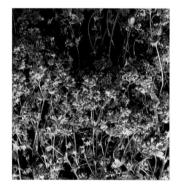

Pale yellow flowers, mixed with lavender and oregano, give a lovely springtime feeling.

This lovely little bunch of cinnamon sticks and dried flowers is an excellent alternative to pot-pourri. Extra stems of nigella, poppy seed heads and *Achillia ptarmica* are used in the steps, while the main picture is more simple.

1 Separate the flowers into bunches according to variety. Take 4–5 cinnamon sticks and place the first flowers so that their heads align with one end of the sticks. Add more flowers so that there are flowerheads at both ends, with the stems meeting in the middle. Build up the flowers so that they run down the entire length of the cinnamon sticks from both ends and almost meet in the centre.

2 Tie the completed bundle around the middle with a wire. Cut away any excess wire and push the ends in among the stalks.

3 Tie a thick raffia bow around the middle of the bundle and trim any straggling stalks. Soak a piece of moss in perfumed oil and tie it to the bunch with a wire.

AUTUMN PERFUMED BUNCH

. . .

A rich selection of warm colours is combined here with long, golden brown cinnamon sticks, to bring cheer in autumn months. Add a few drops of a spicy perfumed oil to capture the essence of autumn.

MATERIALS

. . .

dried flowers, e.g. red amaranthus, echinops, carthamus, yellow roses, blue larkspur, nigella, solidago

. . .

long cinnamon sticks

. . .

.91 wires

. . .

scissors

. . .

small fir cones

. . .

raffia

. . .

moss

. . .

perfumed oil

Nigella balances nicely against the rounded fir cones.

1 Separate the flowers into bunches, according to variety. Take 4–5 cinnamon sticks and place the first flowers so that their heads align with the sticks. Add more flowers so that there are flowerheads at both ends, with the stems meeting in the middle. Trim the stems.

2 Build up the design so that there are flowerheads running down the length of the cinnamon sticks from both ends and almost meeting in the middle. Tie the bunch around the middle with a wire. Cut off the excess wire and tuck the end in among the stalks.

3 Wire the fir cones (see Techniques). Fix to the centre of the bunch then cover all the wire fixings with a large raffia bow. Soak a piece of moss in perfumed oil and attach to the bunch with a wire.

HAND-TIED POSY

· · ·

The mixture of flowers and herbs makes a beautiful posy, and the draping red amaranthus creates a unique effect.

Hand-tied posies have a fresh, simple, just-picked look about them, but it takes time and practice to perfect the technique of spiralling the stems to create a free-standing bouquet. The long trailing strands of rich, red amaranthus add more interest to this neat, round arrangement.

1 Select your first stem of hydrangea and thread a single rose through the centre. The two stems should cross one another diagonally.

2 Begin to add the amaranthus and oregano stems symmetrically to the core, angling the stems at diagonals. This is very important to achieve the dome shape and to allow the posy to stand by itself once finished.

3 With one hand, continue to add further stems of each material diagonally to the bunch. Hold the bunch securely in the other hand, creating a spiralled effect as you add more material.

4 Build up the posy until you can no longer hold the stems comfortably in your hand. Trim the stems to an even length – the length of the stems should be in proportion to the size of the posy.

A free-standing posy makes an impressive display.

5 Tie the bunch tightly with raffia at the narrowest part of the spiral. If the bunch is correctly made, the posy should stand by itself without support.

6 Make a loose bow out of several lengths of raffia and tie round the binding point. Trim and knot or bind the ends for a neat finish.

ROPE-TIED BUNCH

· · ·

MATERIALS

· · ·

*dried materials, e.g. blue
larkspur, pink roses, poppy
seed heads, wheat*

· · ·

scissors

· · ·

silver reel (rose) wire

· · ·

sea-grass rope

*Large poppy seed heads are
attractive when they protrude
from an arrangement of tall,
thin grasses.*

Mix dried grasses and wheat with country cottage garden flowers to make this lovely tied display. Large poppy seed heads stand out against the smaller materials to help create a full and rounded effect. Complete the country look with an unusual bow of sea-grass rope or, if you prefer, raffia.

1 Separate the materials into piles. Trim any waste material from the stems. Select 2–3 stems of each variety and make a small bunch, holding them tightly in one hand with all the flower and seed heads level.

2 Add extra stems, changing the angle a little each time. As the display builds up, lower the flower and seed heads slightly to create a dome shape. When the bunch is complete, wind silver reel (rose) wire firmly around the stems 5–6 times. Trim the stems level. Tie the rope in a bow, to conceal the wire.

Tied Pink Peony Bouquet

· · ·

MATERIALS

· · ·

15 dried dark pink peonies

· · ·

30 dried dark pink roses

· · ·

1 bunch dried marjoram

· · ·

twine

· · ·

scissors

· · ·

ribbon

This lovely bouquet demonstrates how, by the use of modern preserving techniques, the strong natural colours of flowers can be retained after drying.

The spiralled bouquet is a loose, slightly domed arrangement that uses its flowers on long stems. The colours are extraordinarily rich for dried flowers, with deep pink roses and peonies and purple marjoram.

1 Lay all the materials in separate groups for easy access when working. Split the marjoram into 15 small bunches. Start building the bouquet by holding a dried peony in your hand about two-thirds the way down its stem. Add two stems of roses, then a small bunch of marjoram and another single peony, turning the bunch in your hand with every addition to make the stems form a spiral. Continue adding materials in this sequence, always turning the bunch in your hand to produce a spiral of stems. Occasionally vary your hand position to create a slightly domed shape.

As a gift, the bouquet would be a beautiful alternative to fresh flowers and since it is already arranged it can be put straight into a container.

2 When all the materials have been incorporated in the bunch, tie twine tightly around the binding point – the point where all the stems cross. Trim the stem ends so they are even and, below the binding point, make up about one-third of the overall height of the bouquet. Finally, tie a ribbon around the binding point and finish in a decorative bow.

SUMMER DISPLAYS
· · ·

MATERIALS
· · ·
10 stems dried purple larkspur
· · ·
2 pitchers
· · ·
10 stems dried pink larkspur
· · ·
*10 stems blue globe thistle
(small heads)*
· · ·
*10 stems dried green
amaranthus (straight)*
· · ·
*16 stems dried deep pink
peonies*
· · ·
scissors

*Use the displays in a pair to
achieve the maximum impact.*

The majority of people buying fresh summer cut flowers would think of doing no more than informally arranging them in a vase or pitcher of water. These two matching displays in similar pitchers are loosely arranged in what is almost the dried flower equivalent of this informal approach to flower arranging.

The two displays are characterized by their use of summer flowers in typical summer colours: purple and pink larkspur, blue globe thistle, deep pink peonies and green amaranthus.

Creating the displays requires only the most relaxed approach to dried-flower arranging – you just need to consider carefully the visual balance of the materials to their containers.

1 Split the materials into two equal groups. Cut the purple larkspur so that the stems are approximately three times the height of pitchers. Arrange five stems of purple larkspur loosely in each pitcher. Cut the stems of the pink larkspur to a similar length to the purple larkspur.

2 Arrange the pink larkspur in each pitcher. Break off any offshoots on the globe thistle stems to use separately. Cut the main globe thistle stems to three times the height of the pitchers and arrange in each. Separate the offshoots of globe thistle and arrange in each pitcher.

3 Cut the stems of amaranthus to three times the height of the pitchers and arrange five stems in each.

4 Cut the peony stems to different heights, the tallest being 2.5 cm (1 in) shorter than the larkspur, and the shortest being 20 cm (8 in) shorter than the larkspur. Arrange the peonies evenly throughout the other materials.

RED DISPLAY IN A GLASS CUBE

• • •

This display uses dried oranges to create a coloured base within the glass container itself on which an arrangement using only shades of red is built

The arrangement is a dome of massed materials with contrasting textures: the spikes of globe thistles, the velvet cushions of achillea, and the papery petals of roses. The materials and colours are classical but because of the container used the overall effect is very contemporary.

MATERIALS

20 cm (8 in) glass cube

• • •

20 dried oranges

• • •

knife

• • •

1 block plastic foam for dried flowers

• • •

florist's tape (stem-wrap tape)

• • •

scissors

• • •

2 bunches dried bottlebrush

• • •

2 bunches dried red-dyed achillea

• • •

2 bunches dried red-dyed globe thistle

• • •

2 bunches dried red roses

The display is easy to make but clever in that the mechanics of its construction are hidden when it is completed.

1 Three-quarter fill the glass cube with dried oranges. Cut the plastic foam block so that it fits into the glass cube snugly above the oranges. Only about a third of the depth of the block should be inside the container. Hold the plastic foam securely in place by taping over it and on to the glass (no more than 2.5 cm/1 in down its sides).

2 Cut the bottlebrush stems to 10 cm (4 in) and create the overall outline of the display by pushing their stems into the plastic foam.

3 Cut the dried achillea to a stem length of 10 cm (4 in) and evenly distribute through the bottlebrush by pushing the stems into the foam.

4 Cut the globe thistle stems to 10 cm (4 in) and position evenly throughout the display, pushing their stems into the foam.

5 Cut the dried rose stems to 10 cm (4 in) in length and, in groups of three, fill the remaining spaces evenly throughout the display.

DRIED FLOWER TUSSIE MUSSIES

• • •

These tussie mussies are easy to make, although, to achieve a satisfactory result, they will use a lot of material in relation to their finished size.

These tussie mussies are made of small spiralled bunches of lavender-scented dried flowers. Embellished with embroidered and velvet ribbon bows, they have a medieval look and would make delightful gifts or could be carried by a young bridesmaid.

1 To make Tussie Mussie A, on the right of the main picture, cut all the materials to a stem length of approximately 18 cm (7 in). Set out all the materials in separate groups for easy access. Start by. holding a single rose in your hand and add the other materials one by one.

2 Add, in turn, stems of *Nigella orientalis,* lavender and rose to the central stem. Continue this sequence, all the while turning the bunch in your hand to ensure that the stems form a spiral. Hold the growing bunch about two-thirds of the way down the stems.

3 When all the materials are in place, secure the bunch by tying twine around the binding point of the stems. Trim the bottoms of the stems even. Tie a ribbon around the binding point and finish in a neat bow. (Follow the same method for Tussie Mussie B).

FRESH TUSSIE MUSSIE

In bygone days, ladies carried herbal tussie mussies with them as a form of personal perfume. They were usually made of several varieties of fresh herbs arranged in concentric circles. White lavender makes a delightful tussie mussie contrasted with the more conventional blue.

MATERIALS

· · ·

deep blue lavender

· · ·

white lavender

· · ·

green raffia or twine

· · ·

scissors

· · ·

wide ribbon

White and blue lavender look very pretty together and need no other decoration.

1 Arrange a circle of deep blue lavender stems around a small bunch of white lavender. Secure with a piece of raffia or twine.

2 Arrange the remaining white lavender around the blue. Secure the complete bunch with raffia or twine. Trim the stalks to an even length.

3 Cover the raffia with wide ribbon, tying the ends in a generous bow.

GARLANDS
AND SWAGS

· · ·

Decorate your home with these traditional
symbols of hospitality and welcome. They can
be a simple mixture of flowers and herbs, or an
impressive display for a special occasion. Hang a
garland on a wall or place it flat on a table as an
attractive centrepiece. For a grand effect, drape a
swag along a mantelpiece, fireplace surround or
down the centre of a party table.

INTRODUCTION

· · ·

*Above: A Geometric Garland
above a bundle display*

Below: Mixed Swag

Floral garlands and wreaths are always popular throughout the year. A beautifully scented blue pine (spruce) wreath decorated with red roses and amaranthus makes a wonderful winter decoration for your front door. Simple garlands decorated with dried roses, pot-pourri, lavender and herbs will bring the colours and scents of summer into your home, even in winter. More unusual garlands can be made using a single dramatic dried material such as massed dahlia heads or giant sunflowers, to create a very modern look.

Whatever the finished design, all garlands are built on a base, which you can buy from a florist's or make yourself. Ready-made rings woven from natural materials such as hop vine or willow are available from florists in many different sizes. If you like the idea of weaving your own ring, use vines or twigs cut when they are green so that they are pliable. Leave the ring to dry out naturally before adding the decoration. You can also make your own hay ring by simply binding the hay with silver reel (rose) wire. Another, more expensive base is a copper or steel ring, which consists of two wire circles. This can be covered with hay or moss, or in some garland designs one of the wire circles is used on its own. You can even construct unusual shapes such as triangles or squares, using sticks or canes bound together at the corners.

Above: Fabric-decorated Swag

Left: Romantic Herb Garland

Swags are also built on to a base, which can be a length of rope (or even string), a hay rope or a sausage of chicken wire stuffed with hay or moss. They are technically quite straightforward to create but their sheer size often makes them a challenge. The most important thing is to have plenty of space and to lay all the dried materials out in a very orderly fashion. Work along the whole length of the swag, or around the circle of a garland, to keep an even balance of materials and so that they appear to flow together. Stand back frequently to check the design as it progresses and add delicate flowers such as roses and peonies at the end. Large swags are often made in two or more sections, making them much easier to transport to their finished location. If you are making a single length, work from either end towards the centre; if necessary, you can disguise the point where they meet with a ribbon or raffia bow.

Traditional swags made of winter foliage look wonderful displayed along the length of a fireplace, table or mantelpiece. Mixed summer swags made of flowers and herbs are ideal for summer parties. More unusual designs featured here include a hanging swag incorporating fabric to match your decor, and an outdoor swag studded with shells and starfish. Swags do not have to be large and impressive; a small swag makes a very attractive, novel feature and is much quicker to make.

Below: Pine Garland

ROSE AND POT-POURRI GARLAND

· · ·

Keep the decoration of this garland light and delicate.

This pretty garland uses a hop vine ring as its base. These are fairly inexpensive and can be purchased from most florists. If you prefer to make your own ring, use vines or twigs cut when green so that they are pliable. Weave them together into a circle then leave to dry completely.

1 Steam the roses if necessary (see Techniques). Cut off the stems and glue the heads to the ring, some in pairs and others as single roses to achieve a good balance. Glue moss in the gaps between the roses.

2 Apply generous quantities of glue directly on to the ring. Sprinkle on pot-pourri to cover the glue completely. Finally, add the fir cones. Tie strands of raffia in a trailing bow and glue to the top of the garland.

FROSTED WINTER GARLAND
• • •

This design is very simple and quick to make as you can use a glue gun to attach all the materials to a ready-made base. Leave the garland in its natural state or spray it with a light coat of silver, white or gold paint for a festive effect.

MATERIALS
• • •
glue gun and glue sticks
• • •
fir cones
• • •
hop vine or twig ring
• • •
assorted nuts, e.g. brazil nuts,
hazelnuts (filberts), walnuts
• • •
cinnamon sticks
• • •
wide red paper ribbon
• • •
silver, white or gold spray paint

Graduate the fir cones and nuts from a thin layer at the top of the ring to a thicker layer at the bottom.

1 Glue the fir cones to the ring in groups of 4–5, leaving a large space between each group. Attach the larger fir cones at the bottom of the ring.

2 Glue the nuts and cinnamon sticks between the fir cones, individually or in groups, again with the larger nuts at the bottom. Tie the ribbon in a large bow and glue to the top of the ring. Spray the whole design lightly with paint.

GIANT SUNFLOWER GARLAND

· · ·

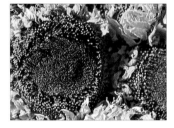

The large size of this garland is in proportion to the giant sunflowers.

This wonderfully flamboyant garland celebrates the vivid colour and dramatic shape of sunflowers. Attach all of the sunflower heads as low down their stems as possible so that they stand proud of the other material – you should be able to push your fingers easily around each flower. The other materials provide a range of other bright colours which contrast nicely with the yellow of the sunflowers.

1 To make a loop for hanging the finished garland, bend a strong wire into a U-shape. Push it through the hay ring as shown.

2 Check the size of the loop and adjust it by pulling or pushing the wire through the hay to make the loop larger or smaller.

3 Twist the ends of the wire together and tuck them neatly into the hay. If necessary, you can add another loop when the garland has been completed and you know which way up it will look best when it is hung in its final position. Begin to separate the smaller material into mixed bunches and lay them aside.

4 Trim the stems of the smaller bunches to about 20 cm (8 in). Lay them in position and wind around silver reel (rose) wire to bind the stems tightly to the ring.

5 Wire the sunflowers (see Techniques). Push the wired stems through the ring from the front then twist the wire ends and tuck into the back. Fill small gaps with small bunches of material.

Use this large garland to decorate a door or window.

CORN-ON-THE-COB GARLAND

· · ·

*The spiky, textured
appearance of the corn-on-the
cob leaves helps to give this
display its rustic charm.*

Dried corn-on-the cob comes in attractive shades ranging from pale yellow to rich orange, which make a lovely kitchen display. Here the base of the garland is an old wooden sieve, and dried hops add to the charming rustic effect.

1 Thread a length of wire through a hole in the sieve frame and around the wire mesh. Repeat on all four sections of the sieve where there is an existing hole.

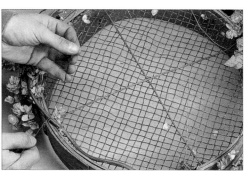

2 Cut four short lengths of hop stems and attach the ends to the wires. Twist the wire ends together to secure. Repeat to cover the whole sieve edge.

3 Choose three corn heads of similar length and tie them together with a length of wire. Holding the cluster of corn tightly together with one hand, fold the wire over the leaves of all three cobs.

4 Twist the wire ends together. To conceal the wire, fold down a few of the corn leaves and wrap them neatly around the wire.

5 Tie the ends of the leaves with another length of wire to form a tuft. Trim excess wires and leaves.

6 Attach the groups of corn around the sieve by threading the wire through the mesh and on to the hop garland. Twist the wire ends together. Stagger the corn at regular intervals around the sieve.

7 Trim excess wires and corn leaves, but don't over-trim as this will detract from the charm of the arrangement.

The wire mesh and wooden frame of an old sieve blend perfectly with the colours and textures of the natural dried materials.

HEART OF WHEAT

. . .

Fashioning simple decorations out of wheat is a traditional country custom, and very satisfying to do.

M̲ake this endearing "token of affection" at harvest-time, perhaps for a delightful decoration to place on a kitchen wall or dresser. It is quite robust and should last for many years. You can make the base any size you wish.

1 Cut three long lengths of wire and bend them into a heart shape. Twist the ends together at the bottom.

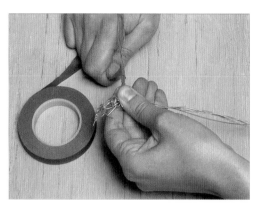

2 Use florist's tape (stem-wrap tape) to cover the wire.

3 Using silver reel (rose) wire, bind together enough small bunches of wheat to cover the wire heart densely. Leave a short length of wire at each end.

4 Starting at the bottom, tape the first bunch of wheat stalks to the heart.

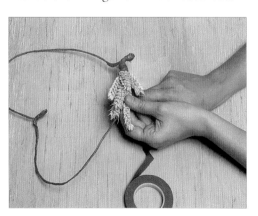

5 Tape the second bunch further up the heart shape, behind the first. Continue to tape the bunches until the whole heart is covered.

6 For the bottom, wire together about six bunches of wheat stalks, twist the wires together and wire them to the heart. Neaten with florist's tape (stem-wrap tape).

WHITE DAHLIA GARLAND
· · ·

MATERIALS
· · ·
silver reel (rose) wire
· · ·
large wicker garland base
· · ·
moss
· · ·
scissors
· · ·
glue gun and glue sticks
· · ·
dried white dahlia heads
· · ·
sea-grass rope

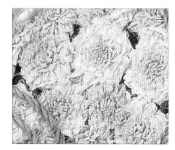

The starkness of using all creamy-white flowers is quite eye-catching.

Large, creamy-white dahlia flowers make a stunning garland, loosely looped with bleached rope for a fresh summer feeling. Trim the stems before you start so the flowerheads can be glued directly on to the base.

1 Attach one end of the silver reel (rose) wire to the outside edge of the garland base and tie securely.

2 Add layers of moss on to the top of the garland base. Wind the reel (rose) wire around the base to secure the moss.

3 Continue to add the moss until the whole garland base has been covered. Cut the wire and tie securely.

4 Squeeze some glue on to the underside of a dahlia head and press it firmly on to the moss-covered garland. Continue, leaving no gaps. Overlap the flowerheads if necessary.

5 Continue until the whole garland is covered. Place the flowers deep into the inner ring, and as far down the outer edge as possible.

6 Attach a length of sea-grass rope to the outer edge of the underside of the garland base. Tie in a secure knot and trim the end.

Massing together one flower creates a sumptuous effect. You could make the same design using bright red or yellow dahlias for quite a different look.

7 Wind the rope loosely over the garland. Taking care not to damage the flowers, position it diagonally at regular intervals around the circle.

8 Turn the garland over and make a substantial hanging loop in the rope. Tie a secure knot quite low down where it will not be seen.

9 To finish, wind the end of the rope around the base of the hanging loop several times in a neat spiral then tuck it into the back of the garland.

LAVENDER AND HERB GARLAND

· · ·

MATERIALS

· · ·

scissors

· · ·

.91 wires

· · ·

dried lavender

· · ·

dried artemisia

· · ·

dried lovage

· · ·

dried tarragon

· · ·

glue gun and glue sticks

· · ·

small wicker garland base

· · ·

dried French lavender

Sweet-smelling herbs and flowers are always a delight to work with, and they make the finished garland very fresh and summery.

This pretty garland is composed of mixed herbs and two kinds of lavender, all of which are highly scented. French lavender has large flowerheads, so place these individually at the end to stand out against the smaller-flowered materials.

1 Trim and wire all the dried herbs and flowers, except the French lavender, into small bunches (see Techniques).

2 Using a glue gun, glue the first bunch of the dried lavender neatly on to the garland base.

3 Next glue a bunch of artemisia to the garland base between the lavender.

4 Work around the garland, adding a bunch of lovage.

5 Continue all round the garland, interspersing the different bunches of herbs to cover it completely.

6 Finally, add the individual French lavender flowerheads, positioning them regularly around the garland.

DRIED ROSE WREATH

· · ·

MATERIALS

· · ·

dried red rosebuds

· · ·

dried cream rosebuds

· · ·

paper-covered wire plant twists

· · ·

scissors

· · ·

loosely woven ring of twigs

· · ·

dried lavender

· · ·

dried hydrangea heads

· · ·

essential rose oil

· · ·

red ribbon

The materials in this dried floral wreath will look wonderful as a wall-hanging.

Many flowers, including roses, dry beautifully and can be enjoyed for months after fresh flowers would have perished. Kept away from strong sunlight, which will fade the petals, dried flowers need gentle dusting and a few drops of essential oils to keep them perfumed. As dried flowers are very fragile and easily broken, a wall-hanging wreath is an ideal way of arranging them and makes a country-style alternative to a picture.

2 Tie the hydrangea heads to the ring of twigs using the wire twists so that they conceal any stems and cover the twigs. Add just a few drops of essential rose oil.

1 Divide the rosebuds into five bunches and tie with the plant twists. Cut the the stems to 5 cm (2 in) and use the ends of the plant twists to attach the bunches to the wreath. Repeat with the lavender.

3 Attach the ribbon firmly with a bow and use it to loop the wreath over a picture hook. Refresh with essential oil when it loses its scent and dust carefully from time to time.

TWIG GARLAND

. . .

When covering a whole garland with twigs it is best to use fresh, green twigs; dry ones will be very brittle and liable to snap in your hands. The twigs will dry naturally to an attractive brown shade. A large green paper bow balances the decoration at the bottom of the garland.

MATERIALS

. . .

secateurs

. . .

willow or other similar twigs

. . .

.91 wires

. . .

copper or steel garland ring

. . .

glue gun and glue sticks

. . .

dried materials, e.g. fir cones, fungi, twigs, pomegranates

. . .

wide green paper ribbon

With the twig garland as a base, you can add whatever woodland materials you have to hand.

1 Trim the willow twigs to an even length then wire them into small bunches (see Techniques). Tie the wires to the garland ring to give a sweeping, circular outline. This will create a basic twig garland design to which the other materials can be added.

2 Glue the dried materials in a decorative group at the bottom of the garland, wiring smaller materials such as twigs in small bunches as necessary.

3 Cut a long length of green paper ribbon. Tease the ribbon open then scrunch it back up again. Fold the length in half and pull down the centre to make an M-shape.

4 Holding the two loops, cross them over each other, tie in a knot and pull tightly. Adjust the size of the bow, open out the ribbon and glue to the top of the garland.

GEOMETRIC GARLAND

· · ·

MATERIALS

· · ·

strong canes or sticks

· · ·

strong florist's wires

· · ·

pliers

· · ·

glue gun and glue sticks

· · ·

moss

· · ·

silver reel (rose) wire

· · ·

twigs

· · ·

.91 wires

· · ·

dried fungi

· · ·

fir cones

If you make a triangular frame, the resulting garland is even more unusual.

Most garlands are round, but they can also be square or triangular. Experiment with different shapes created with canes or sticks – they do not have to be completely straight to create an interesting variation.

1 If the canes or sticks are thin, wire 5–8 together to make one stronger length for each side of the frame. Use pliers to twist the wire around the ends. Make a square frame, tying the canes or sticks in each corner with a wire. Add a dab of glue to the wires to fix them firmly.

2 Cover the frame with moss, holding it in place with silver reel (rose) wire. Try to keep an even amount of moss on all sides and avoid leaving any gaps. Make the base secure, as this is what the remaining material will be attached to.

3 When the frame is completely covered with moss, tie the twigs on to it with wire. Add as many as you think look good, remembering what materials you have to come. Then glue the fungi and fir cones in position, placing them in small groups. Hide any wires that show with extra moss.

TRAY DECORATION
· · ·

This pretty little garland was specially designed to decorate a tray, to cheer up an invalid confined to bed. Use small flowers so that you can keep the depth of the garland fairly low, otherwise it might get in the way. A copper or steel ring is made up of two separate rings, only one of which you need for this project.

MATERIALS
· · ·
copper or steel garland ring
· · ·
hay or moss
· · ·
silver reel (rose) wire
· · ·
dried miniature pink roses
· · ·
scissors
· · ·
*small dried flowers, e.g.
Achillea ptarmica,
bupleurum, hydrangea,
marjoram*
· · ·
glue gun and glue sticks

On a small garland such as this, the best effect is created by mixing the different varieties of dried flowers all over the ring.

1 Cut off the cross-wires between the two rings and retain one circle for this project. Cover it with hay or moss, attaching it by winding around silver reel (rose) wire. Leave gaps of about 2.5 cm (1 in) between each turn of the wire.

2 Steam the roses if necessary and set aside (see Techniques). Trim the other flower stems to about 5 cm (2 in).

3 Tie silver reel (rose) wire to the covered ring and begin to wind it around the stems, working from the inside outwards. The flowers should hang down to touch the work surface.

4 Trim the rose stems close to the flowerheads and glue them to the garland, together with extra material if necessary to fill any gaps.

GOLD CONE GARLAND

· · ·

MATERIALS

· · ·

wire cutters

· · ·

copper or steel garland ring

· · ·

pliers

· · ·

larch twigs, with cones

· · ·

.91 wires

· · ·

2 small terracotta pots

· · ·

dried red chillies

· · ·

glue gun and glue sticks

· · ·

green moss

· · ·

rope

· · ·

gold spray paint

*E*ven simple materials such as
rope look festive with a dusting
of gold paint.

This winter garland is made from an unusual selection of materials, including larch cones, rope, chillies and small terracotta pots. Leave some of the larch branches longer than you need so that they stick out at interesting angles, and place extra material at the bottom of the garland to give it balance. It will look striking when hung on a door or window frame outside.

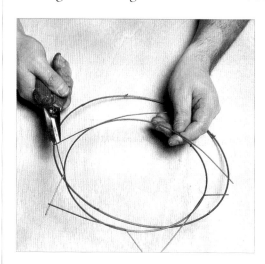

1 Cut off the cross-wires between the two rings and discard them. Cut the wire as close to the ring as possible or, using pliers, pull the wire away from the ring so that no sharp ends are left. Use either of the rings, depending on the size you want.

2 Tie a larch twig to the ring, using a short wire, so that the fixing is close to one end of the twig. Bend the twig gently to the shape of the ring and repeat the fixing on the other end. Repeat this all around the ring.

3 Make sure that the entire ring is covered and neatly packed. If some of the larch twigs are small or thin, add more than one at a time, crossing the ends over each other.

4 Wire each terracotta pot to the ring by passing a wire through the drainage hole and top of the pot and the ring. Twist the loose ends together and tuck the wire ends away.

5 Centre-wire three bunches of chillies (see Techniques). Attach in the same way as the pots, pushing the wire ends back into the display. Glue small pieces of moss to cover the fixings. Spray the rope gold. Tie in a bow with long ends and glue to the top of the garland. Frost the garland lightly with gold spray paint.

All the materials used here are fairly weather-resistant, so this garland will be quite happy on an exterior door.

269

PINE GARLAND

· · ·

MATERIALS

· · ·

copper or steel ring

· · ·

moss

· · ·

silver reel (rose) wire

· · ·

secateurs (garden clippers)

· · ·

blue pine (spruce)

· · ·

dried amaranthus, dyed red

· · ·

.91 wires

· · ·

dried red roses

· · ·

dried lavender

· · ·

raffia

· · ·

twigs

· · ·

sweet chestnuts

· · ·

fir cones

· · ·

dried fungi

· · ·

strong florist's wire

Blue pine (spruce) instantly evokes a wintry feel.

I n this garland, blue pine (spruce) is used fresh and left to dry out later. It releases a glorious fresh scent as you work with it and makes a magnificent decoration. Here it is used with red roses and amaranthus for a traditional look. You could also add fresh apples or tangerines for a lively, if less long-lasting, arrangement – pierce each fruit with a wire to fix it in place.

1 Cover the ring very roughly on both sides with moss – this need not be thick but should be fairly even. Secure in place by winding with silver reel (rose) wire, leaving a space of about 5 cm (2 in) between each loop.

2 Trim the blue pine (spruce) to lengths of about 15–20 cm (6–8 in). Divide into four piles and begin to tie each stem to the ring with wire, using one pile for each quarter of the ring. Work outward from the inner edge in a zigzag fashion.

3 Trim the amaranthus stems to 20 cm (8 in) and wire into four small bunches (see Techniques), leaving the wires untrimmed. Treat the roses in the same way, but cut the stems to 10 cm (4 in). In each quarter of the ring, push a bunch of roses and a bunch of amaranthus, tying the wires into the back of the ring.

4 Trim the lavender to 20 cm (8 in) and wire into four bunches. Keep a long length of wire hanging from each bunch and wind a bow of raffia around the stems. Push each wire through the blue pine (spruce) and tie to the back of the ring.

5 Wire bunches of twigs, chestnuts, fir cones and fungi. Tie bows of raffia around the bunches of twigs. Add these materials in small mixed groups, linking each group around the ring. Add a loop of strong wire to the back of the garland for hanging and tie a raffia bow at the top.

Hung outside the front door, a pine garland provides a beautiful welcome for visitors.

271

SPICY STAR WALL DECORATION

• • •

MATERIALS

• • •

*15 cinnamon sticks, 30 cm
(12 in) long*

• • •

raffia

• • •

scissors

• • •

75 lavender stems

• • •

ribbon

*If a Christmas look is
required, substitute dried fruit
slices and gilded seed heads for
the lavender. Similarly, any
sturdy straight twigs can be
used instead of cinnamon.*

This star-shaped wall decoration is constructed from groups of long cinnamon sticks. It is embellished with bunches of lavender to add colour, texture, contrast and a scent which mixes with the warm, spicy smell of the cinnamon.

Its construction requires a bit of patience but is a simple matter of binding the materials together. Take care when handling the cinnamon as it can be brittle.

1 Separate the cinnamon sticks into five groups of three. Interlace the ends of two groups of sticks to form a point and secure firmly by tying them together with raffia. Trim the ends of the raffia.

2 Continue interlacing and binding together groups of cinnamon sticks to create a star-shaped framework. Also, bind together the sticks where they cross each other to make the frame rigid.

3 Separate the lavender into bunches of 15 stems each. Turn the star shape so that the binding knots are at the back and attach the bunches of lavender to the front of the frame, using raffia at the cross points of the cinnamon sticks.

4 When all the lavender bunches have been secured, make a small bow from the ribbon and tie it to the decoration at the bottom crossing point of the cinnamon sticks.

ROSE AND STARFISH WREATH

· · ·

MATERIALS

· · ·

10 small dried starfish

· · ·

.71 wires

· · ·

scissors

· · ·

florist's adhesive

· · ·

plastic foam ring for dried flowers, 13 cm (5 in) diameter

· · ·

45 shell-pink dried rose heads

· · ·

velvet ribbon

The construction of this wreath involves a small amount of wiring, but is otherwise straightforward.

The design of this visually simple wall decoration involves massing a single type of flower and framing them with a halo of geometric shapes, in this case stars. The prettiness of its soft peach colours makes it suitable for a bedroom wall, in which case sprinkle it with scented oil.

1 Double leg mount the starfish as an extension of one of their arms with a .71 wire. Cut the wire to about 2.5 cm (1 in) and apply florist's adhesive to both the tip of the starfish arm and wire. Push the wired arm into the outside edge of the plastic foam ring. Position all the starfish around the ring. Leave a gap of 3 cm (1¼ in) for attaching the ribbon.

2 Cut the stems of the rose heads to about 2.5 cm (1 in) and put florist's adhesive on their stems and bases. Push the glued stems into the plastic foam to form a ring around its outside edge on top of the starfish. Working towards the centre of the ring, continue forming circles of rose heads until the ring is covered apart from a gap for the ribbon.

3 Pass the ribbon through the centre of the ring and position it so that it sits in the gap between the roses and starfish to cover the foam. This can be used to hang up the wreath or just tied in a bow for decoration.

ROMANTIC HERB GARLAND

· · ·

Mix herbs and flowers to create a sweet-smelling garland for a wall or table centrepiece. This design is made using a simple hay ring base, which you can make yourself. Divide the ring into sections and add the dried material evenly to make sure you end up with a nicely balanced effect.

MATERIALS

· · ·

dried herbs and flowers,
e.g. Achillea ptarmica,
bay leaves, lavender,
marjoram, mint, poppy
seed heads, oregano

· · ·

scissors

· · ·

silver reel (rose) wire

· · ·

hay-covered copper garland
ring (see Techniques)

The Achillea ptarmica *adds splashes of white to the display, which contrast nicely against the green herbs.*

1 Separate the dried materials and trim the stems to equal length. Wire 4–6 stems at a time to the hay ring, winding the wire around to hold them in place. Continue until you have covered the whole hay ring.

2 Cut the end of the wire and tuck it neatly into the ring.

DIAMOND, HEART, SPADE AND CLUB WREATHS

• • •

These light-hearted wall decorations are instantly recognizable and would make a strong display either grouped together, perhaps in a line, or even individually framed and used separately.

Each decoration uses a single type of material in one colour and has its own distinctive texture. This reinforces the shape of each wreath. The diamond decoration has scented blue lavender spires used directionally to emphasize its simple shape. Appropriately, the heart display incorporates papery-textured red roses. The outline of the spade is formed from pale brown, oval poppy seed heads with distinctive star-shaped crowns and a lovely grey bloom. And bulbous, ribbed nigella seed heads in pale green and burgundy stripes define the shape of the club wreath.

Quite apart from any other consideration, making these decorations is an excellent exercise in taping and wiring techniques. It teaches valuable lessons about the versatility of stay wires in achieving relatively complex shapes, and how the choice of material affects the form of a floral decoration. Begin with the diamond, the simplest of the shapes, and work through the progressively more complex sequence of heart, spade and club and you will encounter an increasing number of factors to take into account to achieve a successful display. It is particularly important to grade the size of materials for both practical considerations, such as decorating difficult corners, and to emphasize features of outline shape.

Making these decorations will increase your understanding and experience of flower arranging and at the same time you will have created unusual and attractive displays.

LAVENDER DIAMOND WREATH

. . .

MATERIALS

. . .

.71 wires

. . .

florist's tape (stem-wrap tape)

. . .

scissors

. . .

105 stems dried lavender

. . .

.38 silver wires

Ensure that all the lavender spires point in the same direction to give this simple wreath maximum impact.

1 Make a stay wire from .71 wire on which the decoration can be built. Cover with florist's tape (stem-wrap tape). Form the stay wire into a diamond shape about 22 cm (8¾ in) high with the two ends meeting at the bottom point.

2 Cut the lavender to an overall length of approximately 5 cm (2 in) and group it in threes. Double leg mount these groups with .38 wires, then tape the 35 wired groups with florist's tape (stem-wrap tape).

3 Start at the top point of the diamond shape and attach the groups of lavender by taping around their wired stems and the stay wire. Slightly overlap one group with the next to achieve a continuous line around one half of the shape, finishing at the bottom open end of the stay wire. Start covering the second half of the diamond shape from the bottom open end of the stay wire. When covered, tape the two open ends together.

Twig Heart Door Wreath

· · ·

Welcome guests with a door wreath that's charming in its simplicity. Just bend twigs into a heart shape and adorn the heart with variegated ivy, a white rose and clusters of red berries.

MATERIALS

· · ·

secateurs (garden clippers)

· · ·

pliable branches, such as buddleia, cut from the garden

· · ·

.71 wire

· · ·

seagrass string

· · ·

variegated trailing ivy

· · ·

white rose

· · ·

golden twine

· · ·

red berries

Red berries add a special final touch to this simple heart wreath.

1 Cut six lengths of pliable branches about 70 cm (28 in) long. Wire three together at one end. Repeat with the other three. Cross the two bundles over at the wired end. Wire the bunches together in the crossed-over position.

2 Holding the crossed, wired ends with one hand, ease the long end round and down very gently, so the branches don't snap. Repeat with the other side, to form a heart shape. Wire the bottom end of the heart.

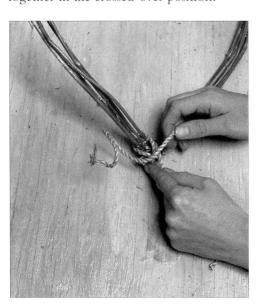

3 Bind the wiring with seagrass string at top and bottom and make a hanging loop at the top.

4 Entwine trailing ivy around the heart shape. Make a posy of ivy leaves and a white rose. Tie the posy with golden twine and wire it to the heart.

NIGELLA CLUB WREATH

· · ·

MATERIALS

· · ·

.71 wires

· · ·

florist's tape (stem-wrap tape)

· · ·

scissors

· · ·

*57 stems dried nigella seed
heads of similar size*

· · ·

.38 silver wires

*This wreath makes an eye-
catching and fun decoration.*

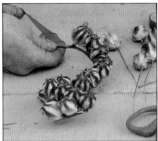

1 Make a stay wire from .71 wire on which the decoration can be built. Cover with florist's tape (stem-wrap tape). Form the stay wire into a club shape about 22 cm (8¾ in) high with the two ends of the wire meeting in a line at the centre at the bottom of the shape.

2 Cut the stems of the nigella to a length of approximately 2.5 cm (1 in) and double leg mount the individual nigella seedheads on .38 silver wires. Tape the wired stems with florist's tape (stem–wrap tape).

3 Starting at the beginning of the stay wire, tape the wired heads of nigella to the stay wire. Slightly overlap the nigella heads to achieve a continuous line. Continue until the stay wire is covered and then join the two ends of the wire together by taping.

ROSE HEART WREATH

· · ·

MATERIALS

· · ·

.71 wires

· · ·

florist's tape (stem-wrap tape)

· · ·

scissors

· · ·

50 stems dried red roses

· · ·

.38 silver wires

This effective heart would make an unusual and long-lasting Valentine's day gift.

1 Make a stay wire from .71 wire on which the decoration can be built. Cover with florist's tape (stem-wrap tape). Form the stay wire into a heart shape about 22 cm (8¾ in) high with the two ends of the wire meeting at its bottom point.

2 Cut the stems of the dried roses to a length of approximately 2.5 cm (1 in) and double leg mount them individually on .38 silver wires, then tape the wired stems with florist's tape (stem-wrap tape) to hide the wire.

3 Starting at the top, tape the rose stems to the stay wire. Slightly overlap the roses to achieve a continuous line of heads, finishing at its bottom point. Starting back at the top, repeat the process around the other half of the heart. Tape the two ends of the wire together.

POPPY SPADE WREATH

· · ·

MATERIALS

· · ·

.71 wires

· · ·

florist's tape (stem-wrap tape)

· · ·

scissors

· · ·

50 stems dried poppy seed heads

· · ·

.38 silver wires

It is important to tape the poppy seed heads closely together so that they can rest against each other and not "flop" down.

1 Make a stay wire from .71 wire on which the decoration can be built. Cover with florist's tape (stem-wrap tape). Form the stay wire into a spade shape about 22 cm (8¾ in) high with the two ends of the wire meeting in a line at the bottom of the shape.

2 Cut the stems of the poppy seed heads to a length of approximately 2.5 cm (1 in) and double leg mount the individual poppy seed heads on .38 silver wires, then tape the wired stems with florist's tape (stem-wrap tape) to hide the wire.

3 Starting at the pointed top of the shape, tape the poppy seed heads to the stay wire starting with the smallest. Slightly overlap the seed heads to achieve a continuous line. The size of the heads should be increased as you work towards the bulbous part of the shape, after which the heads should be decreased. When you have completed one side, repeat the whole process on the opposite side, again starting from the point at the top. Tape the two ends of the stay wire together with tape.

DRIED AROMATIC WREATH

· · ·

An aromatic wreath is a decorative way to scent a room naturally. Here, the subtle pinks and purples of dried marjoram and lavender, matched by coloured string, add up to a delightful tonal colour scheme.

MATERIALS

· · ·

.32 silver reel (rose) wire

· · ·

dried lavender stems

· · ·

dried marjoram

· · ·

willow wreath base, 38 cm (15 in) diameter

· · ·

1 skein each of deep pink and blue twine

· · ·

scissors

The bands of alternating herbs lend impact to this easy-to-make wreath.

1 Wire the lavender into small bunches. Repeat with the marjoram.

2 Lay a row of marjoram bunches across the width of the wreath base and tie into position using the pink twine. Lay a row of lavender bunches just below the marjoram and tie them on with blue twine. Repeat, alternating the marjoram and lavender, until the wreath is covered.

CRESCENT MOON WREATH

· · ·

This novelty decoration is designed to be hung on the wall of a nursery or child's bedroom. The golden-yellow of *Craspedia globosa* and the pale gold sheen of the linseed seed heads give the decoration a luminosity which children will love.

It is made like a garland headdress, on a stay wire but shaped to the outline of a crescent rather than a circle.

MATERIALS
· · ·
35 Craspedia globosa *heads*
· · ·
scissors
· · ·
.38 silver wires
· · ·
1 bunch dried linseed
· · ·
florist's tape (stem-wrap tape)
· · ·
.71 wires

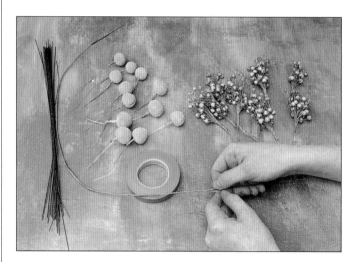

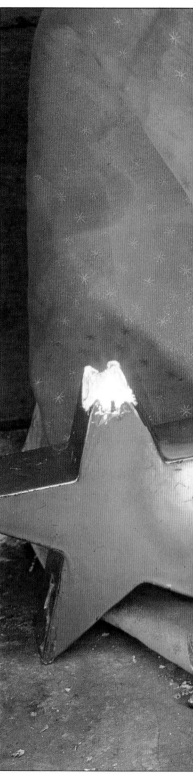

1 Cut the *Craspedia globosa* heads to a stem length of approximately 2 cm (¾ in) and double leg mount them on .38 silver wires. Split the dried linseed into very small bunches, each approximately 4 cm (1¾ in) long, and double leg mount them on .38 wires. Tape all the wired materials with the florist's tape (stem-wrap tape). Create a stay wire about 60 cm (24 in) long from the .71 wire.

2 Cover the stay wire with florist's tape (stem-wrap tape) Bend the stay wire into the outline of a crescent shape, taking care to ensure an even arc and pointed ends.

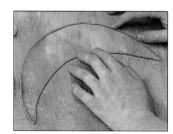

3 At one open end of the stay wire, tape on a bunch of linseed, followed by a small head of the *Craspedia globosa* slightly overlapping. Use the smaller heads of the *Craspedia globosa* at the pointed ends of the crescent and the larger heads at its centre. As you get towards the centre of the crescent, increase the width of the line of materials by adding material to the sides of the wire. Decrease the width again as you work towards the far point.

4 When the outside edge of the crescent outline has been completed, repeat the process on the inner edge but this time working from the bent point of the crescent down towards the open end of the stay wire. When the inner wire has been decorated, join the two open ends of the stay wire by taping them together, then cut off any excess wires and tape over their ends. This joint will be hidden by the dried materials.

To make the crescent shape accurately – narrower at its points – requires a degree of skill and like all wired decorations, time and patience.

TEXTURED FOLIAGE RING

· · ·

MATERIALS

· · ·

scissors

· · ·

10 stems dried natural coloured honesty

· · ·

5 branches glycerine-preserved beech leaves

· · ·

5 branches glycerine-preserved adiantum

· · ·

60 cm (24 in) length dried hop vine

· · ·

twisted wicker wreath ring, approximately 30 cm (12 in) diameter

· · ·

twine

Very easy to construct from commercially available materials, this foliage ring makes a wonderful autumn wall decoration for a hall or, if protected from the weather, a front door.

Some types of foliage can be successfully air dried but many others cannot and need to be glycerine preserved.

This decoration mixes both types of foliage to create a feast of textures and subtle colours that succeeds without the enhancement of flowers.

1 Cut all the foliage stems to around 12 cm (4¾ in) long. You will need 21 lengths of each type of foliage to cover your ring. Start by securely tying a group of three stems of honesty to the wicker ring with twine.

2 Making sure it slightly overlaps the honesty, bind on a group of three glycerined beech stems with the same continuous length of twine. Repeat this process with a group of three stems of hops followed by a group of three stems of glycerined adiantum.

3 Continue binding materials to the ring in the same sequence until the ring is completely covered. Cut off any untidy stems and adjust the materials to achieve the best effect if necessary. Finally, tie off the twine in a discreet knot at the back of the ring.

HERB AND DRIED FRUITS WREATH

· · ·

Lavender and rosemary provide two of the most popular essential oils used in aromatherapy, and the scents of both combine well with citrus oils. As the fragrance of the fresh herbs in this wreath begins to fade it can be refreshed with a couple of drops of essential oil.

MATERIALS

· · ·

rosemary

· · ·

secateurs (garden clippers)

· · ·

blue raffia

· · ·

ready-made twig wreath

· · ·

slices dried orange

· · ·

.71 wires

· · ·

lavender

· · ·

dried poppy seed heads

· · ·

glue gun and glue sticks

1 Divide the rosemary branches into sprigs approximately 15 cm (6 in) long using secateurs (garden clippers). Tie one end of the raffia to the wreath and bind the rosemary sprigs to the top and sides.

2 Thread two or three slices of dried orange on to a wire, leaving enough wire at either end to bind around the wreath. Repeat to make five groups.

3 Using raffia, tie the stems of lavender together in groups of eight to ten to make tiny posies approximately 5 cm (2 in) long.

4 Place the orange slices in position and then take the wire around the sides and twist the two ends together at the back of the wreath. The wire will also help to keep the rosemary firmly in place.

Tie a length of raffia to the top of the wreath. Hang from a picture hook that is securely fixed to the wall as the finished ring is quite heavy.

5 Position the lavender bunches between the groups of orange slices, making sure the flower heads follow the line of the rosemary sprigs; secure firmly with raffia.

6 Cut the stems off the poppy seed heads. Glue each seed head to the base of the wreath wherever there is a space around the oranges, or to conceal any wire that may be showing.

LAVENDER AND SUNFLOWER GARLAND

· · ·

Sunflowers and lavender provide striking, contrasting colours to brighten up the kitchen dresser.

Spread a little scented sunshine with a vibrant dried garland. Use it as a celebration decoration, then drape it above shelves, kitchen cupboards or wardrobes to perfume the room decoratively for the rest of the year.

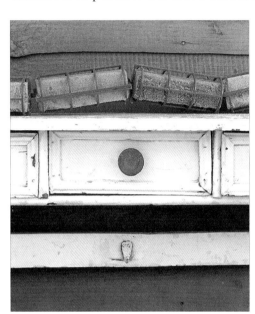

1 The garland base consists of plastic cases that link together using a hook-and-eye system.

2 Cut the foam to fit inside the plastic cases, then link them together to make the desired length of garland.

3 Position the garland base on the shelf. Cut the sunflower stems to 5 cm (2 in). Insert groups of sunflowers at intervals along the length of the garland. Add dried curry flowers around the sunflower heads.

4 Trim the lavender stems to 5 cm (2 in) and add them to the garland. Start by working outwards from one group of sunflowers, making sure that whole area of plastic foam is covered before moving to work round the next group of sunflowers.

CONTEMPORARY WREATHS

· · ·

MATERIALS

· · ·

RED AND YELLOW
MATERIALS
scissors

· · ·

34 red roses

· · ·

33 yellow roses

· · ·

florist's adhesive

· · ·

plastic foam ring for dried
flowers, 10 cm (4 in) diameter

· · ·

ribbon

· · ·

BLUE AND WHITE
MATERIALS
scissors

· · ·

25 white roses

· · ·

26 small heads blue globe
thistle

· · ·

glue

· · ·

plastic foam ring for dried
flowers, 10 cm (4 in) diameter

· · ·

ribbon

The wreaths are simple to
make but will require a lot of
material and a little patience to
achieve the neat checker-board
patterns that characterize them.

These two wall-hanging decorations show how massed dried flowers in strong contrasting colours can create a striking contemporary display.

One display couples white roses with blue globe thistles, the second red roses with yellow roses; but alternative materials can be used provided all the flower-heads used in any display are about the same size as each other. Consider using green *Nigella orientalis* with white roses, bleached white poppy seed heads with bright yellow helichrysums or blue sea holly with bright orange carthamus.

1 For the red and yellow wreath, cut the rose stems to 2.5 cm (1 in). Around the outside edge of the foam ring, form a circle of alternating yellow and red roses by gluing on their stems and pushing them into the foam. Leave a small gap in the rose circle for a ribbon. Inside the first circle, construct a second circle, offsetting the colours against the first ring.

2 Continue building circles of roses until the ring is covered. Pass the ribbon through the centre and around the gap on the plastic foam ring. Use the ribbon to hang the wreath or tie in a bow. Follow the same method for the second wreath.

LAVENDER WREATH

· · ·

Lavender is an important plant in the traditional cottage garden and has been widely cultivated over centuries for the perfume of its purple flowers. Its healing powers are used in aromatherapy to ease headaches and stress, and this wreath will fill any room in which it hangs with the rich scent of summer. The florist's technique of spiral-binding is used to attach the lavender stalks to a ready-made foundation wreath.

MATERIALS

· · ·

natural seagrass rope or coarse string

· · ·

ready-made twig wreath, 30 cm (12 in) diameter

· · ·

dried lavender stems

The colour and texture of rope goes well with spiky lavender stems.

1 Tie one end of the rope or string securely to the wreath.

2 Take a bunch of lavender and with one hand hold it across the wreath with the flowers pointing outwards. Hold the rope or string in the other hand and wind it around the stems, then over the wreath and spiral-bind the stems in place.

3 Place a second bunch of lavender to the right of the first bunch, and bind in place, wrapping the rope once or twice around the stems to secure them in place. The next bunch goes to the right of the second, with the flowers pointing away from the wreath. Continue to spiral-bind small bunches in the same way, making sure that the twig wreath is concealed. When the ring is completely covered, tie off the end of the rope securely and finish off with a loop for hanging.

CINNAMON AND ORANGE RING

. . .

This lovely ring would make an ideal gift – perhaps as a house-warming present, or for someone who loves cooking.

The warm colours, spicy smell and culinary content of this small decorated ring make it perfect for the wall of a kitchen.

The display is not complicated to make but requires nimble fingers to handle the very small pieces of cinnamon used. These pieces have to be tightly packed together to achieve the right effect and great care must be taken because attaching so much cinnamon to the plastic foam may cause it to collapse. To help avoid this happening you can glue the foam ring to stiff card cut to the same outline, before starting work.

1 Apply glue to the bases of the dried oranges and fix them to the plastic foam ring, equally spaced around it. Break the cinnamon sticks into 2-4 cm (¾-1½ in) pieces.

2 Apply glue to the bottom of the pieces of cinnamon and push them into the foam between the dried oranges, keeping them close together to achieve a massed effect.

3 Glue a line of the cinnamon pieces around both the inside and outside edges of the ring to cover the plastic foam completely.

HYDRANGEA CIRCLET

• • •

Hydrangea heads remain beautiful when dried but they do not necessarily dry well when hung in the air. Thus, while it might seem a contradiction in terms, it is best to dry hydrangea whilst they are standing in shallow water. This slows down the process and avoids the hydrangea florets shrivelling.

There is an enormous range of hydrangea colours, from white through pinks, greens, blues and reds to deep purples and in most cases they keep these colours when dried so are ideal for dried flower arranging.

MATERIALS

• • •

12 full dried hydrangea heads

• • •

scissors

• • •

.71 wire

• • •

.32 silver reel (rose) wire

• • •

*1 vine circlet, about 35 cm
(14 in) diameter*

1 Break down each hydrangea head into five smaller florets. Double leg mount each one individually with .71 wire.

2 Take a long length of .32 silver reel (rose) wire and attach a hydrangea floret to the vine circlet by stitching the wire around one of the vines and the wired stem of the hydrangea, pulling tight to secure. Using the same continuous length of wire, add consecutive hydrangea florets in the same way, slightly overlapping them until the front surface of the vine surface is covered.

This circlet is a celebration of the colours of dried hydrangeas and the soft, almost watercolour look, of these hues make it the perfect decoration for the wall of a bedroom.

3 Finish by stitching the silver reel (rose) wire several times around the vine.

293

EVERGREEN TABLE SWAG

· · ·

MATERIALS

· · ·

knife

· · ·

rope

· · ·

secateurs (garden clippers)

· · ·

fresh blue pine (spruce)

· · ·

silver reel (rose) wire

· · ·

fir cones

· · ·

.91 wires

· · ·

dried red chillies

· · ·

glue gun and glue sticks

· · ·

dried fungi

· · ·

dried pomegranates

· · ·

reindeer moss

· · ·

dried lavender

· · ·

dried red roses

Decorate the blue pine (spruce) swag with crossed bunches of red roses and lavender.

This seasonal table decoration is made in two halves so it is easier to handle. Conceal the join with large dried materials such as extra pomegranates and fir cones. Use the blue pine (spruce) fresh; it will dry out naturally without losing its colour or needles, and has a wonderful scent. Take great care when using the hot glue gun; any glue that gets on to the display by accident can be covered with the addition of a little moss. If you want to place your swag above an open fire, make sure it is well away from the heat.

1 Cut two lengths of rope: their combined length should be the length you want the swag to be. Cut the blue pine (spruce) stems to about 20 cm (8 in) long. Using silver reel (rose) wire, bind the stems to the rope.

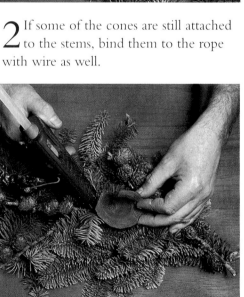

2 If some of the cones are still attached to the stems, bind them to the rope with wire as well.

3 Continue the process until the whole length of both ropes has been well covered. Do not leave any gaps along the edges. Centre-wire the chillies (see Techniques), and fix them along the length of the swag.

4 Using a glue gun, glue the fungi, extra fir cones and pomegranates in place, at well-balanced intervals and to create an attractive design. Then add the reindeer moss to fill any spaces and to create extra colour and interest.

5 Centre-wire the lavender and roses. Fix them in groups, crossing a bunch of roses with a bunch of lavender. Twist the wire ends under the swag and tuck the sharp ends back into the bottom. You can decorate the point where the ends of the swag meet, if you like, by placing candles in terracotta pots in the centre of the display.

This evergreen swag will look wonderful decorating the table for a simple meal for two, or as the feature of an elaborate feast.

MIXED SWAG

· · ·

· · ·

hay

· · ·

silver reel (rose) wire

· · ·

scissors

· · ·

*dried flowers, e.g. pink
larkspur, marjoram, nigella,
oregano, small pink roses*

· · ·

.91 wires

· · ·

raffia

· · ·

glue gun and glue sticks

*Place the flowers so that the
different varieties seem to flow
through the swag.*

This gorgeous summery swag is quite simple to make, but you do need to be careful to get the balance of materials right. If you are making a very long swag, it is easier and safer to make it in short sections and cover the joins with ribbon, otherwise you may have trouble carrying it.

1 Make a hay rope to the length required (see Techniques). Separate the flowers, ideally placing them in a semicircle within arm's reach. Trim the stems to about 18 cm (7 in).

2 Tie silver reel (rose) wire to one end of the hay rope. Bind on bunches of each flower variety in a zigzag fashion, winding the wire well down the stems.

3 Continue to the end of the rope then bind the stems together and tie a knot. Wire small bunches of a filler flower in any gaps (see Techniques). Tie and glue a large raffia bow to one end.

FABRIC-DECORATED SWAG

. . .

With a design incorporating fabric, it is important to consider the final location of the display and to co-ordinate it with the decor. The terracotta pots add a rustic touch, but the design would work just as well without them. Leave the pots empty or fill them with horse chestnuts, fir cones and nuts.

MATERIALS
. . .
wire cutters
. . .
chicken wire
. . .
sphagnum moss
. . .
.91 wires
. . .
small terracotta pots
. . .
pliers
. . .
fabric
. . .
mossing (floral) pins
. . .
glue gun and glue sticks
. . .
scissors
. . .
dried lavender
. . .
dried roses
. . .
dried peonies
. . .
green moss

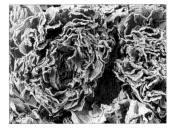

1 Make a chicken wire swag approximately 10 cm (4 in) in width, 2.5 cm (1 in) in depth and 60–90 cm (2–3 ft) in length (see Techniques). Attach the terracotta pots at random angles, by passing a wire through both the pot and the chicken wire. Twist the ends together with pliers.

2 Fold a strip of fabric lengthways into three to make a band about 10 cm (4 in) wide. Scrunch up one end and pin it to the top of the swag, using a mossing (floral) pin. Wrap the fabric down the length of the swag and around the pots, letting it hang fairly loosely. Every 15 cm (6 in), fix it with another pin. Make sure the raw edges are at the back. Pull the fabric into shape, scrunch up the other end, tuck it under the last pot and pin.

3 Make a fabric bow (see Techniques). Glue it to the top of the swag, using a glue gun. Trim the lavender and roses to 15 cm (6 in) then centre-wire them in bunches (see Techniques). Push the wires into the swag, with a little of the flowers covering the fabric. Criss-cross the bunches at random until the frame and moss are covered. Cut the peony heads from their stems and glue down the length of the swag. Fill any spaces with moss.

Peonies have a striking pink colour, so try to choose a fabric that matches the flowers well.

FLOWERPOT SWAG

· · ·

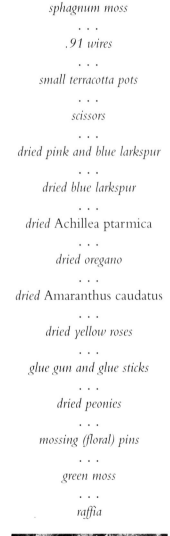

Trailing amaranthus flowers work very well in this swag, giving it a natural country feel.

This lovely design has a chicken wire swag, filled with moss, for its base. Tiny terracotta pots are suspended along its length, blending well with the colourful selection of flowers. Add the large peony heads at the end, using them to adjust the balance of the design and also to cover any wires.

1 Make a chicken wire swag about 1.2 m (4 ft) long (see Techniques). Attach the terracotta pots by passing a wire through the drainage hole in the base and over the rim. Pass the two ends through the swag and twist them firmly together. Push the twisted ends of wire back into the swag.

2 Trim and centre-wire the larkspur, *Achillea ptarmica* and oregano (see Techniques). Starting with the pink larkspur, push the ends of the wires firmly into the swag base. Work the whole length of the swag, adding one variety at a time and criss-crossing the materials to create a balanced look.

3 Trim the amaranthus, leaving only 5 cm (2 in) of stem, and wire it into bunches (see Techniques). Add them along each edge of the swag, plus a few bunches along the centre between the other materials.

4 Wire small bunches of yellow roses. Put a little glue on the stems and push them into some of the terracotta pots.

5 Cut the peony heads from the stems directly under the flowers. Glue in groups of 2–3, to cover any stems or wires. Using mossing (floral) pins, attach the moss in any gaps. Tie a raffia bow and glue it to one end of the swag.

SEASIDE SWAG

• • •

MATERIALS

• • •

wire cutters

• • •

chicken wire

• • •

sphagnum moss

• • •

.91 wires

• • •

small terracotta pots

• • •

dried Eryngium alpinum

• • •

glue gun and glue sticks

• • •

dried echinops

• • •

dried Eucalyptus spiralus

• • •

shells

• • •

starfish

• • •

mossing (floral) pins

• • •

reindeer moss

• • •

dried yellow roses

• • •

raffia

The materials used in this swag make it ideal for damp conditions.

This large swag is made from a wide collection of materials, combining dried flowers and leaves with seashells, starfish and small flowerpots. It makes an exuberant summer decoration to display outdoors.

1 Make a chicken wire swag about 1.2 m (4 ft) long (see Techniques). Fix several pots along its length, by passing a wire through the drainage hole in the base and over the rim. Pass the ends of the wire through the swag, then twist firmly together and push back into the swag.

2 Centre-wire the eryngium (see Techniques). Push the ends of the wire firmly into the swag. Work gradually along the whole length, criss-crossing the bunches of eryngium.

3 Glue small bunches of echinops on to the swag. Space them along the whole length of the swag, covering both the sides and the top. Wire the eucalyptus (see Techniques) and place in bunches along the swag and around the pots.

4 Attach the shells and starfish, making sure that the glue comes into contact with the chicken wire frame, the stems and the wires.

5 Using mossing (floral) pins, fix reindeer moss into any gaps. Finally, bunch the roses and push 4–5 into some of the pots. Tie the raffia into a large bow and glue it to one end of the swag.

STARFISH SWAG

· · ·

This small swag is full of character, with an unusual and interesting mix of materials. It can be viewed from both sides, making it ideal for placing against a window or mirror. The starfish swag would be ideal for a bathroom, where dried flowers and herbs are less suitable.

The distinctive shapes of starfish make this swag very appealing.

1 Cut a length of rope 1–1.2 m (3–4 ft) long. Randomly tie knots along its length and make a loop at one end.

2 Place a blob of glue on one side of a starfish and lay the rope across it, between two knots.

3 Glue a second starfish over the top of the first, trapping the rope between the two. Tuck some tillandsia moss around the edges of the two starfish, so that some of it hangs out of the sides. Repeat at several points along the rope.

4 Trim the eucalyptus to 20 cm (8 in) lengths. Using wires, fix several pieces to the rope in one place. Repeat along the rope about every 25 cm (10 in).

5 Glue a shell at the base of the eucalyptus bunches. Work around the rope until the bases of the stems and the wires are covered. Attach a little lichen moss and add occasional pieces of branch. Repeat along the whole length of the rope at varying intervals.

String makes an unusual base for such an impressive swag, and also makes it very flexible.

6 Wire the fir cones between the natural "teeth" of the cone, as close to the base as possible. Add the fir cones in groups of three at regular intervals.

7 To prepare the chillies, take three at a time and wire the stalks together. Introduce these into the swag in large clusters between the other main groups of materials.

8 To finish, feed rope or ribbon between the various groups. Secure it to the swag at strategic points with pins made of short lengths of bent wire. Do not pull the rope or ribbon too tightly – just a little slack will look far more natural.

WINTER FIREPLACE SWAG

· · ·

MATERIALS

· · ·

knife

· · ·

thick rope

· · ·

secateurs

· · ·

dried red amaranthus

· · ·

dried marjoram

· · ·

dried holly oak

· · ·

fresh blue pine (spruce)

· · ·

silver reel (rose) wire

· · ·

.91 wires

· · ·

dried red roses

· · ·

dried lavender

· · ·

dried red chillies

· · ·

dried kutchi fruit

· · ·

glue gun and glue sticks

· · ·

fir cones

· · ·

dried oranges

· · ·

green moss

· · ·

raffia

When you are working with a large number of materials it is easy to forget one or two, so check the design frequently.

This attractive swag is created from a rich mixture of many different materials. The blue pine (spruce) is used fresh, providing a soft base for the other dried materials. The swag will look good throughout the winter, and for Christmas you can add dark red ribbons and gold-sprayed fir cones. Remember to position the swag on the fireplace but well away from an open fire.

1 Cut the rope to the required length. Trim the amaranthus, marjoram, holly oak and blue pine (spruce) and make a pile of each. Using silver reel (rose) wire, tie small bunches to the rope, alternating the materials. Work in a zigzag fashion, leaving no spaces along the bottom, until the rope is covered.

2 Wire the roses and lavender, and centre-wire the chillies and kutchi fruit, both in small bunches (see Techniques). Attach these to the swag, to create a pleasing design. Glue the fir cones and oranges at intervals. Fill small gaps with moss, using glue. Tie a large raffia bow and glue to the centre of the swag.

FLOWER AND HERB TABLE SWAG

• • •

Make a long swag by joining two shorter swags that have flowers running in opposite directions. Use the space where the swags join for a collection of candle pots, as a central focal point. The candle pots can be surrounded by some tillandsia moss and dried pomegranates, for a warm, sumptuous feeling. Include some of these materials in and around the swag, to co-ordinate the table.

MATERIALS

• • •

scissors

• • •

dried red amaranthus

• • •

dried oregano

• • •

dried red roses

• • •

dried lavender

• • •

silver reel (rose) wire

• • •

rope

• • •

.91 wires

• • •

cinnamon sticks

• • •

raffia

• • •

dried pink peonies

• • •

glue gun and glue sticks

• • •

green moss

• • •

fir cones

This arrangement benefits from the combination of materials and their vibrant mix of colour.

1 Trim all the stems of the various flowers to 15–20 cm (6–8 in). Using the silver reel (rose) wire, bind the red amaranthus and oregano in small bunches down the length of the rope, evenly spacing the bunches, with plenty of space between them.

2 Wire the roses, lavender and cinnamon sticks in small bunches (see Techniques), and decorate the cinnamon sticks with raffia bows. Push the wires through the swag, twist together and push back the sharp ends. Space the bunches evenly.

3 Cut the stems from the peony heads and glue them to the swag, spacing them evenly. Fill small gaps with moss or fir cones, gluing them in place.

SECTION SEVEN

· · · ·

TOPIARY DISPLAYS

· · ·

Creating a perfect topiary tree or ball is quite a challenge but very rewarding and fun to do. Your efforts will certainly be noticed and admired, and should last a long time. The classic image of topiary is a sculptural shape in green foliage, but there are many variations on this theme. Experiment with different dried materials to achieve some spectacular results.

INTRODUCTION

· · ·

Above: Frosted Rose Tree

Below: Fir Cone Trees

A topiary display is the ideal solution if you do not have space for a traditional arrangement which would take up a lot of room on a flat surface. A tall topiary tree will fill an awkward space, and a tree decorated with flowers will give colour and interest to a dark corner. For a really elegant effect, place a matching pair of topiary trees either side of a doorway or on a mantelpiece.

The other most popular topiary design is a hanging ball, which is simply a round tree shape without the trunk. Often decorated with sweet-smelling roses, small flowers or herbs, these look very attractive suspended by a ribbon from a beam across a ceiling or in an alcove, again in positions where other dried arrangements would not be suitable.

The base of any topiary arrangement is a geometric shape, usually a ball or cone. For a less formal finish, you can make a ball yourself out of chicken wire filled with plastic foam offcuts and dried moss. Always make sure that the moss is fully dried out, especially if you intend to add flowers to the design, as fresh moss contains thousands of tiny mould spores which would ruin your display. To save time and effort, and for a perfect shape, ready-made plastic foam balls and cones are available from florists' suppliers in a wide range of sizes. The foam can be trimmed with a knife to fit into the pot you are using, or to create an unusual shape for a particular project.

Above: Rose Tree

Left: Marjoram and Bay Tree

Below: Protea Tree

If you are making a topiary tree, the first stage is to fix the pot, the trunk and the ball or cone firmly together to make a solid base to work on. The trunk is often a branch or a group of canes tied together; in some designs, a twisted trunk of contorted willow may add to the overall sculptural effect. A common fault is to make the trunk too thin – a short, thick trunk is preferable to one that is long and thin, which could look unbalanced. Always keep the size and height of the finished tree in proportion to the pot, standing back frequently as you work to check the shape.

If you do not want to display a topiary tree in a terracotta pot, it is still a good idea to have a pot as the base. Use a plastic pot and conceal it inside a decorative container; if the container is made of clear glass, surround the pot with pot-pourri to complement the colours in the topiary.

To create a more adventurous topiary design, experiment with unusual dried materials such as preserved (dried) leaves or ferns, eucalyptus, blue pine (spruce), poppy seed heads, spices, protea flowers or ata fruit. Often a single material looks most dramatic on its own, without any other decoration. The main requirement is that the material you choose should be long-lasting, so that you can create a permanent display to be proud of.

MOSS BALL

· · ·

MATERIALS

· · ·

wire cutters

· · ·

large-gauge chicken wire

· · ·

*offcuts of plastic foam for dried
flowers*

· · ·

dried moss

· · ·

strong florist's wire

· · ·

pliers

· · ·

silver reel (rose) wire

· · ·

scissors

*The dense green of the moss
creates a rich effect that is very
attractive, but you can use
different kinds of moss, too.*

A piece of foam covered with moss is one of the easiest topiary displays to make. It looks very effective if you place a good-sized mossy globe on a terracotta pot. Making a moss ball is the cheaper alternative to buying ready-made foam spheres, but naturally involves more work.

1 Cut a square of chicken wire, about 10–15 per cent larger than the finished moss ball. Make a pile of foam in the centre. Bend the wire up around the foam to form a roughly round shape. Add more foam pieces to fill any gaps.

2 Push dried moss into the gaps between the foam, through and behind the wire, so that the foam is hidden by moss as much as possible.

3 Gather the ends of the chicken wire together. The ball should have a fairly round shape by now. Secure the loose ends of chicken wire with a strong wire, twisting it firmly in place with pliers. Cut off any excess chicken wire.

4 Tie the end of the silver reel (rose) wire to the mesh. Pad out the ball with plenty more moss to fill any gaps. Keep winding the reel (rose) wire around the ball to hold the moss in place. Cut off any straggly bits of moss.

MOSS TREE

• • •

This simple tree is the base for many more elaborate topiary designs. If it is possible, collect the moss yourself, including different kinds of moss as well as small woody items. Always gather moss from more than one area.

MATERIALS
• • •
silver reel (rose) wire
• • •
*plastic foam cone, with trunk
and pot attached
(see Techniques)*
• • •
moss
• • •
wire cutters
• • •
.91 wires
• • •
mossing (floral) pins (optional)
• • •
scissors
• • •
glue gun and glue sticks
• • •
dried fungi

As the moss dries it will contract slightly, so apply it generously to cover the tree shape. Allow extra moss around the base of the tree as this will shrink also.

1 Tie the end of the silver reel (rose) wire to the tree trunk. Wind it a couple of times around the foam cone then start adding moss under the wire, altering the angle of the wire to give a good coverage.

2 When the cone is completely covered, cut the wire. Tie the end to a florist's wire bent in half and push into the cone. Secure the moss with more bent wires, or use mossing (floral) pins.

3 Trim the tree to create a good pyramid shape. Glue dried fungi at random on to the surface. Cover the base of the tree with plenty of moss.

ROSE TREE

· · ·

MATERIALS

· · ·

silver reel (rose) wire

· · ·

plastic foam ball, with trunk and pot attached (see Techniques)

· · ·

scissors

· · ·

.91 wires

· · ·

dried roses

· · ·

dried oregano

· · ·

moss

You can use any colour combination you like for the rose tree, such as red and pink roses, and herbs, as shown here.

Dried roses make stunning topiary trees but you always need more flowers than you think. To create a perfectly round shape, it is important to wire the roses to the same height and balance them evenly with the other materials. You can add a few drops of perfumed rose oil to the moss, but don't put it directly on to dried flowers or this will make the petals soft and they will become mouldy.

1 Tie the end of the silver reel (rose) wire to the tree trunk then wind it around both the trunk and the ball to hold them together. Secure the end with a wire bent in half and inserted into the foam.

2 Steam the roses if necessary (see Techniques). Trim the stems about 8–10 cm (3–4 in) from the base of each rose head. Wire small bunches of 3–4 roses, with the leaves attached (see Techniques). Attach extra leaves from the discarded stems if necessary. Wire the oregano into small bunches (see Techniques). Begin to push the rose bunches into the foam ball.

3 Use the rose bunches to create the basic shape of the tree. When you have added 10–12 bunches, start to fill in the spaces with the oregano. Support the foam with your other hand on the opposite side of the ball, but don't hold the trunk. Complete the design then fill any small spaces with moss. Finally, cover the base of the trunk and the clay in the pot with generous handfuls of extra moss.

FROSTED ROSE TREE

· · ·

After a couple of years the colours of a rose tree will inevitably fade. Instead of discarding the display, give it a new lease of life by spraying it with a fine dusting of white paint, to make an enchanting winter decoration.

MATERIALS

· · ·

faded rose tree

· · ·

hair-dryer

· · ·

6 mm (¹⁄₄ in) wide paintbrush

· · ·

white spray paint

To accentuate the winter theme, spray paint a few fir cones and add them around the base of the tree.

1 First clean the dust carefully off the old display, using a hair-dryer (set on cold) and a paintbrush. Take care not to break any materials in the display.

2 Spray the whole display, including the pot, with a fine coat of white paint. Keep the paint can moving while spraying so that the layer of paint is even.

POPPY SEED TREE

· · ·

MATERIALS

· · ·

terracotta pot

· · ·

setting clay

· · ·

branches

· · ·

reindeer moss

· · ·

mossing (floral) pins

· · ·

wire cutters

· · ·

large-gauge chicken wire

· · ·

plastic foam offcuts

· · ·

dried moss

· · ·

strong florist's wire

· · ·

pliers

· · ·

silver reel (rose) wire

· · ·

secateurs

· · ·

large dried poppy seed heads

Poppy seed heads will keep for years, but don't spray them with clear florist's lacquer or they will lose their grey-white bloom.

This informal design is made very simply and cheaply from large poppy seed heads inserted into a moss ball. The splayed-out branches round the trunk add to the rustic effect. If necessary, support the poppies with wires wound around the stems before you insert them into the ball.

1 Fill the pot with setting clay. Push a branch into the centre, through to the bottom of the pot. Fix reindeer moss around the base of the branch, using mossing (floral) pins. Leave the clay to set until rock-hard.

2 Cut a square of chicken wire slightly larger than the finished ball shape. Pile the foam offcuts in the centre then wrap the chicken wire around them to make a roughly round shape. Add smaller pieces of foam to fill the gaps. Cover the foam with dried moss.

3 Gather the ends of the chicken wire together and secure with a strong wire, twisting the ends together with pliers. Tie the silver reel (rose) wire to the chicken wire mesh then begin to wrap it around the ball.

4 Working at right angles to the ball, insert the poppy seed heads into the dried moss to make an overall round shape. Push the ball on to the top of the trunk. Add extra branches at irregular heights around the trunk.

PROTEA TREE

• • •

This strong-coloured topiary tree is ideal for a beginner because protea is such a sturdy material to work with. Cover the foam base with a good layer of moss to prevent any foam showing through under the flowerheads. The tree will last very well and only needs dusting to keep it looking good.

MATERIALS

· · ·

terracotta pot

· · ·

setting clay

· · ·

bundle of tied canes, for the trunk

· · ·

reindeer moss

· · ·

mossing (floral) pins

· · ·

plastic foam ball

· · ·

green moss

· · ·

silver reel (rose) wire

· · ·

secateurs

· · ·

dried protea

The brightly-coloured flower heads make a very unusual topiary design.

1 Fill the pot with setting clay. Push the canes into the centre, through to the bottom of the pot. Fix reindeer moss around the base using mossing (floral) pins. Leave the clay to fully set.

2 Cover the foam ball with plenty of green moss, attaching it with mossing (floral) pins. Push the ball firmly on top of the canes and tie securely in place with silver reel (rose) wire.

3 Trim the protea stems to the same length. Insert them at right angles into the foam until they cover the ball completely.

OREGANO TREE
· · ·

*The beauty of oregano is that
its colour and scent last a very
long time.*

Most dried materials will slowly fade over a period of time, especially if they are exposed to bright sunlight. Oregano, however, retains both its soft grey-green colour and beautiful scent well. This makes it an ideal material to use for a large display, because you know it will last a long time.

1 Fill the pot with setting clay. Push the trunk through to the bottom of the pot. Fix reindeer moss around the base of the trunk, using mossing (floral) pins.

2 Leave the clay to set then push the foam ball on top of the trunk. Tie the end of the silver reel (rose) wire to the trunk then wind it around both the trunk and the foam ball to hold together.

3 Trim and wire the oregano into bunches, with the stems 10 cm (4 in) long (see Techniques). Push them into the foam ball, holding the stems as far down as possible.

4 Add the bunches close together and hold the opposite side of the ball with your other hand to support the foam. Keep adding bunches until the whole ball is covered.

EUCALYPTUS TREE

· · ·

This attractive topiary tree is well worth making because the strong scent and unusual colour of the eucalyptus will last for a long time. For a fuller, more compact tree, wire small extra bunches of eucalyptus and push them into the foam ball between the longer single stems.

MATERIALS

· · ·

terracotta pot

· · ·

setting clay

· · ·

*piece of tree trunk or branch,
for the trunk*

· · ·

reindeer moss

· · ·

mossing (floral) pins

· · ·

plastic foam ball

· · ·

silver reel (rose) wire

· · ·

scissors

· · ·

dried Eucalyptus spiralus

1 Fill the pot with setting clay. Push the trunk through to the bottom of the pot. Fix reindeer moss around the base of the trunk, using mossing (floral) pins.

2 Leave the clay to set then push the foam ball on top of the trunk. Tie the end of the silver reel (rose) wire to the trunk then wind it around both the trunk and the foam ball to hold them together.

Eucalyptus leaves have a lovely white bloom which is destroyed by the use of clear florist's lacquer.

3 Trim the eucalyptus into 10 cm (4 in) lengths, removing the lower foliage to leave about 2.5 cm (1 in) bare stem. Push the eucalyptus stems individually into the foam ball, holding the opposite side with your other hand to support the foam.

4 Continue to add more stems in the same way. Stand back every so often to check that the ball is evenly covered and is a perfectly round shape.

MARJORAM AND BAY TREE
. . .

MATERIALS
. . .

terracotta pot

. . .

setting clay

. . .

*piece of tree trunk or branch,
for the trunk*

. . .

reindeer moss

. . .

mossing (floral) pins

. . .

plastic foam ball

. . .

silver reel (rose) wire

. . .

scissors or secateurs

. . .

dried marjoram

. . .

.91 wires

. . .

fresh bay stems

. . .

dried oregano

. . .

twigs

*When this display looks a
little tired, you can spray it
with clear florist's lacquer to
bring back some of the colour
and the natural glossy shine of
the bay leaves.*

Herbs make excellent topiary trees. If you have access to fresh bay leaves, add them straight from the bay tree and they will slowly dry out in the display. Most of the materials are added in blocks, but a few pieces of each are mixed with the bulk, to tie the whole design together.

1 Fill the pot with setting clay. Push the trunk into the centre, through to the bottom of the pot. Fix reindeer moss around the base of the trunk, using mossing (floral) pins. Leave the clay to set until rock-hard then push the foam ball on top of the trunk. Tie silver reel (rose) wire to the trunk then wind it around the ball to attach it securely.

2 Trim and wire the marjoram in bunches, with stems about 10 cm (4 in) (see Techniques). Push the bunches one at a time into the foam ball, holding the opposite side of the foam to which the flowers are being added, to ensure that you don't push the ball off the top of the trunk. Stand back from the display so that you can check the shape.

3 Keep adding bunches of marjoram until the whole ball is covered.

4 Cut the bay stems vertically to separate sprays of 1–2 leaves. Wire in bunches or leave individually; also wire the oregano (see Techniques).

5 Turn the whole display upside-down and push the bay stems and oregano into the foam, all around the base of the trunk. There should be no bay stalks showing. Centre-wire the twigs into bundles (see Techniques) and place through the arrangement.

LAVENDER TREE

· · ·

MATERIALS

· · ·

knife

· · ·

*2 plastic foam balls, about
20 cm (8 in) diameter*

· · ·

*container, same diameter as the
foam balls*

· · ·

secateurs

· · ·

contorted willow

· · ·

scissors

· · ·

dried lavender

· · ·

.91 wires

· · ·

reindeer moss

*Contorted willow makes an
unusual and very attractive
trunk for a topiary tree.*

Make a beautiful, scented dried lavender tree with a contorted willow trunk. You could even make a pair of trees and place them on either side of your mantelpiece mirror or fireplace for an elegant architectural effect.

1 Cut one of the foam balls in half and place in the container. Use extra foam if necessary to fill the container. Cut two 50 cm (20 in) lengths of contorted willow and insert into the foam.

2 Push the other foam ball on to the top of the willow. Trim the lavender stalks to 2.5 cm (1 in). Insert a ring of lavender around the foam ball then repeat in the opposite direction.

3 Fill in each section with lavender, working evenly in rows until full. Bend wires into U-shapes and use to pin reindeer moss at the base of the tree in the container, to conceal the foam.

OAK-LEAF TOPIARY

. . .

Preserved (dried) foliage is an excellent display material in its own right, as well as a useful filler with other materials. By experimenting with different leaves you can create unusual designs with great impact. Oak, copper and beech leaves are the most common type of preserved (dried) leaf.

MATERIALS

. . .

silver reel (rose) wire

. . .

plastic foam cone, with trunk and pot attached (see Techniques)

. . .

moss

. . .

secateurs

. . .

.91 wires

. . .

preserved (dried) oak leaves

You could also try pinning individual oak leaves to a foam ball or cone with mossing (floral) pins. Work from the top downwards, placing the next leaf to hide the previous pin. Alternatively, you can use a glue gun to attach the leaves.

1 Wind silver reel (rose) wire 2-3 times around the pot to secure. Continue to wind from the bottom of the pot upwards, trapping hanks of moss under the wire as you work.

2 Trim and wire small bunches of 6-8 oak leaves (see Techniques). Push them into the foam cone at random, so that they fan out. Use smaller bunches of 2-3 leaves to fill the gaps.

MINI WRAPPED TREES

. . .

MATERIALS

· · ·

small terracotta pot

· · ·

setting clay

· · ·

*bundle of cinnamon sticks or
small branch, for the trunk*

· · ·

moss

· · ·

mossing (floral) pins

· · ·

large preserved (dried) leaves

· · ·

plastic foam cone

· · ·

*glue gun and glue sticks
(optional)*

· · ·

raffia

· · ·

*extra cinnamon sticks or
dried lavender*

*Tie raffia bows around the
decorative bundles to blend in
nicely with the tree design.*

These stunning little trees are very simple to make, using just a few materials. The large leaves create an interesting contrast in scale to the small pot. The raffia looks as if it is holding the leaves in place but in fact it is purely decorative.

1 Fill the pot with setting clay. Push the trunk into the centre. Fix moss to trail around the base of the trunk, using mossing (floral) pins. Leave the clay to set until rock-hard.

2 Pin the preserved (dried) leaves to the foam cone, using mossing (floral) pins. Overlap each leaf so that it hides the pins. Use a glue gun as well as pins, if you prefer.

3 Wind long strands of raffia around the tree then tie the ends in a bow at the bottom. Push the cone on to the trunk. Decorate with cinnamon sticks or lavender bundles.

FERN TREES

· · ·

Preserved (dried) ferns turn an attractive colour and are worthy of a display in their own right. In this case the aim is not to create a perfect topiary shape, but you should still stand back as you work to check the overall balance.

MATERIALS

· · ·

terracotta pot

· · ·

setting clay

· · ·

bundle of canes, for the trunk

· · ·

moss

· · ·

mossing (floral) pins

· · ·

plastic foam cone or ball

· · ·

silver reel (rose) wire

· · ·

.91 wires

· · ·

preserved (dried) ferns

Give the display as much movement as you can by adding the ferns at angles, so that they appear to flow into each other.

1 Fill the pot with setting clay. Push the bundle of canes into the centre of the pot. Fix moss around the base of the trunk, using mossing (floral) pins. Leave the clay to set until rock-hard.

2 Fix the foam cone or ball to the trunk, tying it in place with silver reel (rose) wire. Attach a rough layer of moss to the foam, using bent wires or mossing (floral) pins, so the foam will not be seen.

3 Wire the stems of the preserved (dried) ferns (see Techniques). Insert the stems into the foam at angles to create a natural, flowing design.

FIR CONE TREES

· · ·

MATERIALS

· · ·

FOR THE BALL TREE
silver reel (rose) wire

· · ·

plastic foam ball, with trunk
and pot attached
(see Techniques)

· · ·

.91 wires

· · ·

fir cones

· · ·

moss

· · ·

FOR THE CONE TREE
knife

· · ·

1 block plastic foam for dried
flowers

· · ·

terracotta pot, the same
diameter as the cone

· · ·

glue gun and glue sticks

· · ·

plastic foam cone

· · ·

.91 wires

· · ·

silver reel (rose) wire

· · ·

fir cones

· · ·

moss

You should be able to find
the materials for these trees
on woodland walks or in
specialist shops.

Use very dry fir cones for these displays because fresh, wet ones will open up as they dry out, distorting the shape. Similarly, do not keep the tree in a damp place or the reverse will happen and the fir cones will close up. As an alternative to wiring, you could attach the fir cones with a glue gun, if you prefer.

1 To make a ball tree, tie the end of the silver reel (rose) wire to the trunk then wind it around both the foam ball and the trunk. Loop about 10 cm (4 in) of wire around each fir cone as close to the base as possible. Secure the wire by twisting the ends neatly together.

2 Push the wired fir cones into the foam, working from the bottom upwards. Add hanks of moss to fill any gaps and firmly secure with wires.

3 To make a cone tree, trim and fit the foam in the pot. Glue the cone on top and secure with two wires bent in half, by pushing them through the sides of the cone and down into the foam.

4 Tie silver reel (rose) wire around the base of the cone and wind round to the top, adding moss. Push wired fir cones into the cone.

PINE TREE

• • •

MATERIALS

• • •

silver reel (rose) wire

• • •

plastic foam ball, with trunk and pot attached (see Techniques)

• • •

secateurs

• • •

blue pine (spruce)

• • •

moss

• • •

.91 wires

• • •

small dried red roses

• • •

fir cones

• • •

nuts, e.g. chestnuts, walnuts

• • •

cinnamon sticks

• • •

dried rosemary

• • •

raffia

The thinner stems of blue pine (spruce) will tend to droop as the display dries out, so use them on the lower half of the display.

Blue pine (spruce) is an excellent material for topiary and the branches release a wonderful aroma when you cut into them. This design can be displayed throughout winter. If kept in a warm place it will gradually dry out, making an attractive dried arrangement. You can make the tree small or large. To create the large tree use a trunk that is at least 8 cm (3 in) in diameter.

1 Tie the end of the silver reel (rose) wire to the tree trunk then wind it around both the foam ball and the trunk to hold them together. Cut the blue pine (spruce) into 15 cm (6 in) lengths, trimming the foliage to expose about 2.5 cm (1 in) bare stem. Push the stems into the foam ball, filling small gaps with moss.

2 Wire the roses into bunches of 3–4 flowerheads, leaving a long length of wire (see Techniques). Add them to the tree at random, so that there is plenty of blue pine (spruce) between each rose.

3 Wire the fir cones. Add them to the display, standing back frequently to check the balance of the materials is even.

4 Wire the nuts (see Techniques). Add them to the tree, again checking the balance as you work.

5 Tie wires around the cinnamon sticks and rosemary stalks to make small bundles then cover the wire with strands of raffia and tie in a bow. Add them to the tree.

6 Cover the base of the trunk and the pot with handfuls of moss.

The large outdoor tree is decorated with a bunch of garden canes cut to length and tied with a fabric bow.

SEASHELL TOPIARY

· · ·

MATERIALS

· · ·

silver reel (rose) wire

· · ·

*plastic foam ball with trunk
and pot attached (see
Techniques)*

· · ·

glue gun and glue sticks

· · ·

assorted seashells

· · ·

moss

*You can buy seashells from
specialist shops or collect them
on the beach, but always check
that your source is not harming
the environment. Rinse the
shells in a bowl of water
before using.*

A seashell tree makes an unusual decoration for the bathroom, where the atmosphere is too damp for dried materials. If you are collecting your own seashells take care not to break any conservation laws.

1 Tie the end of the silver reel (rose) wire to the tree trunk then wind it around both the foam ball and the trunk to hold them together.

2 Glue the shells in place on the ball, allowing the glue to cool slightly so it doesn't melt the foam. Mix colours and shapes to create an attractive design.

3 Add just a little moss to fill gaps between the shells; too much will look heavy. Finish by covering the foam in the pot with a generous amount of moss.

LAVENDER OBELISK
. . .

Evoke the sumptuous style of the seventeenth century with this magnificent ribboned obelisk. It is very easy to make, but it does use a lot of lavender and can work out quite costly if you do not have access to home-grown lavender.

MATERIALS
. . .
knife
. . .
plastic foam cone
. . .
antique metal urn
. . .
dressmaker's pins
. . .
*wire-edged ribbon, 5 cm
(2 in) wide*
. . .
dried poppy seed heads
. . .
scissors
. . .
dried lavender

The different textures of lavender, poppy seed heads and ribbon look gorgeous against the weathered metal of an antique urn.

1 Using a knife, carefully trim the bottom of the foam cone, shaping it so that it will fit snugly into the urn.

2 Using dressmaker's pins, attach the ribbon to the cone, starting at the bottom and working around to the top, then working back down to make a criss-cross trellis. Scrunch the ribbon slightly as you go. Insert one large poppy seed head at the top and others at various, balanced intervals.

3 Cut the lavender stalks to within 2.5 cm (1 in) of the heads. Insert them in a ring at the bottom of the cone where it meets the rim of the urn. Working methodically in rings and lines, fill in each section outlined by the ribbons. As you reach a poppy seed head, remove it to insert a lavender stalk near the hole, then replace.

DRIED FRUIT TOPIARY URN

· · ·

MATERIALS

· · ·

glue gun and glue sticks

· · ·

antique metal urn

· · ·

plastic foam ball

· · ·

moss

· · ·

.91 wires

· · ·

dried ata fruit, with stalks

Ata fruit is quite an unusual material to use, which makes it all the more satisfying.

This elegant urn is simply filled with a foam ball then decorated with ata fruit to create an effect similar to a giant pineapple. Like fir cones, this fruit comes with stalks ready for arranging. You could use dried limes and small dried oranges instead, but they would need to be wired first.

1 Using a glue gun, inject a generous line of glue all around the inside edge of the antique metal urn.

2 Place the foam ball over the urn and press down firmly. Hold for at least 30 seconds to allow the glue to set.

3 Cover the surface of the foam with a good layer of moss. Pin it securely in place with pins made from wires bent in half. This will hide the foam and help to position the ata fruit.

4 Begin to add the ata fruit to the moss-covered foam. For added anchorage, squeeze a few drops of glue on to the base of each ata fruit before inserting the stalk firmly into the foam.

The combination of ata fruit and an antique urn makes a striking display.

5 Place two lines of fruit in the shape of a cross on the foam. Ensure that the heads are level with one another and that the cross shape is even.

6 Fill in each quarter with more fruit. Look at the size of each ata fruit to decide where it will be best placed, as some are smaller than others.

333

FRUIT TOPIARY

· · ·

Choose the plumpest, reddest fruits for the best effect.

Strawberries and raspberries do not grow together, nor do they grow on trees. However, you can create your own fantasy fruit trees with dried fruits and a little imagination. Why not make a pair of matching trees to flank a door or to adorn a mantelpiece?

1 Trim the plastic foam to fit snugly inside the basket. Should you require two pieces, secure these together with pins made from short lengths of .71 wire. For added security, you can glue the base of the foam to the basket itself, using a glue gun.

2 Completely cover the foam pyramid with tillandsia moss, fastening it with small wire pins. Trim off any stray pieces of moss to maintain a neat pyramid shape.

3 Place the pyramid centrally over the top of the basket and secure using long .90 wire pins pushed diagonally through the base of the pyramid and into the foam below. Use as many as necessary until you feel confident that the structure will hold in position.

4 Using a glue gun, begin to stick small pieces of lichen randomly over the pyramid. This material is introduced to add new texture and to give the display a frosted look. The lichen is very delicate and should be handled gently.

5 Using a sharp knife, cut the strawberries in half and begin to glue to the pyramid structure at regular intervals. Hold each strawberry firmly against the pyramid until the glue has dried.

6 Glue on clusters of raspberries between the strawberry halves wherever necessary, to ensure even coverage.

· · ·

MATERIALS
· · ·

terracotta pot, 15 cm (6 in) diameter

· · ·

cellophane (plastic wrap)

· · ·

sand

· · ·

knife

· · ·

1 block plastic foam for dried flowers

· · ·

glue

· · ·

1 piece preserved (dried) root with two branches

· · ·

2 plastic foam balls, 12 cm (4¾ in) diameter

· · ·

60 slices preserved (dried) apple

· · ·

.71 wires

· · ·

150 stems natural phalaris

· · ·

scissors

· · ·

30 stems cream dried roses

· · ·

50 stems Nigella orientalis

· · ·

20 stems natural ti tree

· · ·

150 stems dried lavender

· · ·

12 short stems preserved (dried) eucalyptus

Decorative trees are often referred to as topiary trees, and whether made from fresh or dried materials can be designed to match the colour scheme and image of any room.

This dried flower and fruit example has soft soothing colours: pale green phalaris and *Nigella orientalis,* dusty blue lavender, white ti tree, soft grey eucalyptus and the creamy tones of the dried roses and apple slices.

Topiary trees have a tendency to be top heavy, especially if they have more than one branch. To counterbalance this, make sure that the container is weighted with wet sand or, as a more permanent measure, plaster of Paris.

1 Line the terracotta pot with cellophane (plastic wrap) or polythene (plastic sheeting) and three-quarters fill it with wet sand. Cut the block of plastic foam to fit the pot, firmly wedge it in on top of the sand and level it with the rim of the pot.

2 Put a few drops of glue on the base of the piece of root. With its branches pointed upwards, push the root into the centre of the plastic foam in the terracotta pot. Apply a few drops of glue on to the top of the branches and push one of the plastic foam balls on to each branch.

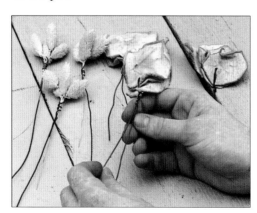

3 Form the apple slices into 20 groups of three. Push a .71 wire through the flesh of a group and bring the ends down, twisting together to form a double leg mount. Cut the phalaris stems to a length of about 3 cm (1¼ in) and form 30 groups of five, double leg mounting each group with .71 wire.

4 Cut the wires of the phalaris groups to approximately 4 cm (1½ in) and distribute them evenly all over the two balls by pushing the wired stems into the plastic foam. Cut the roses to a stem length of approximately 5 cm (2 in) and push the stems into the foam, distributing them evenly among the phalaris.

5 Cut the wire stems of the groups of apple slices to a length of approximately 4 cm (1½ in) and push them in to the foam, distributing them evenly around both balls. Cut 40 stems of the *Nigella orientalis* and all the stems of ti tree to a length of approximately 5 cm (2 in). Push the stems into the foam, distributing both evenly over the two balls.

6 Cut the lavender to an overall length of approximately 5 cm (2 in), form them in to 40 groups of three and push the stems of these groups into the foam. Position them evenly among the other materials on both balls.

7 Cut the eucalyptus stems and the remaining *Nigella orientalis* and lavender stems to varying lengths. At the base of the tree push these stems into the plastic foam to create an arrangement that covers the foam completely.

This tree is relatively intricate to make as it involves wiring and a large quantity of different materials. However, a more unusual effect can be achieved by the use of only one or two materials, for example the roses and the apple slices.

FRUITED TREE

· · ·

MATERIALS

· · ·

secateurs (garden clippers)

· · ·

*3 branches glycerined beech
leaves*

· · ·

.71 wires

· · ·

dried pear slices

· · ·

*1 plastic foam ball for dried
flowers, about 13 cm
(5 in) diameter*

· · ·

flowerpot, 18 cm (7 in) tall

*Golden dried pears make a
beautiful and unusual focus for
this opulent topiary design.*

Glycerined leaves make a perfect foundation for any dried topiary. You can buy them in branches, ready glycerined for use, or glycerine your own garden prunings. Here, they have been wired into bunches for a fabulous, full look.

1 Cut the leaves off the branches and trim the stalks. Wire up small bunches of four or six beech leaves and twist the ends of the wires together.

2 Pass a wire through the top of each pear slice and twist the ends together. Completely cover the portion of the ball that will show above the pot with beech leaves.

3 Add the pear slices and put the ball into the pot.

FLOWER CONE
· · ·

This unusual design employs a series of stacked rings around a cone shape, each ring containing massed flowers of one type and colour to create a quirky display with a strong geometric pattern.

One side of the container is higher than the other so its rim is an ellipse rather than a circle and this is exploited by making the rings of the flowers follow this elliptical shape to form lines of colour sweeping down from back to front.

MATERIALS
· · ·
plastic foam cone for dried flowers, 28 cm (11 in) high
· · ·
galvanized metal container, approximately 11 cm (4½ in) diameter
· · ·
scissors
· · ·
20 stems dried floss flower
· · ·
40 stems dried pink rose heads
· · ·
20 stems dried marjoram
· · ·
10 stems small dried globe thistle heads
· · ·
ribbon

1 Wedge the plastic foam cone firmly into the galvanized container. Cut the floss flower stems to about 2.5 cm (1 in) long and arrange a ring around the bottom of the cone to follow the ellipse of the rim of the container. Cut the rose stems to about 2.5 cm (1 in) long and, tight to the first ring, arrange a second ring with the rose heads again following the elliptical shape.

The pretty colours of the display and finishing ribbon make it ideal for a dressing-table where a mirror at its back will show the arrangement in the round.

2 Cut the stems of the marjoram and globe thistle to about 2.5 cm (1 in). Tight to the ring of rose heads, form a third elliptical ring with the marjoram. Tight to the marjoram, form a fourth elliptical ring with the globe thistle. Repeat this sequence of rings until all the cone is covered. At the tip, fix a single rose head.

3 Wrap the ribbon around the galvanized metal container and finish it in a small tied bow at the front of the display.

SPICE CONE
· · ·

MATERIALS
· · ·
knife
· · ·
cinnamon sticks
· · ·
small terracotta pot
· · ·
glue gun and glue sticks
· · ·
2 small plastic foam cones, 1 to fit the pot, 1 slightly larger
· · ·
.91 wires
· · ·
whole star anise
· · ·
scissors
· · ·
cloves

Star anise, together with the other spices, look as delicious as their wonderful rich scent.

This unusual little cone is studded with cloves and star anise, both of which are highly aromatic. A cinnamon stick cross completes the design and the pot is also decorated with cinnamon sticks. Place it near the entrance to your home so that the scent will welcome you on arrival.

1 Cut the cinnamon sticks carefully to the height of the pot. Glue them at regular intervals around the pot.

2 Trim off the top of the larger cone and work it into a less regimented shape. Cut the smaller cone to fit the pot.

3 Put four wires upright into the pot so they project above the foam. Fix the sculpted cone on top of the pot.

4 Pass a wire over the front of the first star anise, in one direction then in another direction to make a cross. Twist the wires together at the back and trim to about 1 cm (½ in).

5 Arrange the star anise in rows down the cone, to quarter it. Add two more vertically between each line. Fill the remaining area of cone with cloves, packing them tightly. Glue two short pieces of cinnamon stick into a cross. Wire and place on top of the spice cone.

TOPIARY BALLS

. . .

MATERIALS

. . .

long florist's wire

. . .

plastic foam ball

. . .

pliers

. . .

scissors

. . .

dried materials, e.g. achillea, larkspur, nigella, marjoram, oregano, miniature roses

. . .

.91 wires

. . .

wide ribbon

*T*opiary balls can be made
with a wide combination of
different flowerheads, for a
colourful effect.

*T*hese are made using the same techniques as a round topiary tree but hang from ribbons instead of standing on a surface. Small dried flowers or herbs look best, massed together to make a perfectly round shape. A single material is very effective or you can use a combination of mixed colours.

1 First attach a wire for hanging the topiary ball. Bend a long florist's wire in half and push it through the foam ball, leaving about 2.5 cm (1 in) of the looped end sticking out. Twist the ends of the wire neatly together underneath the ball.

2 Trim all the stalks to the same length. Wire the material in small bunches, with flowerheads and foliage in separate bunches (see Techniques). Push the bunches into the foam, turning the ball gently as you work. When complete, trim to achieve a perfect round shape. Thread the ribbon through the loop for hanging.

ROSE BALL

· · ·

The rose ball is a simple variation on a topiary ball, using one single flower variety and colour. It looks very similar to an old-fashioned pomander. To achieve a perfectly round ball, trim the stalks to the same length before you start then adjust them as you work so the rose heads are all at the same height.

MATERIALS

· · ·

long florist's wire

· · ·

plastic foam ball

· · ·

pliers

· · ·

dried roses

· · ·

scissors

· · ·

.91 wires

· · ·

wide ribbon

Choose a ribbon to match the colours of the roses, or to add extra colour.

1 First attach a wire for hanging the rose ball. Bend a long florist's wire in half and push it through the foam ball, leaving about 2.5 cm (1 in) of the looped end sticking out. Using pliers, twist the ends of the wire neatly together underneath the ball, so that it is not visible. Steam the roses if necessary (see Techniques).

2 Trim all the rose stalks to the same length then wire them in bunches of 3–4 (see Techniques). Wire the foliage from the roses in separate bunches (see Techniques). Push the bunches alternately into the foam, turning the ball gently as you work. Thread the ribbon through the wire loop for hanging.

SPICED POMANDER

· · ·

MATERIALS

· · ·

cloves

· · ·

*plastic foam ball, about 8 cm
(3 in) diameter*

· · ·

glue gun and glue sticks

· · ·

green cardamom pods

· · ·

raffia

· · ·

91 wire

*Cloves and cardamom smell
delicious and look
very decorative.*

Pomanders are Nature's own air fresheners. The traditional orange pomanders are fairly tricky to make because the critical drying process can easily go wrong, leading to mouldy oranges. A foam ball, decorated with spices such as cloves and cardamom pods in soft, muted colours, makes a refreshing change.

1 Press in a single line of cloves all around the circumference of the ball. Make another line in the other direction, to divide the ball into quarters.

2 Following the same pattern, press in a line of cloves on both sides of the original lines to make broad bands of cloves quartering the ball.

3 Starting at the top of the first quarter, glue cardamom pods over the foam, working in rows to create a neat effect. Repeat on the other three quarters.

4 Tie a bow in the centre of a length of raffia. Pass a wire through the knot then twist the ends together, leaving them to stick out.

5 Attach the bow to the top of the pomander ball, using the wire.

6 Join the two loose ends in a knot, for hanging the pomander.

LAVENDER POMANDER

· · ·

MATERIALS

· · ·

.71 wire

· · ·

*1 plastic foam ball for dried
flowers, about 9 cm
(3½ in) diameter*

· · ·

ribbon

· · ·

scissors

· · ·

2 bunches dried lavender stems

*Hang this pomander in
the bedroom, where it will
release a relaxing aroma while
you sleep.*

This delightful lavender version of a spice pomander makes an aromatic room decoration at any time of the year.

1 Bend the wire in half and fix through the centre of the foam ball. Pass the ribbon through the top loop and push down so that it is fixed firmly to the ball. Trim the ends of the wires. Bend the wires at the bottom flat against the foam to secure the ribbon.

2 Select similar-size lavender heads, and, starting at the bottom of the ball, push the stems into the foam, making a circle around the circumference of the ball.

3 When the first circle is complete, make another circle of lavender around the circumference at right angles to the first. This will divide the pomander into quarters.

4 Working in lines, fill in one quarter. Repeat with the others. Tie a bow at the top of the ribbon.

ORNAMENTS AND GIFTS

⸱ ⸱ ⸱

Special occasions such as dinner parties and
birthdays call for special displays and gifts.
Ornamental displays can be made from simple
materials, to give a country effect, or you can
indulge in grand theatrical gestures. Chandeliers
and dramatic table centrepieces make wonderful
ornamental displays, and pomanders and
pot-pourris are always loved as gifts.

INTRODUCTION

· · ·

Above: Formal Table Centrepiece

Below: Candle Rings

Floral arrangements such as candle rings, table centrepieces and napkin rings always add a lovely ornamental touch to your dining table, and candle pots, garlands and pot-pourris are ideal to give as special gifts. The ideas shown here cover a wide range of ornaments and gifts, most of which are very easy to make.

The ornamental displays are often designed to be dismantled afterwards, so this is an excuse to create something extravagant and spontaneous instead of a display which needs to be long-lasting. Several of the table centrepieces in this chapter are designed to be taken apart and reassembled on another occasion, each time adding to or adjusting the arrangement to keep it interesting. They incorporate numerous candle pots and a wealth of different dried materials to create large, exuberant displays which are still essentially based on simple techniques.

Candle pillars, however, are definitely intended for grand occasions. They always look elegantly stunning, and are ideal for a formal evening party. Place a single large candle pillar on the floor, or make a matching pair for either end of a mantelpiece or a long dinner table. The success of the design rests on getting the right balance between the candle and the base. They are more vulnerable to accidents than short, fat candles in pots, so do position them very carefully and never leave them unattended when the candle is burning.

Above: Candle Cuff

*Left: Classic Orange
and Clove Pomander*

The gift ideas in this chapter are slightly different in that they are all very quick and simple to make, often requiring no wiring or technical skills and very few materials. Most can be made very inexpensively from individual flowers and materials left over from larger projects. However, like many other handmade presents, they possess great charm and individual character.

Collect decorative gift boxes in which to present your dried flower displays. When you have nothing suitable for a container, you can disguise unattractive cardboard boxes by painting them with a distressed paint effect or wrapping them in remnants of fabric. If you know the room where your gift is likely to be placed, try to choose a co-ordinating paint or fabric to make your present even more special.

A still life display of dried materials, shells and other decorative objects can also be tailor-made to suit an individual person or location. Include in it materials which have special meaning to the recipient, such as favourite flowers, or those which complement their furnishings. Another very personal design is a clipframe containing a photograph: decorate this with flowers and leaves which suit the personality of the person you are giving it to.

All these attractive ornaments and gifts are so easy to make that you need never again be stuck for an idea, even at the last minute.

Below: Leaf Napkin Rings

351

CANDLE RING

· · ·

The radiant gold of Achillea filipendulina *has a stunning impact on this display.*

Pink roses, hydrangeas, achillea and peonies make a stunning summer table decoration, and the large flower-heads will cover the garland base very quickly. Plastic candleholders are available from florists; remember never to leave burning candles unattended.

1 Cover the garland ring with hay or moss (see Techniques). Push in the candleholders at evenly spaced intervals, then add the candles to check they stand straight. Remove the candles and glue the holders to the ring. Trim and wire the hydrangeas in small bunches (see Techniques). Push the wires into the ring and glue in place, covering both the inside and outside of the ring.

2 Cut the achillea stems to about 5 cm (2 in), push them directly into the ring and glue in place.

3 Add the roses and peonies in the same way, handling them gently. Steam the roses if necessary (see Techniques).

4 Fill small gaps with green moss, attaching it with mossing (floral) pins. Glue the candles into the candleholders.

This lovely candle-lit ring of summer flowers doesn't take long to make but looks very impressive.

353

CANDLE PILLAR

· · ·

The yellow flowerheads contrast well with the blue, to make a bold, modern design.

Covered in dark green moss, this pillar looks stunning, an ideal decoration for a grand dinner party. A pair of these above the fireplace or on the dinner table would add atmosphere to any occasion. Choose a candle that balances the thickness of the floral base. Because of its height, a candle pillar is much more vulnerable to accidents, so make sure you place it in a secure position and never leave it unattended when the candle is lit.

1 Make a topiary base using the medium terracotta pot (see Techniques). Glue the small pot to the top of the trunk, making sure that it is completely straight.

2 Tuck moss into the base of the larger pot and wrap it around the trunk, tying it in place with silver reel (rose) wire. Keep the moss as even as possible and not too thick.

3 Continue to add the moss until the whole trunk has been covered, and so that the area around the small pot at the top of the trunk also has a good layer of moss.

4 If the roses are small, steam them (see Techniques). Trim the stems off the rose heads then glue the heads in small groups on to the moss, in various positions around the trunk.

5 Repeat with the echinops until the whole of the moss is covered. Fill any small gaps with moss, fixing it in place with a glue gun or mossing (floral) pins. Fix the candle in the small pot, either by gluing or by packing the pot tightly with moss.

FLORAL CHANDELIER
· · ·

*This mix of flowers will keep
its colour for a long time, but
you may need to replace the
moss after a few months.*

This unusual chandelier is designed to hang fairly low, so no flowers are added to the base. Hold it up every so often while you are making it to see how it looks from that angle. The flowers look enchanting in the candlelight; remember never to leave the chandelier unattended when lit.

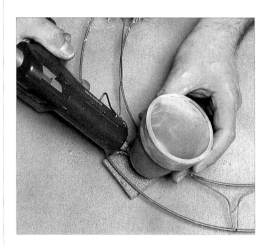

1 Flatten the garland ring by pushing or pulling the triangular wires towards each other. Glue a small piece of foam under the ring and to one of the pots, so that at least one of the wires crosses the centre of the foam; change the angle of the wire if necessary. Attach all four pots in the same way, spacing them evenly around the ring.

2 Wrap sphagnum moss around the ring, holding it in place with silver reel (rose) wire. The moss needs to be about 2.5 cm (1 in) thick. Pay particular attention to the base of the ring, making sure that the foam base and the area around the pots are covered.

3 To create a hanging loop, push both ends of a strong wire through the ring, between two pots on the inner edge. Make sure that it crosses the ring frame under the moss. Twist the ends together and tuck into the moss. Repeat at even intervals to make four loops for hanging.

4 Centre-wire bunches of larkspur, roses and achillea (see Techniques). Push the wire into the moss frame. Angle the flowers so that they are pointing from the inside of the frame to the outside.

The chandelier will look dramatic when lit, and should last a fair while with such thick candles.

5 Continue to add these three materials, criss-crossing them. Place them in the same order in each quarter of the ring, to give balance to the design.

6 Cut the stems off the peonies and glue the heads in place. Using mossing (floral) pins, attach the dark green moss to the ring, filling any gaps. Attach four hanging ropes to the wire loops. Fit the candles into the pots, wedging them in place with foam and moss.

WOODLAND CANDLE RING

· · ·

MATERIALS

· · ·

copper or steel garland ring

· · ·

glue gun and glue sticks

· · ·

offcuts of plastic foam for dried flowers

· · ·

4 small terracotta pots

· · ·

sphagnum moss

· · ·

silver reel (rose) wire

· · ·

.91 wires

· · ·

preserved (dried) oak leaves

· · ·

twigs

· · ·

dried eucalyptus seed heads

· · ·

dried fungi

· · ·

fir cones

· · ·

dark green moss

· · ·

mossing (floral) pins

· · ·

4 candles

Pile the woodland materials around the pots to create a natural display.

Here, a copper or steel garland ring is flattened to form the circular base for an autumnal table decoration. Preserved (dried) oak leaves are used to cover the ring then fungi, twigs, fir cones and seed heads are added on top, as on a woodland floor. Never leave the lit candles unattended.

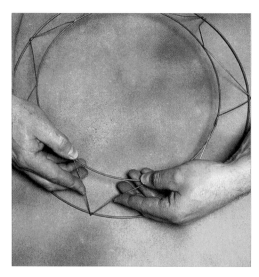

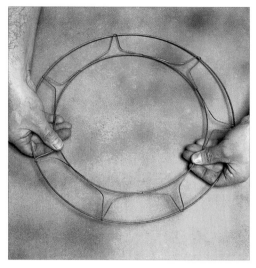

1 Push or pull the triangular wires of the ring towards each other, working all the way round, to flatten the ring.

2 Lay the ring on the clear work surface and flatten it out completely with your fingers.

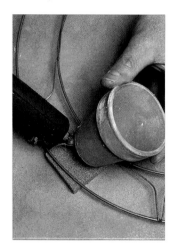

3 Glue a small piece of foam under the ring. Glue a pot on top so that at least one of the wires crosses the centre of the foam, changing the angle of the wire if necessary. Space all four pots evenly around the ring.

4 Cover the ring with plenty of sphagnum moss, holding it in place with silver reel (rose) wire. The moss needs to be about 2.5 cm (1 in) thick. Pay particular attention to the base of the ring, making sure that the foam base and the area around the pots are well covered.

5 Centre-wire bunches of oak leaves (see Techniques), then push the wires into the moss base. They should not go through the ring but run along its length. Fill each section between the pots, using plenty of oak leaves.

6 Repeat with wired bundles of twigs, adding one bundle next to each pot. Add a second bundle of twigs to cross the first. If the wire is not long enough to hold the bundle firmly in place, use a glue gun to secure it. Add the other materials in the same way, gluing or wiring them in place to fill the spaces.

7 Fill small gaps with green moss using mossing (floral) pins. Place candles in the pots and pack them with moss.

Eucalyptus seed heads make an attractive addition to the other woodland materials.

PINK LARKSPUR PILLAR

· · ·

MATERIALS

· · ·

glue gun and glue sticks

· · ·

small terracotta pot

· · ·

tree trunk

· · ·

medium terracotta pot

· · ·

setting clay

· · ·

moss

· · ·

silver reel (rose) wire

· · ·

scissors

· · ·

dried pink larkspur

· · ·

dried lavender

· · ·

green moss

· · ·

mossing (floral) pins

· · ·

tall candle

*Pink larkspur is the dominant
flower in this candle pillar,
blending nicely with the
other materials.*

This lovely display is fairly easy to make, but only add as much material as you can comfortably hold in one hand, fixing it in place with the silver reel (rose) wire before trying to add more. Experimentation will tell you the best position to hold the pillar – you may find it easier to lay it down while you add the materials. When the display is finished, go back to the top and if there are any gaps push a few stems between those already in place.

1 Glue the small pot to the top of the trunk, making sure that it is completely level. Set the trunk in the medium pot, using setting clay.

2 Tuck moss into the base of the medium pot and wrap it around the trunk, tying it in place with silver reel (rose) wire. Keep the moss even.

3 Continue until the whole trunk is covered with moss. Make sure that the area around the pot at the top of the trunk also has a good layer.

4 Trim the flower stems to about 13 cm (5 in). Starting at the top of the trunk, tie the larkspur in place with silver reel (rose) wire.

5 Add the lavender, working down the whole length of the trunk. Each layer should cover the workings of the last. Wrap green moss around the stems and wire of the final layer, and fix in place with mossing (floral) pins. Glue the candle into the small pot.

ARTICHOKE CANDLEHOLDER

• • •

MATERIALS

• • •

large dried globe artichoke

• • •

gold spray paint

• • •

glue gun and glue sticks

• • •

plastic candleholder

• • •

dark green moss

• • •

mossing (floral) pins

• • •

fir cones

• • •

.91 wires

• • •

twigs or cinnamon sticks

• • •

candle

• • •

gold cord

Dried artichokes have a stunning impact, but you can use dried fruit if they are too hard to find.

Sprayed gold, the distinctive shape of the artichoke makes an exotic table decoration. Choose artichokes with a flat bottom so that the candle will stand safely. Make sure that you never leave a burning candle unattended.

1 Spray the artichoke with gold paint and leave to dry for a few minutes. Put some glue in the centre of the artichoke and push the candleholder into the soft glue.

2 Cover the top of the artichoke with moss, fixing it in place with mossing (floral) pins. Make sure the moss covers the sides of the candleholder, but leave the hole at the top clear.

3 Using a glue gun, glue the fir cones firmly on top of the moss. Try to create a pleasing, balanced arrangement as a base for the other materials.

4 Decorate with wired bunches of twigs or cinnamon sticks or, as shown here, fir cones on a twig. Fit the candle into the candleholder and arrange the cord.

This display makes a perfect dinner-table decoration.

LEAF-WRAPPED CANDLES

· · ·

MATERIALS

· · ·

glue gun and gun sticks

· · ·

*large preserved (dried) leaves,
e.g. magnolia leaves*

· · ·

candle

· · ·

scissors

· · ·

raffia

*These naturally dark magnolia
leaves are very attractive in a
display, but can also be bought
dyed a beautiful rich burgundy
colour, as for this project.*

These handsome candles are simple to make yet sophisticated enough for a grand occasion. Thin candles will burn too quickly so make sure that you choose ones that are at least 8 cm (3 in) in diameter and about 15 cm (6 in) tall. Remember never to leave burning candles unattended.

1 Place a little glue on the back of a leaf, near the base. Press the leaf firmly on to the side of the candle. Repeat all round the candle.

2 Trim the base of the leaves, so that the candle stands straight. Tie a few strands of raffia tightly around the bottom of the leaf-wrapped candle.

CANDLE RINGS

· · ·

Any small-headed flowers would be suitable for these attractive decorations but dried miniature roses are perfect. If you are using more than one shade of rose on a candle ring, glue them in pairs of different colours and position the heads so that they are facing outwards. Small leaves discarded with the unwanted rose stems make useful fillers, but take care that they are not too tall and may become a fire hazard. Never leave lighted candles unattended.

MATERIALS

· · ·

glue gun and glue sticks

· · ·

moss

· · ·

small cane ring

· · ·

scissors

· · ·

dried flowers, e.g. miniature roses, bupleurum

· · ·

candle

· · ·

moss

*M*ake the candle ring any size, depending on the width of your candle.

1 Glue a light covering of moss to the cane ring. Try to make sure that no glue is visible.

2 Trim the rose heads from their stems, leaving as little stalk as possible. Glue them in place in a balanced and symmetrical design.

3 Fill the spaces between the roses with other flowers or foliage, leaving enough room for the candle. Fill any remaining gaps with moss.

SUMMER CANDLE SACK

· · ·

MATERIALS

· · ·

plastic bag

· · ·

sand

· · ·

knife

· · ·

*1 block plastic foam for dried
flowers*

· · ·

fabric remnant

· · ·

.91 wires

· · ·

silver reel (rose) wire

· · ·

preserved (dried) leaves

· · ·

scissors

· · ·

dried pink roses

· · ·

dried blue larkspur

· · ·

dried flowering mint

· · ·

plastic candleholder

· · ·

wide green paper ribbon

· · ·

scented candle

*Mint gives off a delicious
aroma, especially when the
candle is lit.*

Mint flowers are an unusual material in this pretty candle sack, mixed with pink roses and blue larkspur. The scented candle and aromatic mint are perfect for evening meals in the garden. Remember never to leave the candle unattended when it is burning.

1 Fill the plastic bag with sand to a depth of 2.5 cm (1 in) and a diameter of 13 cm (5 in). Tie a knot to close the bag. Cut a cylinder of foam slightly smaller than the bag of sand. Place the sand bag on top of the fabric and the foam on top of the bag. Gather the fabric up around the foam, also bringing the sand bag up a little around the base.

2 Fix the fabric in place with wires bent into U-shapes. Attach the silver reel (rose) wire to the fabric by winding it 2–3 times around the neck of the base. Add the preserved (dried) leaves, holding them in place with the wire.

3 Trim the stalks of the roses, larkspur and mint to about 15 cm (6 in) and wire them into small mixed bunches (see Techniques). Push the candleholder into the centre of the foam. Add the wired bunches, leaning them slightly outwards, until the foam is covered. Fill any gaps with individual flowers or leaves. Tie a ribbon bow around the base and place the candle in the candleholder.

WINTER TABLE DECORATION
· · ·

Red chillies, roses and pomegranates mingle with the earthy colours of some terracotta pots and cinnamon sticks in this tumble of materials falling away from a large central candle pot. Gluing the candle pots to canes gives them a solid fixing, but never leave the candles unattended when lit.

MATERIALS
· · ·
1–2 blocks plastic foam for dried flowers
· · ·
canes
· · ·
glue gun and glue sticks
· · ·
small and medium terracotta pots
· · ·
tall and short candles
· · ·
green moss
· · ·
mossing (floral) pins
· · ·
dried materials, e.g. pomegranates, red chillies, red roses, cinnamon sticks
· · ·
extra terracotta pots, in various sizes
· · ·
gold cord

The terracotta pots add a chunky effect that works well in this unstructured display.

1 Trim two pieces of foam to produce bases large enough to stand the pots on. For each candle pot, push a piece of cane about 8 cm (3 in) long into the foam, leaving 1 cm (½ in) protruding. Glue around the cane at the base then push the candle pot on to the cane.

2 Glue the candles into the appropriate size pots. Surround the base of each candle with green moss, fixing it in place with mossing (floral) pins.

3 Arrange all of the materials and the extra pots on top of the moss, spilling around and on to the tablecloth. Twine or tie gold cord loosely around the candles.

WINTER CHANDELIER
. . .

MATERIALS
. . .

dried oranges

. . .

gold spray paint

. . .

knife

. . .

small screwdriver

. . .

.91 wires

. . .

glue gun and glue sticks

. . .

moss

. . .

starfish

. . .

rope

. . .

ready-made hop vine or twig garland

. . .

green moss

. . .

4 florist's candleholders

. . .

4 candles

Starfish, dried oranges and moss make very unusual decorations.

This quirky chandelier consists of a moss-covered ring, from which hang gold-sprayed dried oranges decorated with gold starfish. To dry the oranges, place them on a wire rack over a stove or in an airing cupboard for several weeks until they are very hard. Remember to never leave a burning candle unattended.

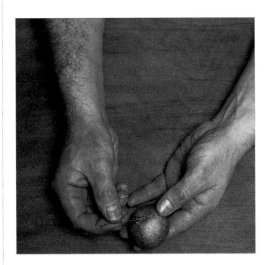

1 Spray the oranges with gold paint. Cut them in half and make a hole in each half with a screwdriver. Push the two ends of a bent wire through the hole, to make a hanging loop. Turn the orange over and bend the ends of the wire up, to prevent the loop from falling out.

2 Using a glue gun, coat the inside of the orange with glue and push moss into the open space, until you have completely filled it up.

3 Take a starfish. Place glue on the moss and around the edge of the orange, where the starfish touches it. Hold in place until the glue sets. Dab a little glue on two or three more starfish and place them on the top and sides of the orange.

4 Bend the top and bottom of a long wire and hang the orange on one end. Spray it gently and carefully with gold paint, so that it provides a frosting rather than solid colour, allowing a little of the orange colour to show through.

5 Tie four lengths of rope firmly to the ring, so that the chandelier hangs horizontally. At this stage, keep the ropes fairly long so that you can adjust them afterwards.

The whole chandelier is brought together by the gold frosting on the ring and the rope.

6 Push a handful of green moss on to the ring between two of the ropes. Make a small hole in the centre of the moss with your fingers.

7 Put some glue in the hole and push a candleholder in, keeping it straight. Put a candle into the holder. Add the oranges when the chandelier is positioned.

WINTER CANDLE SACK

• • •

. . .

plastic bag

. . .

sand

. . .

knife

. . .

*1 block plastic foam for dried
flowers*

. . .

fabric offcut

. . .

.91 wires

. . .

silver reel (rose) wire

. . .

preserved (dried) ferns or leaves

. . .

scissors

. . .

*dried flowers, e.g. carthamus,
marjoram*

. . .

plastic candleholder

. . .

raffia

. . .

candle

*Marjoram adds a full look
and attractive texture to
displays, and is an ideal
background for brightly
coloured flowers.*

This unusual candle base is simply a plastic bag filled with sand to balance the tall candle. Two alternatives are shown here: deep red roses, marjoram, ferns and leaves in the main photograph, or orange carthamus, marjoram and ferns in the step-by-step photographs. Never leave a burning candle unattended.

1 Fill the plastic bag with sand to a depth of 2.5 cm (1 in) and a diameter of 13 cm (5 in) when the sand is patted down into a round. Tie a knot to close the bag, squeezing out all the air. Cut a cylinder of foam slightly smaller than the bag of sand. Place the sand bag on the piece of fabric, and the foam cylinder on top of the bag.

2 Gather the fabric up around the foam, while also bringing the sand bag up a little around the base of the foam. Fix the fabric in place with wires bent into U-shapes. Wind the silver reel (rose) wire 2–3 times round the neck of the bag to make a firm starting point. Add the ferns or leaves, holding them in place with the wire around the neck of the bag.

3 Trim the flower stalks to about 15 cm (6 in) then wire the flowers into small mixed bunches (see Techniques). Push the candleholder into the centre of the foam. Add the wired bunches, so that the flowers lean outwards and away from the candleholder.

4 Continue to add the wired bunches of flowers until the foam is completely covered and the bunches are evenly arranged. Fill any small gaps with individual flowers or leaves. Tie a raffia bow around the base. Place the candle firmly in the candleholder.

FORMAL TABLE CENTREPIECE
. . .

MATERIALS

. . .

small wire urn

. . .

moss

. . .

knife

. . .

1 block plastic foam for dried flowers

. . .

.91 wires

. . .

florist's tape (stem-wrap tape)

. . .

candle

. . .

mossing (floral) pins

. . .

dried hydrangeas

. . .

scissors

. . .

freeze-dried roses

Large roses and hydrangeas are a lovely and very elegant combination.

Hydrangeas dry beautifully and only a few are needed to create a stunning effect. Combined here with large white freeze-dried roses, they make a brilliantly simple arrangement that will look good all year round. Do not let the candle burn down too near to the dried flowers, or leave a lit candle unattended.

1 Cover the inside of the urn with a very thin layer of moss.

2 Cut a piece of foam and place it in the urn. Hold it in position with wires bent into U-shaped pins and threaded through the urn and pushed into the foam.

3 Tape several bent wires around the base of the candle to form pegs.

4 Insert the candle in the centre of the foam. Holding the base of the urn, press the candle down firmly until it fits securely and so that it is straight.

5 Cover the surface of the foam with a thin layer of moss, securing it in place with wires bent into U-shapes or mossing (floral) pins. Select a few choice stems of hydrangea and cut the stalks to leave at least 5 cm (2 in). Begin to insert the heads around the base of the candle so that they are nicely touching the moss.

6 Take a short length of wire and make a hook by bending the top of the wire over. Thread the hook through the centre of a rose and pull down gently until the head of the hook is hidden within the petals and the stalk is protruding sufficiently out of the base. Place the roses between the hydrangea heads in small clusters by inserting the wire stalks firmly into the foam.

7 Move the arrangement round as you insert the materials until fully covered.

The centrepiece has a neat, formal, domed shape.

MIXED CONE CENTREPIECE

• • •

MATERIALS

• • •

knife

• • •

1 block plastic foam for dried flowers

• • •

2 terracotta pots

• • •

glue gun and glue sticks

• • •

2 candles

• • •

green moss

• • •

mossing (floral) pins

• • •

.91 wires

• • •

4 larch branches, with cones

• • •

large piece of felt

• • •

fir cones

The irregular shapes of the fir cones blend well with those of the larch branches, to create a very natural effect.

Terracotta candle pots, cones and moss make a simple but very effective decoration for a table. Collect a good variety of cones from different trees, including small larch cones still on their branches. Make sure the cones and moss are dry before you use them. Never leave a burning candle unattended.

1 Cut a foam block in two and trim both pieces to produce bases large enough to stand the pots on. Glue the candles into the pots. Surround the base of the candles and the sides of the foam with green moss, fixing it in place with mossing (floral) pins.

2 Centre-wire the larch branches (see Techniques). Push the ends of the wires into the foam base. Place larch branches on each side of the foam, so that the ends cross each other. Move the arrangement to its final position, putting felt underneath to protect the table. Place the other fir cones so that they appear to cascade away from the centre of the display.

SEASIDE TABLE CENTREPIECE
· · ·

MATERIALS
· · ·
knife
· · ·
1 block plastic foam for dried flowers
· · ·
large terracotta candle pot
· · ·
various types of moss, including reindeer, tillandsia and green moss
· · ·
mossing (floral) pins
· · ·
scissors
· · ·
.91 wires
· · ·
dried Eryngium alpinum
· · ·
dried yellow roses
· · ·
raffia
· · ·
small terracotta candle pots
· · ·
starfish
· · ·
shells

You could elaborate on the design with whatever seaside materials you can find.

This impromptu collection of materials can be assembled very quickly for dinner on the beach or an informal buffet, then packed away for another time. The large candle pot gives height and structure to the display, with the rest of the materials cascading away from the centre.

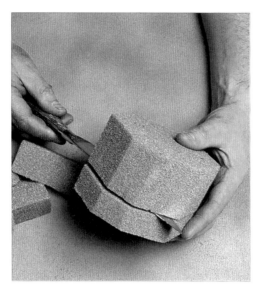

1 Trim the block of foam to produce a base large enough to stand the large candle pot on top.

2 Surround the base of the pot and sides of the foam with green moss, fixing it in place with mossing (floral) pins.

3 Trim and centre-wire bunches of eryngium (see Techniques). Push the wires through the moss into the foam base, placing one bunch on each side of the candle pot.

4 Repeat with the roses, tying them with raffia to cover the wire twisted around each bunch. Move the arrangement to its final position on the table. Place candle pots around the centrepiece and fill the spaces in between with a selection of different mosses. Decorate with starfish and shells.

LEAF NAPKIN RINGS

. . .

MATERIALS

. . .

*large preserved (dried) leaves,
e.g. cobra leaves*

. . .

glue gun and glue sticks

. . .

dried red roses

. . .

green moss

*You could use a variety of
other flowers here. Bright
yellow roses, for example,
would add a further variation
on the same theme.*

This simple idea uses just two leaves for each napkin, decorated with a few flowers. You can make all the napkin rings to match, or use a different flower for each place setting. Other large preserved (dried) leaves would also be suitable.

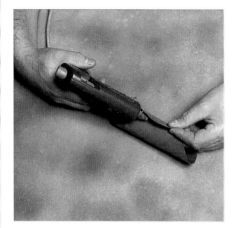

1 Roll a large leaf to form a neat tube, with a diameter large enough to allow for a rolled napkin. Using a glue gun, glue the edge down and hold it in place until the glue sets.

2 Choose another leaf that is about the same length as the rolled leaf. Glue the tube to the flat leaf along its centre spine.

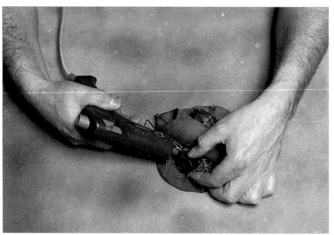

3 Steam the roses if necessary (see Techniques). Either side of the rolled leaf, glue two or more rose heads, depending on their size. Trim the roses with a little green moss, carefully gluing it in place.

TABLE-EDGE SWAG

· · ·

MATERIALS

· · ·

knife

· · ·

rope

· · ·

secateurs

· · ·

fresh conifer

· · ·

silver reel (rose) wire

· · ·

dried pale pink roses

The pale pink roses make this an ideal arrangement for a wedding table display.

This swag is very simple to make, but looks very impressive hanging in a short loop along the edge of a table for a special occasion. The fresh conifer isn't longlasting, so if you have to make it a few days before the event it is best to store it by hanging it in a cool, dry, dark place.

1 Cut the rope to the required length and make a loop at each end for hanging. Trim the conifer to short lengths and bind it to the rope, covering it all the way round, with silver reel (rose) wire.

2 Continue in the same way but adding the roses in twos and threes with a handful of conifer stems at regular intervals. Pack the conifer fairly tightly to produce a thick swag.

LEAF PLACE SETTING

. . .

This table decoration is very simple and quick to make. You can use any large leaves, with leftover flowers from other displays for the leaf cones. Place the circle so that the flowers are facing across the table to the guest opposite.

MATERIALS

. . .

dinner plate

. . .

brown paper

. . .

pencil

. . .

scissors

. . .

large preserved (dried) leaves, e.g. cobra leaves

. . .

glue gun and glue sticks

. . .

wires

. . .

dried miniature roses

. . .

dried pink larkspur

The flower-filled leaf cones decorate the side of each guest's plate.

1 Place the dinner plate on paper, draw a circle and cut out. Place the first leaf on the paper, with its tip overlapping the edge. Glue its edge and lay a second leaf on the glue. Repeat around the circle.

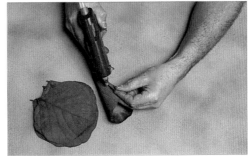

2 Fold a leaf into a cone shape and glue the edge so that it keeps its shape. Repeat three times.

3 Glue two leaf cones on to the edge of the leaf circle. Glue the third on top.

4 Wire three bunches of mixed roses and larkspur and push into each cone.

AUTUMNAL MIRROR BORDER

· · ·

MATERIALS

· · ·

wire cutters

· · ·

chicken wire

· · ·

sphagnum moss

· · ·

wooden frame, with mirror

· · ·

.91 wires

· · ·

dried materials, e.g. yellow and red roses, solidago, peonies, lavender, wheat, Achillea ptarmica *and poppies*

· · ·

dried fungi

· · ·

cinnamon sticks

· · ·

pomegranates

· · ·

small terracotta pots

· · ·

glue gun and glue sticks

· · ·

green moss

· · ·

mossing (floral) pins

The rich textures of all the different materials create a very opulent effect.

Because of its size, this is a fairly adventurous project, but the techniques are the same as for making a swag, so it is still a reasonably straightforward display to put together. It is important to try to make the fixings as strong as possible so that they will support the weight of the heavy mirror; if the moss is still damp, store the frame in a warm, dry place before putting it up on the wall.

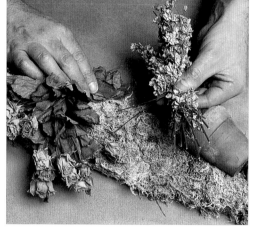

1 Make chicken wire swags to fit round the mirror frame (see Techniques). Group and centre-wire all the dried materials into separate bunches, trimming the flower stems to about 15 cm (6 in) (see Techniques). Push a wire through each pot and over its rim then push the ends into the moss frame and twist them together. Attach the materials to the frame one at a time, spacing them evenly.

2 Push the ends of the wires through the frame and twist them together.

3 Continue until nearly all the frame has been covered. Completely remove the stems of some of the flowers and glue them directly on to the framework or over the wires of centre-wired materials. Make sure the glue is in contact with the wire as well as the moss. Work with one material at a time, ensuring that each is evenly distributed throughout the frame.

4 Trim the frame with moss, using mossing (floral) pins to hold it in place. Pay particular attention to the edges that hang nearest to the wall, which are often forgotten when the frame is flat on the work surface.

STARFISH AND ROSE TABLE DECORATION

• • •

MATERIALS

• • •

9 small dried starfish

• • •

.71 wires

• • •

*church candle, 7.5 x 22.5 cm
(5 x 9 in)*

• • •

*plastic foam ring for dried
flowers, 7.5 cm (3 in) diameter*

• • •

scissors

• • •

reindeer moss

• • •

40 dried rose heads

*The cream roses complement
the colour of the candle and
contrast is provided by the
apricot colour and strong
geometric shape of the small
dried starfish.*

This is an alternative decoration for a large church candle using dried rose heads and starfish. The result is a table centre decoration with a seaside feel. This is a simple and quick decoration to make, but is very effective nonetheless.

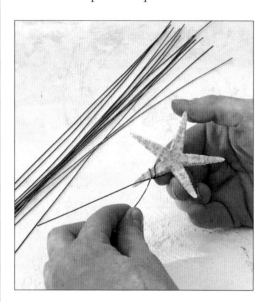

1 Double leg mount all the starfish individually through one arm with .71 wires to extend their overall length. Cut the wires to approximately 2.5 cm (1 in) in length and put to one side.

2 Position the candle in the centre of the plastic foam ring. Make 2 cm (1¾ in) long hairpins from cut lengths of .71 wires. Use these to pin the reindeer moss around the edge of the ring.

3 Group the wired starfish into sets of three and position each group equidistant from the others around the foam ring. Push their wires into the foam to secure.

4 Cut the stems of the dried rose heads to about 2.5 cm (1 in) and push the stems into the foam to form two continuous tightly packed rings of flowers around the candle.

ARTICHOKE PINHOLDER DISPLAY

· · ·

This otherwise traditional line arrangement is unusual in that dried materials are used on a pinholder. Dried stems are hard and it is not easy to push them on to the spikes of a pinholder. There is also the heaviness of the artichokes to consider and they have to be carefully positioned to avoid disrupting the physical balance of the arrangement. Make sure that all the stems are firmly pushed on to the pinholder's spikes.

Use naturally trailing stems of hazel at the front of the pinholder and bring it down over the pedestal to the right of its centre line to create a natural trailing effect.

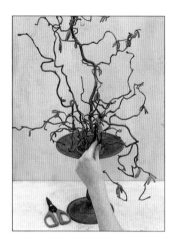

1 Push the hazel stems, cut to 45 cm (18 in) on to the spikes of the pinholder, positioning the tallest stem at the back.

2 Arrange the artichoke heads throughout the hazel. Use the smallest head on the longest stem centrally at the back. Work away from this with progressively shorter stems. Position the largest artichoke head about two-thirds down from the top of the display.

3 Arrange the poppy seed head stems throughout the display. Position the longest stem at the back, making sure it is shorter than the tallest hazel stem but taller than the tallest artichoke. Work away from this point with progressively shorter stems, with some stems trailing over the front to the right of centre.

SEASHELL MIRROR FRAME

· · ·

Decorate a bathroom mirror with this spectacular border. If you are not sure how the shells will look, place them alongside the frame and move them around before gluing them in position. Use the small terracotta pots to hold extra features such as a candle or starfish.

MATERIALS

· · ·

glue gun and glue sticks

· · ·

selection of shells

· · ·

plain wooden frame

· · ·

small terracotta pots

· · ·

reindeer moss

This starfish is simply balanced in one of the terracotta pots.

1 Beginning in a corner, glue the first shells to the frame. Apply the glue to each shell before pressing it on to the frame. Remove any excess glue as you work.

2 Continue around the frame, adding shells as you go, so that they almost flow into each other. Use smaller shells to fill the larger gaps and glue shells on to each other.

3 Apply glue to the side of a pot and stick it directly to the frame (not on to any shells). Build up shells so that they come right to the edge of the pot and glue smaller shells on to the pot itself, so that all the elements blend together.

4 When you have finished adding the shells, fill any gaps with reindeer moss, gluing it in place. Fill some of the pots with extra loose shells.

PEONIES AND ARTICHOKES IN AN URN

· · ·

MATERIALS

· · ·

knife

· · ·

1 block plastic foam for dried flowers

· · ·

small cast-iron urn

· · ·

florist's adhesive tape

· · ·

scissors

· · ·

5 stems dried heads of flowering artichoke

· · ·

8 stems dried pale pink peonies

· · ·

16 stems dried poppy seed heads

The aim of this arrangement is to show off the attractive container, so the normal rules of proportion have been turned on their head: the vase accounts for two-thirds of this arrangement.

Some containers merit an arrangement specifically designed to show them off and in order to do this, the floral display should neither be too high nor too wide and certainly should not trail down over it.

The particular attraction of this small cast-iron urn is its tall, elegant outline and the grey bloom of its surface. To make the most of the container, the arrangement has been kept low and compact in low-key colours. Pale pink peonies and brown artichokes with purple tufts are set against poppy seedheads with a grey bloom to match the urn.

1 Cut the block of plastic foam so that it can be wedged into the urn level with the rim. Secure the foam in place using florist's adhesive tape.

2 Cut the artichoke stems to about 13 cm (5¼ in). Push one stem into the foam at its centre. Position the other stems around the central stem by pushing them into the foam so that they are slightly shorter, creating a domed outline.

3 Cut the peony stems to about 13 cm (5¼ in) long and push them into the foam evenly and tightly massed throughout but slightly recessed below the artichoke heads.

4 Cut the poppy stems to about 13 cm (5¼ in) long and push them into the plastic foam evenly throughout the artichokes and peonies with their heads level with the artichoke heads.

EXOTIC ARRANGEMENT

· · ·

*T*ake care when building the arrangement because the stems are hard and will damage the plastic foam if pushed in and pulled out too often.

This display is designed to produce an interesting counterpoint between the unusual floral materials and the traditional way in which they are arranged in a classic cast-iron urn. The rusting surface of the container beautifully complements the brown, pink and orange colouring of the materials.

The forms and textures of the individual contents of the arrangement are strong and hard but the overall effect is softened by the delicate twisting stems of contorted willow which work with the rest of the materials to create harmony within the display.

1 Cut the plastic foam to fit neatly into the urn with a 6.5 cm (2¾ in) projection above its rim. Secure it in place with florist's adhesive tape.

2 Make hairpins from the .71 wires and pin the reindeer moss to the plastic foam around the rim of the urn so that it tumbles over its edge.

3 Establish the overall height, width and fan shape of the arrangement with stems of contorted willow pushed into the plastic foam.

4 Arrange the *Protea compacta* amongst the willow, with the tallest at the back and shorter stems towards the sides and front. Position the *Banksia hookerana* stems in the same way, starting with the tallest at the back.

5 Position the dried bean stems adjacent to the *Banksia hookerana,* reducing their height towards the front. Place the *Banksia coccinea* stems evenly through the display at varying heights.

6 Push the stems of the *Protea compacta* buds into the foam, evenly arranging them throughout the display and decreasing their height from the back to the front and sides.

MANTELPIECE DISPLAY
· · ·

MATERIALS
· · ·

knife

· · ·

1 block plastic foam for dried flowers

· · ·

florist's adhesive tape

· · ·

string of hops

· · ·

5 branches glycerined beech

· · ·

3 dried corn cobs

· · ·

12 stems dried sunflowers

· · ·

12 stems dried green amaranthus (straight)

Using dried flowers is more practical than a fresh display because the arrangement will last far longer and require little maintenance.

When a fireplace is not in use it can lose its status as the focal point of a room but decorating its mantelpiece and grate with dramatic floral arrangements will ensure it remains a major feature. The material contents of this mantelpiece arrangement give it a high summer look; it incorporates bright yellow sunflowers, green amaranthus and green hops with corn cobs used as the focal material.

Construction is relatively straightforward provided you maintain the physical as well as visual balance of the display. So, to prevent the arrangement falling forwards make sure the majority of the weight is kept at the back and, whether the plastic foam is in a tray or sitting directly on the mantelpiece, make sure it is firmly secured.

1 Cut the block of plastic foam in half, position one half at the centre of the mantelpiece and secure it in place with adhesive tape. If using a plastic tray, first secure the foam to the tray with adhesive tape, then tape the tray to the mantelpiece.

2 Lie the string of hops along the full length of the mantelpiece and secure it to the ends of the shelf with adhesive tape. The hops on the vine should lie on and around the plastic foam without covering it completely.

3 Push the stems of beech into the plastic foam, distributing them evenly to create a domed foliage outline that also trails into the hops. Push the three stems of the corn cobs into the foam towards the back, one at the centre with a slightly shorter cob at either side.

4 Distribute the sunflowers evenly throughout the plastic foam following the domed shape. Place longer stems towards the back and shorter stems towards the front. Arrange the amaranthus throughout the other materials in the plastic foam to reinforce the outline shape.

CLASSICAL URN

· · ·

MATERIALS

· · ·

knife

· · ·

*2 blocks plastic foam for dried
flowers*

· · ·

cast-iron urn

· · ·

florist's adhesive tape

· · ·

scissors

· · ·

10 stems preserved eucalyptus

· · ·

10 stems bleached honesty

· · ·

2 bunches linseed

· · ·

2 bunches natural phalaris

· · ·

20 stems dried white roses

· · ·

1 bunch natural ti tree

A lovely shallow urn in rust-tinged cast iron is the inspiration for this display. The classic shape of the container is a major feature of the display and is echoed by a dried flower arrangement of traditional elegance.

Predominantly white and yellow, with contrasting greens, the display is a dense dome of roses, honesty, ti tree, eucalyptus, linseed and phalaris.

1 Cut the blocks of plastic foam to fit into the cast iron urn and wedge it in, securing it with adhesive tape.

2 Cut the eucalyptus stems to 15 cm (6 in) long and push them into the plastic foam to create an even domed foliage outline.

3 Cut the honesty stems to about 20 cm (8 in) in length and push them into the plastic foam, distributing them throughout the foliage with longer stems towards the centre of the urn.

4 Separate the linseed into 18 smaller bunches, each cut to a length of 15 cm (6 in). Push the bunches into the plastic foam evenly throughout the other materials.

The luminosity of the arrangement's pale colours would lighten a dark corner of a room.

5 Cut the phalaris and the rose stems to approximately 15 cm (6 in) in length and individually push into the plastic foam evenly throughout the display.

6 Cut the ti tree stems to approximately 15 cm (6 in) in length and arrange them evenly throughout the display.

MASSED STAR-SHAPED DECORATION

• • •

The decoration is simple to make, although it does call for a substantial amount of material.

This display has a huge visual impact of massed colour and bold shape with the added bonus of the delicious scent of lavender.

Built within a star-shaped baking tin and using yellow and lavender colours, the display has a very contemporary appearance. It would suit a modern style interior.

1 Cut the plastic foam so that it fits neatly into the star-shaped baking tin and is recessed about 2.5 cm (1 in) down from its top. Use the tin as a template for accuracy.

2 Cut the lavender stems to 5 cm (2 in) and group them into fives. Push the groups into the plastic foam all around the outside edge of the star shape to create a border of approximately 1 cm (½ in).

3 Cut the dried roses to 5 cm (2 in). Starting at the points of the star and working towards its centre, push the rose stems into the foam. All the heads should be level with the lavender.

CLASSIC ORANGE AND CLOVE POMANDER

· · ·

This classic pomander starts as fresh material that, as you use it, dries into a beautiful old-fashioned decoration with a warm spicy smell evocative of mulled wine and the festive season.

Make several pomanders using different ribbons and display them in a bowl, hang them around the house, use them as Christmas decorations or even hang them in your wardrobe.

MATERIALS

· · ·

3 small firm oranges

· · ·

3 types of ribbon

· · ·

scissors

· · ·

cloves

Pomanders are easy and fun to make, and ideal as gifts. Remember to tighten the ribbons as the pomanders dry and shrink.

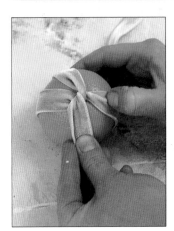

1 Tie a ribbon around an orange, crossing it over at the base.

2 Finish off at the top of the orange by tying the ribbon into a bow. Adjust the position of the ribbon as necessary to ensure the orange is divided into four equal-sized areas.

3 Starting at the edges of the areas, push the sharp ends of the exposed cloves into the orange skin and continue until each quarter is completely covered.

DECORATED CLIPFRAME

· · ·

MATERIALS

· · ·

*clipframe, 25 x 20 cm
(10 x 8 in) or larger*

· · ·

scissors

· · ·

large preserved (dried) leaves

· · ·

epoxy resin glue

· · ·

glue gun and glue sticks

· · ·

preserved (dried) ferns

· · ·

dried pale pink roses

· · ·

dried pale pink peonies

· · ·

.91 wire

· · ·

dried lavender

· · ·

raffia

*The soft colours of the flowers
will complement old
sepia photographs.*

Transform a simple clipframe into a special gift with preserved (dried) leaves, ferns and a few carefully chosen flowers. If you are including a photograph, place it in the frame first so that you can position the materials around it. Scraps of lace can also be incorporated into the design. You can of course buy any sized frame, according to the size of your photograph, and adapt the design accordingly.

1 Clean the glass of the frame, removing any grease and fingermarks. Cut the leaves horizontally in half. Apply epoxy resin glue to the back of each leaf in turn then lay the straight cut edge along the edge of the frame. Continue placing leaves all around the frame.

2 Using a glue gun, attach ferns on top of the leaves in two opposite corners. Use more ferns in one corner so that the design is not symmetrical.

3 Steam the roses and peonies, if necessary (see Techniques). Centre-wire a bunch of lavender (see Techniques). Tie a raffia bow around the lavender, to hide the wire. Position the flowers to create a pleasing design, gluing them in place.

SEASHELL SOAP DISH

· · ·

If you do not live close to the seaside, you can buy seashells from specialist shops.

A large, attractive shell makes a perfect soap dish, especially if it already has some natural drainage holes. If not, shells are quite easy to drill, either with an electric drill or by hand. Place a handful of small rounded shells in the bottom of the dish so that the soap does not sit in water.

1 Put some glue into the middle of the base of the large shell. Make a coil of rope and press it firmly into the glue, before it begins to set hard. Continue coiling the rope around, adding glue to the shell as you work. Cover about a third of the shell, to provide a soft, stable base. Cut the rope-end at a sharp angle and glue to the edge of the coil.

2 Turn the large shell over and glue another piece of rope in place all round the outer edge. If the shell is wide enough, repeat to provide a lip on which to fix small shells.

3 Put some glue on the rope and press the first of the small shells firmly in place. Continue this process, working around the dish. Add the largest shells first then return to the spaces and fill them with smaller shells. Glue the shells not just on the rope, but to each other. Fill any gaps with tiny pieces of moss.

DECORATED DISPLAY BOX

· · ·

Disguise an ordinary cardboard box with a distressed paint finish then fill it with a collection of dried materials and shells to make a very attractive ornament. Vary the contents of the box to suit the recipient.

MATERIALS

· · ·

decorator's paintbrush

· · ·

dark green paint

· · ·

cardboard box

· · ·

medium-grade sandpaper

· · ·

knife

· · ·

1 block plastic foam for dried flowers

· · ·

secateurs

· · ·

willow sticks

· · ·

string

· · ·

glue gun and glue sticks

· · ·

dried materials, e.g. echinops, seed pods, garlic cloves, dried fungi

· · ·

shells

· · ·

reindeer moss

· · ·

candle (optional)

The blue, spiky texture of the echinops contrasts nicely against the smooth brown willow sticks.

1 Paint the cardboard box dark green (or the colour of your choice) and leave to dry. Rub the sandpaper horizontally across the sides of the box, revealing some of the box colour beneath to give a weathered effect.

2 Trim the foam block to fit into the box, slightly lower than the top edge. Cut the willow sticks to length and tie together in two bundles with string. Glue all the materials on to the foam, building up an attractive arrangement. Leave space for a candle if desired. Fill any gaps with reindeer moss, again gluing it in place. Tie string around the centre of the box.

401

FABRIC-COVERED LAVENDER CANDLE POT

· · ·

MATERIALS
· · ·
terracotta pot
· · ·
fabric
· · ·
dressmaker's scissors
· · ·
knife
· · ·
1 block plastic foam for dried flowers
· · ·
candle
· · ·
florist's tape (stem-wrap tape)
· · ·
mossing (floral) pins
· · ·
.91 wires
· · ·
lavender
· · ·
moss
· · ·
raffia

The colour and scent of lavender makes it a perfect choice for gift arrangements.

Lavender makes an ideal gift; with its attractive flowers, rich colour and a long-lasting perfume, it is always welcome. Trim the pot with raffia to give a rustic feel or, for a smarter look, use a bow made of the same fabric. It is best to choose a large candle so that it will last a long time. If you are presenting it to someone, remind them that they should not leave burning candles unattended.

1 Place the pot in the middle of the fabric and cut a circle large enough to wrap up the sides, with 8 cm (3 in) extra all round.

2 Wrap the fabric up over the sides of the pot and tuck it neatly in. Space the creases in the fabric evenly to create a nice folded look.

3 Trim the foam to fit the pot tightly. Push the foam firmly into the pot right to the bottom, so that it holds the fabric in place.

4 Prepare a candle with florist's tape (stem-wrap tape) and mossing (floral) pins (see Techniques). Push it into the centre of the foam.

A pretty pot filled with lavender makes a lovely, special present.

5 Wire the lavender into small bunches (see Techniques). Working round the pot, push the bunches into the foam so that they lean well out, keeping them evenly spaced.

6 Continue until you have made a full circle. Fill the space around the candle with moss, fixing it with mossing (floral) pins. Keep the moss clear of the candle. Tie a raffia bow around the pot.

LAVENDER LINEN HEART

· · ·

MATERIALS

· · ·

1 m (1 yd) garden wire

· · ·

blue-dyed raffia

· · ·

scissors

· · ·

dried lavender

· · ·

glue gun and glue sticks

The strong scent of lavender will deter moths, as well as perfuming linen cupboards and wardrobes beautifully.

A lavender-covered wire heart is a charming and attractive "token of affection" and a welcome change to the perennially popular lavender bag. Raffia, dyed in a variety of colours, is available from a good florist's.

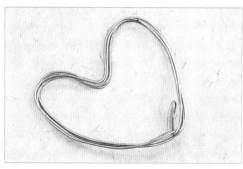

1 Fold the wire in half then in half again. Make a hook at one end and hook into the loop at the other end. Bend a dip in the top to form a heart shape.

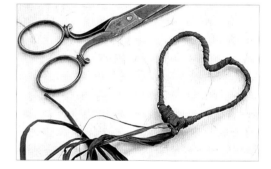

2 Bind the heart with the blue-dyed raffia. Start at the bottom, working round the heart. When the heart is fully covered, tie the ends together.

3 Starting at the dip at the top, bind three stalks of lavender to the heart, with the heads pointing inwards and downwards. Continue to bind the lavender in bunches of three, working down the heart. When you reach the bottom, repeat for the other side.

4 For the bottom, make a larger bunch of lavender and glue in position with the flowerheads pointing upwards. Trim the stalks close to the heads.

SMALL CANDLEHOLDER DISPLAY

. . .

There are many containers in the average household which, because of their colour, shape or material content, are suitable for a flower arrangement. This display was inspired entirely by the small crown-shaped, brass candleholder in which it is arranged.

An elevated position on, for example, a mantelpiece, would be perfect for such a small, neat display. Indeed, it could be used as a wedding-cake decoration.

MATERIALS

. . .

knife

. . .

1 block plastic foam for dried flowers

. . .

crown-shaped candleholder

. . .

scissors

. . .

15 stems poppy seed heads

. . .

20 stems dried pink roses

1 Cut a piece of plastic foam so that it can be wedged firmly into the candle holder, and sits about 2 cm (¾ in) below its top edge.

2 Cut the stems of the poppy seed heads to 9 cm (3½ in) and push them into the foam, distributing them evenly to create a domed shape.

3 Cut the dried rose stems to 9 cm (3½ in) and push them into the foam between the poppy seed heads, to reinforce the domed outline.

Making the display is straightforward and the method is applicable to any arrangement in a similarly small container.

CANDLE CUFF

• • •

MATERIALS

• • •

candle

• • •

plain white paper

• • •

scissors

• • •

thick brown paper

• • •

clear tape (cellophane)

• • •

hessian (burlap)

• • •

glue gun and glue sticks

• • •

rope

• • •

.91 wire

• • •

twigs

• • •

green moss

• • •

dried miniature roses

The combination of dark and pale pink roses is exquisite.

Choose a wide candle so that the cuff is large enough to apply the dried flower materials. The candle must be at least twice the height of the cuff, so that it has plenty of room to burn without any danger of setting the hessian (burlap) alight. Wrap the candle well at the start of the project to ensure that it is kept clean and that the hot glue does not melt the wax.

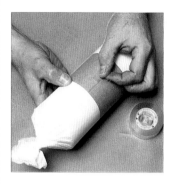

1 Wrap the candle in plain paper. Cut a piece of brown paper approximately 8 cm (3 in) wide and long enough to wrap around the candle. Tape the loose end down; the paper collar must be able to move freely up and down the candle.

2 Cut a piece of hessian (burlap) twice as wide as the brown paper and long enough to wrap round the candle. Fold the two outer quarters up to meet in the middle and glue them down.

3 Lay the candle on the wrong side of the hessian (burlap) and apply a little glue to either side of the candle. Wrap the hessian (burlap) tightly around the candle, smoothing it to fit the paper neatly, and applying glue where necessary.

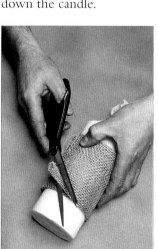

4 Trim the corners of the exposed edge of hessian (burlap) and glue them down sparingly.

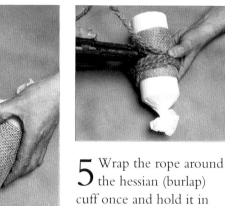

5 Wrap the rope around the hessian (burlap) cuff once and hold it in place. Apply glue all the way around the rope, so that the glue comes into contact with both the rope and the hessian (burlap). Wrap the rope around the candle again, as close as possible to the first wrap. Repeat until the whole cuff is covered.

6 Centre-wire a small bundle of twigs (see Techniques). Glue the bundle and some green moss to the cuff at an angle, using the moss to cover the wire. Cut the heads from the roses and glue them in place around the bundle of twigs.

HEART-SHAPED GARLAND

. . .

MATERIALS

. . .

garden wire

. . .

silver reel (rose) wire

. . .

moss

. . .

scissors

. . .

small dried flowers, e.g. roses, rosebuds, lavender, bupleurum

. . .

glue gun and glue sticks

*R*oses are particularly suited to this heart-shaped garland because they conjure up images of romance and fond memories.

Give this lovely miniature garland as a very special memento, which can be hung on a dresser or bedroom wardrobe. Decorate it either with roses and bupleurum or with lavender and roses. The garland is constructed on a simple wire base; you can buy these ready-made, but it is very easy to make your own.

1 Fold the garden wire in half then in half again. Bend a hook in the wire at one end and hook it into the loop in the folded wire at the other end, to make a circle. Make a dip in the top of the circle to create a heart shape.

2 Using silver reel (rose) wire, bind the wire heart with a thin layer of moss. Trim the moss to neaten the shape.

3 Trim the stems off all the flowers. Glue the flowerheads to the moss heart, working on each side in turn to keep a balance. Add the largest roses last at the top of the heart shape. Glue extra moss to fill any small gaps.

SWEETHEART WALLHANGING
. . .

Create a wallhanging from a heart, roses and lavender – three icons of romance. It is very easy to make, and will be a delightful decoration for any room in the house.

MATERIALS
. . .
3 blocks plastic foam for dried flowers
. . .
heart-shaped copper cake tin, about 30 cm (12 in) across
. . .
knife
. . .
paper
. . .
pencil and scissors
. . .
2 bunches dried rose stems
. . .
4 bunches dried lavender stems

Choose half-open rosebuds and arrange them quite tightly in the centre of the heart.

1 Line up the foam blocks to match the size of the cake tin. Press the cake tin rim on to the foam to make a print of its shape. Using the knife, cut just inside this line so the foam shape will fit tightly into the tin. Use the off-cuts to fill in any spaces.

2 For the rose centre, draw a heart motif on to paper and cut out. Place the heart shape on the foam and draw round with a knife to make a guideline for the roses.

3 Cut the rose stems to 2.5 cm (1 in). Insert a line of them around the rose shape. Here darker roses go round the perimeter and lighter ones in the centre. Finally, add the lavender and fill in, in concentric circles, around the rose heart.

ROSE AND LEMON NOSEGAY
· · ·

MATERIALS
· · ·
*3 dried lemons with splits in
their skin*
· · ·
.71 wires
· · ·
scissors ·
· · ·
15 stems globe thistles
· · ·
15 stems dried yellow roses
· · ·
twine
· · ·
ribbon

*Although the lemons have to
be wired, this is a simple
decoration to make.*

Traditionally a nosegay was a small tight bunch of selected herbs, sometimes with flowers, carried about the person, the scent of which was used to combat bad odours and protect against disease. Effectively it was portable pot-pourri. Today the content of a nosegay is just as likely to be chosen for its appearance as its strong aroma.

This nosegay has whole dried lemons, yellow dried roses and blue globe thistles, and is finished with a ribbon tied in a bow. While the roses and lemons have a faint scent, this can be augmented either by steeping the ribbon in cologne or by sprinkling the materials with perfumed oils.

1 Wire the dried lemons by pushing a .71 wire into a split near the base, through the lemon and out of a split on its other side. Bend the wires downwards and twist the two pieces together under the bases of the lemons.

2 Cut the globe thistle and rose stems to approximately 12 cm (4½ in). Start with a dried rose as the central flower and build a small spiralled posy around it by evenly adding the other ingredients.

3 When all the materials have been formed into a tight round posy, tie it with twine at the binding point. Trim the bottom of the stems. Make a ribbon bow and attach it to the binding point.

SUMMER POT-POURRI
. . .

The traditional pot-pourri is based on rose petals because when fresh they have a powerful fragrance, some of which is retained when they are dried, unlike many other perfumed flowers. Today's pot-pourri does not rely entirely on the fragrance of its flowers since there is a wide range of scented oils available and this means materials can be used just for their visual qualities.

This pot-pourri is traditional in that it uses dried roses, but modern in that whole buds and heads have been included instead of petals. The sea holly heads, apple slices and whole lemons are used entirely for their appearance.

MATERIALS
. . .
20 stems lavender
. . .
15 slices preserved (dried)
apple
. . .
5 dried lemons
. . .
1 handful cloves
. . .
20 dried pale pink rose heads
. . .
2 handfuls dried rose buds
. . .
1 handful hibiscus buds
. . .
10 sea holly heads
. . .
large glass bowl
. . .
pot-pourri essence
. . .
tablespoon

1 Break the stems off the lavender leaving only the flower spikes. Place all the dried ingredients in the glass bowl and mix together thoroughly. Add several drops of pot-pourri essence to the mixture of materials – the more you add the stronger the scent. Stir thoroughly to mix the scent throughout the pot-pourri, using a spoon. As the perfume weakens with time it can be topped up by the addition of more drops of essence.

Predominantly pink and purple, the look and scent of this pot-pourri will enhance any home throughout the summer months.

411

PEONY AND GLOBE THISTLE CANDLE DECORATION

· · ·

The effect of this display relies on the peonies being tightly massed together. Never leave burning candles unattended and do not allow the candles to burn below 5 cm (2 in) of the display.

This beautiful arrangement of dried flowers in a terracotta pot is designed to incorporate a candle. Contemporary in its use of massed flowerheads, the display has the stunning colour combination of deep pink peonies and bright blue globe thistles surrounding a dark green candle and finished with a lime-green ribbon. It would make a wonderful gift.

Simple to construct, you could make several arrangements, using different colours and display them as a group. Alternatively, you could change the scale by using a larger container, more flowers and incorporating more than one candle.

1 Cut a piece of plastic foam to size and wedge it firmly into the terracotta pot. Push the candle into the centre of the plastic foam so that it is held securely and sits upright.

2 Cut the peony stems to 4 cm (1½ in) and the globe thistle stems to 5 cm (2 in). Push the stems of the peonies into the foam. Push the stems of the globe thistle into the foam amongst the peonies.

3 Ensure that the heads of all the flowers are at the same level. Wrap a ribbon around the top of the terracotta pot and tie it in a bow at the front. Shape the ends of the ribbon to avoid fraying.

WINTER POT-POURRI

· · ·

The concept of a pot-pourri probably dates from the Elizabethan period when they were used to produce a fragrance to combat the all-pervading bad smells of the times.

This pot-pourri uses its material content in substantial forms – whole oranges, pomegranates, sunflower heads and rose heads with big pieces of cinnamon – because they are included for how they look, not how they smell.

The pot-pourri is mixed using ready-dried materials and although the cloves and cinnamon give it some added spice, it is also worth adding spicy scented oils. A final dusting with gold dust powder gives it a festive Christmas look.

MATERIALS
· · ·
1 handful cloves
· · ·
1 handful dried hibiscus buds
· · ·
1 handful dried tulip petals
· · ·
1 handful small cones
· · ·
7 dried oranges
· · ·
5 dried sunflower heads
· · ·
1 handful dried red rose heads
· · ·
5 small dried pomegranates
· · ·
10 dried grapefruit slices
· · ·
10 cinnamon sticks
· · ·
large glass bowl
· · ·
pot-pourri spicy essence
· · ·
gold dust powder
· · ·
tablespoon

This pot-pourri is very easy to make, so why not have several large bowls of it around the house in winter?

1 Place all the dried ingredients except the cinnamon in the glass bowl and mix together thoroughly. Break the cinnamon sticks into large pieces and add to the mixture.

2 Add several drops of the essence to the mixture. Scatter a tablespoon of gold dust powder over the mixture and stir it well to distribute the gold dust powder and essence throughout the pot-pourri.

JAM-JAR DECORATIONS
· · ·

MATERIALS
· · ·
3 different-shaped jam jars
· · ·
floral adhesive
· · ·
10 skeletonized leaves
· · ·
scissors
· · ·
18 dried yellow rose heads
· · ·
night-light (tea-light) candles
· · ·
1 bunch dried lavender

Containers decorated with plant materials can be very attractive. This type of external embellishment usually conceals a large part of the container so do not waste money buying special pots and vases, just look around the house for something with an interesting shape that you can use.

Here, three different types and sizes of jam jars are decorated for use as night-light (tea light) holders but they could be used to store pens or bric-a-brac or even in the bathroom for toothbrushes, although the damp will accelerate the deterioration of the materials.

Working on this scale does not use a great deal of material and is an opportunity to use left-over items or materials in some way unsuitable for flower arranging. Use your imagination to vary the type of container and the flower decorations.

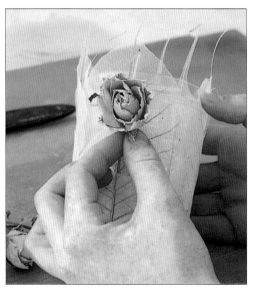

1 Apply adhesive to the sides of the tallest jam jar (approximately 12 cm (4¾ in) high) and stick five upward-pointing, slightly overlapping skeletonized leaves around the jar flush with its base. Higher up the jam jar glue on a second layer of five overlapping leaves, slightly offset from the first layer, to cover the joins between the leaves.

2 Cut the stems completely off four dried yellow rose heads and glue them to the leaf-covered jar at four equidistant points around the top of its outer surface. Place a night-light (tea-light) candle in the jar.

3 Cut the stems completely off approximately 14 dried yellow rose heads, apply the floral adhesive to the base of each head and stick them around the neck of the second more squat jam jar. Place them tightly together to form a continuous ring of flowers. Put a night-light (tea-light) in the jar.

4 Paste adhesive on to the outside of the third jam jar. Separate the lavender into single stems and stick them vertically to the side of the jar so that the flower spikes project about 1 cm (½ in) above its rim. The flower spikes should be tight to each other to completely cover the sides of the jam jar. Apply a second layer of lavender spikes lower down so that their flowers cover the first layer of stems. Trim the stems projecting below the jam jar flush with its base. Place a night-light (tea-light) in the jar, or use as a small vase.

These decorations would make an unusual centrepiece to a dining table.

SUMMER HAT FRUIT DECORATION

. . .

MATERIALS

. . .

30 dried orange slices

. . .

.71 wires

. . .

30 dried lemon slices

. . .

30 dried apple slices

. . .

florist's tape (stem-wrap tape)

. . .

scissors

. . .

10 dried sunflowers

. . .

straw hat

. . .

.32 silver reel (rose) wire

To avoid an embarrassing encounter with someone wearing the same hat as you at that wedding or day at the races, create your own unique headwear.

By the addition of the bright summery colours of dried sunflowers, and orange and lemon slices, a plain straw hat is transformed into a millinery masterpiece.

1 Divide the orange slices into groups of three and double leg mount each group on .71 wire. Repeat the process for the lemon and apple slices. Cover the wired stems with florist's tape (stem-wrap tape). Cut the stems of the sunflowers to 2.5 cm (1 in). Double leg mount on .71 wire and cover the wired stems with the tape.

2 Construct a stay wire by grouping together four .71 wires, each overlapping the next by about 3 cm (1¼ in), and taping them together with florist's tape (stem-wrap tape). Continue adding wires until you have reached the required length – approximately 4 cm (1¾ in) longer than the circumference of the crown of the hat.

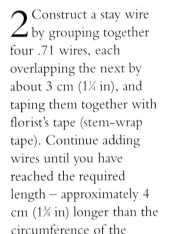

3 Arrange your wired materials into separate groups for easy access while you work. Tape the individual wired materials on to the stay wire in the following repeating sequence: orange slices; apple slices; sunflower heads and lemon slices. Continue this along the whole length of the stay wire bending it into the shape of the crown of the hat as you work and leaving the last 4 cm (1¾ in) undecorated. Take the undecorated end of the stay wire and tape it to the other end through the flowers.

4 Place the completed garland over the crown of the hat so that it sits on the brim, and stitch in position by pushing lengths of .32 reel (rose) wire through the straw and around the stay wire at four equidistant positions around the hat. Once in position, you may want to adjust the wired elements to achieve the best effect.

The hat decoration is similar to a garland headdress and its construction, although involving wiring, is relatively straightforward.

417

FLOWERS FOR SPECIAL OCCASIONS

· · ·

From a luxurious Valentine's posy of deep red roses and an unusual Christmas wreath of clementines and ivy, to lavish bouquets for birthdays and anniversaries, the calendar year presents wonderful opportunities for the flower arranger. Exciting arrangements for weddings, christenings, Easter and Christmas are featured alongside beautiful floral gift-wrappings for every special occasion.

INTRODUCTION
. . .

Traditionally flowers go hand in hand with special occasions – what would a wedding, a christening or a birthday be without celebratory flowers? Throughout the calendar year, from Valentine's Day to Christmas, the flower arranger has opportunity after opportunity to express his or her creativity.

This usually takes the form of a bunch of flowers, but is nonetheless creative for that, especially if you remember that presentation is all. Cellophane (plastic wrap) or tissue paper gift-wrapping will make even the most simple posy of flowers really special, and attention to details such as tying with ribbon or raffia will pay handsome dividends in its effect.

However, it is the big events like weddings which present the flower arranger with the real challenge. The challenge is not just the need for the necessary skills to design, arrange and wire the materials, but also having the skills to organize the project properly by making a series of important decisions correctly.

You must decide exactly what you are going to produce, and calculate the quantities of flowers and foliage necessary. You must avoid buying too much or, worse, buying too little. A carefully considered timetable must be prepared for the event. You must decide when to order the flowers and how long the different varieties will remain in good condition. Remember that some flowers, such as lilies and gladioli, may require a few days before the event to open fully. You must estimate how long it will take to produce each arrangement, headdress and buttonhole. You must consider the time-scale available to you for working with the flowers and, to avoid all-night labouring, how many helpers you will need. Can the large arrangements be made *in situ*, or will they need to be made somewhere else and transported, and if so, how? You must decide what containers, how much plastic foam, and what other sundries you will need.

Clearly, you will need a very long, very comprehensive check-list. And it doesn't even stop there: the participants may wish to have a memento and you will have to consider whether the materials you are using are suitable to preserve. You might even consider the meanings associated with the flowers you are using, so that you can really claim to "say it with flowers".

The Meanings of Flower and Herb Names

Acacia	*Secret love*
Almond blossom	*Sweetness, hope*
Amaranthus	*Immortality*
Amaryllis	*Pride, splendid beauty*
Anemone	*Withered hopes, forsaken*
Angelica	*Inspiration*
Apple blossom	*Preference*
Basil	*Good wishes*
Bay	*Glory*
Bellflower (white)	*Gratitude*
Bluebell	*Constancy*
Broom	*Humility*
Buttercup	*Childhood*
Camellia	*Excellence*
Carnation	*First love*
Chives	*Usefulness*
Chrysanthemum (red)	*"I love you"*
Clematis	*Mental beauty, purity*
Coriander (Cilantro)	*Hidden worth*
Cumin	*Fidelity*
Daffodil	*Deceitful hopes*
Daisy	*Innocence*
Dianthus	*Divine love*
Evergreen	*Life everlasting*
Everlasting flower	*Unfading memory*

Fennel	*Flattery*
Forget-me-not	*Fidelity, true love*
Gardenia	*Femininity*
Gladiolus	*Incarnation*

Hawthorn blossom	*Hope*
Heartsease	*Remembrance*
Hibiscus	*Delicate beauty*
Holly	*Hope, divinity*
Honesty	*Wealth*
Honeysuckle	*Devotion*
Hyacinth	*Loveliness, constancy*
Hyssop	*Cleanliness*
Ivy	*Eternal fidelity*
Jasmine (white)	*Amiability*
Jasmine (yellow)	*Elegance, happiness*
Jonquil	*"I desire a return of affection"*
Laurel	*Triumph, eternity*
Lavender	*Devotion, virtue*
Lemon balm	*Sympathy*
Lilac (purple)	*First emotions*
Lilac (white)	*Youthful innocence*
Lily (white)	*Purity*
Lily (yellow)	*Falsehood, Gaiety*
Lily-of-the-valley	*Return of happiness*
Magnolia	*Grief, pride*
Marigold	*Joy*
Marjoram	*Blushes*
Michaelmas daisy	*Farewell*
Mint	*Eternal refreshment*
Mistletoe	*Love*
Nasturtium	*Patriotism*
Oak	*Forgiveness, eternity*
Olive branch	*Peace*
Orange blossom	*Purity, loveliness*
Oregano	*Substance*

Pansies	*Love, "Thinking of you"*
Parsley	*Festivity*
Peach blossom	*Long life*
Peony	*Bashfulness*
Periwinkle (blue)	*Early friendship*
Periwinkle (white)	*Pleasures of memory*
Pinks	*Love*
Poinsettia	*Fertility, eternity*
Poppy (red)	*Consolation*
Rose (red)	*Love*
Rose (yellow)	*Jealousy*
Rosebud	*Pure and lovely*
Rosemary	*Remembrance*
Rue	*Grace, clear vision*
Sage	*Wisdom, immortality*
Salvia (red)	*"I am thinking of you"*
Snowdrop	*Hope, consolation*

Sorrel	*Affection*
Southernwood	*Jesting*
Stock	*Lasting beauty*
Sunflower	*Haughtiness, false riches*
Sweet William	*Gallantry*
Tansy	*Hostile thoughts*
Tarragon	*Lasting interest*
Thyme	*Courage, strength*
Tulip (red)	*Declaration of love*
Tulip (yellow)	*Hopeless love*
Violet	*Humility*
Wallflower	*Fidelity in adversity*
Zinnia	*"Thinking of absent friends"*

VALENTINE POT-POURRI

• • •

MATERIALS

· · ·

box

· · ·

dried rose leaves

· · ·

dried lavender

· · ·

scissors

· · ·

reindeer moss

· · ·

dried rosebuds

· · ·

*other dried flowers, e.g. pink
larkspur*

· · ·

rose or lavender essential oil

*Sweet-smelling roses and
lavender are very popular pot-
pourri ingredients.*

This is a wonderful way of making use of spare flowers and flower pieces from other displays. Here, an oval cardboard box has been covered with broad red ribbon and a piece of the same ribbon has been cut in half and folded to create the decoration on top. Essential oil will discolour dried materials over a period of time, so only let the drops fall on the moss.

1 Line the bottom of the box with rose leaves and a few lavender stems. Trim the stems of the lavender fairly short, using mostly the flowerheads.

2 Place some reindeer moss in the box, around the lavender flowerheads.

3 Trim the stems from the heads of the remaining flowers and arrange the flowerheads in the box.

4 Gently drizzle a few drops of essential oil over the reindeer moss, but not on the flowers.

FRESH VALENTINE
TERRACOTTA POTS
. . .

MATERIALS
. . .
half block plastic foam
. . .
*2 small terracotta pots,
1 slightly larger than the other*
. . .
cellophane (plastic wrap)
. . .
knife
. . . .
scissors
. . .
ming fern
. . .
ivy leaves
. . .
*5 stems 'Santini' spray
chrysanthemums*
. . .
6 stems purple phlox
. . .
18 dark red roses

*Very quick and easy to make,
the simplicity of these charming
decorations is irresistible.*

With luck, Valentine's Day brings with it red roses, but these small jewel-like arrangements present them in an altogether different way. The deep red of the roses visually·links the two pots: contrasting with the acid lime green of 'Santini' chrysanthemums in one, and combining richly with purple phlox in the other.

1 Soak the plastic foam in water. Line both terracotta pots with cellophane (plastic wrap). Cut the foam into small blocks and wedge into the lined pots. Trim the cellophane to fit. Do not trim too close to the edge of the pot.

2 Build a dome-shaped foliage outline in proportion to each pot. In the larger pot, push the stems of ming fern into the plastic foam and in the small pot push the ivy leaves into the foam.

3 In the larger pot, arrange 'Santini' chrysanthemums amongst the ming fern. In the small pot, distribute the phlox amongst the ivy to emphasize the dome shapes of both.

4 Strip the leaves from the dark red roses, cut the stems to the desired lengths and arrange evenly throughout both displays.

SMALL FRESH ROSE VALENTINE'S RING

• • •

While this delightful floral circlet could be used at any time of the year, the impact created by the massed red roses makes it particularly appropriate to Valentine's Day. It can be hung on a wall or, with a candle at its centre, used as a table decoration for a romantic dinner for two.

MATERIALS

• • •

plastic foam ring,
15 cm (6 in) diameter

• • •

dark green ivy leaves

• • •

.71 wires

• • •

bun moss

• • •

20 dark red roses

• • •

scissors

If you receive a Valentine's Day bouquet of red roses, why not recycle them? After the rose blooms have fully blown open, cut down their stems for use in this circlet to extent their lives. Finally dehydrate the circlet and continue to use it as a dried flower display.

1 Soak the plastic foam ring in water. Push individual, medium-sized ivy leaves into the foam to create an even foliage outline all around the ring.

2 Make hairpin shapes out of the .71 wires and pin small pieces of bun moss on to the foam ring between the ivy leaves. Do this throughout the foliage but to a thinner density than the ivy.

3 Cut the rose stems to approximately 3.5 cm (1½ in) long and push them into the foam until the ring is evenly covered. The ivy leaves should still be visible in-between the rose heads.

Dried Valentine
Decoration in a Box

· · ·

· · ·

*1 block plastic foam
(for dried flowers)*

· · ·

knife

· · ·

heart-shaped box

· · ·

scissors

· · ·

1 bunch dried red roses

· · ·

2 bunches dried lavender

· · ·

*2 bunches dried poppy seed
heads*

· · ·

1 bunch Nigella orientalis

*This arrangement is easy to
make, but to get the best effect
you must not scrimp on
materials. The flowerheads
need to be massed together very
tightly to hide the foam.*

This display, in a heart-shaped box, demonstrates that dried flowers and seed heads look very striking and attractive when massed in groups of one type. Filled with romantic roses and scented lavender, this display can be made as a gift for Valentine's Day or simply as a treat for yourself. It can also be made at any other time of year using a different-shaped box.

1 Stand the block of plastic foam on its end and carefully slice in half down its length with a knife. Then shape both pieces, using the box as a template, so that they will each fit into one half of the box. Fit these two halves into the heart-shaped box ensuring that they fit snugly.

2 Divide the heart shape into quarters, separating each section by a line of the materials to be used. Fill one quarter with rose heads, one with lavender, one with poppy seed heads and the last with *Nigella orientalis*. Make sure that all the material heads are at the same level.

VALENTINE'S HEART CIRCLET
. . .

Instead of the traditional dozen red roses, why not give the love of your life a wall hanging decoration for Valentine's Day?

Set your heart (in this case wooden) in a circlet of dried materials full of romantic associations – red roses to demonstrate your passion, honesty to affirm the truth of your feelings and lavender as sweet as your love.

MATERIALS
. . .
33 dried red rose heads
. . .
scissors
. . .
.38 silver wire
. . .
florist's tape (stem-wrap tape)
. . .
55 stems dried lavender
. . .
10 stems dried honesty
. . .
.71 wires
. . .
*1 small wooden heart, on a
string*

1 Cut the dried rose stems to approximately 2.5 cm (1 in) and individually double leg mount on .38 silver wires, then cover the stems with tape. Group three rose heads together and double leg mount on .38 wire, then cover the stems with tape. Repeat the process for all the rose heads, making in total eleven groups.

Group the dried lavender into bunches of five stems and double leg mount on .38 silver wire, then tape. Repeat the process for all the lavender stems, making in total eleven groups.

Cut individual pods from the stems of dried honesty and group into threes, double leg mounting them together on .38 silver wires and taping. Make eleven groups in total.

Make a stay wire from .71 wires.

2 Lay a group of the honesty pods over one end of the stay wire and tape on securely. Then add, so that they just overlap, a group of lavender stems followed by a group of rose heads, taping each group to the stay wire. Keep repeating this sequence, all the while bending the stay wire into a circle.

3 When the circle is complete, cut off any excess stay wire leaving approximately 3 cm (1¼ in) to overlap. Then tape the two ends together through the dried flowers to secure. Tie the string from the wooden heart on to the stay wire between the dried blooms, so that the heart hangs in the centre of the circlet.

This takes a little more effort than ordering a bunch of flowers from your florist, but that effort will be seen as a measure of your devotion.

CHILDREN'S PARTY PIECES
· · ·

MATERIALS
· · ·
1 block plastic foam
· · ·
knife
· · ·
3 enamel mugs
· · ·
scissors
· · ·
*24 pink and yellow
"mini-gerbera"*

*The gerbera's sugary colouring
means the display can be
integrated with the contents of
the table – surround them with
jelly and blancmange or have
them emerging from a
mountain of sweets!*

Most people probably think that flowers are wasted on a children's party, but if we can make them fun, then why not?

Gerbera are extraordinary in their simple form and bright colours, and look like a child's idea of a flower. In this display the gerbera are arranged upright and apparently unsupported in simple containers, just like a child's drawing.

1 Soak the block of plastic foam in water. Using a knife, cut small pieces of foam and wedge them into the bottom of each mug so that they take up about one third of the depth.

2 Cut the gerbera stems so that they are approximately 5 cm (2 in) taller than the mug. Push the stem ends into the foam, keeping the flowers upright and pushing some in further than others to get slight variations of height.

SIMPLE EASTER DISPLAY

. . .

This display strips away all embellishments and relies entirely on the intrinsic beauty of the flowers themselves for its impact. To heighten the impact, the flowers are massed in one type only in each container.

The displays are appropriate to Easter because they use familiar flowers which are associated with spring and convey the message of rebirth.

MATERIALS
. . .
50 stems pale blue grape hyacinth
. . .
1 tea-cup
. . .
scissors
. . .
4 pale pink 'Angelique' tulips
. . .
2 pitchers (1 larger than the other)
. . .
15 mauve crocus flowers
. . .
30 stems of narcissi (some cream, some white)
. . .
2 jam jars

1 Measure the grape hyacinth against the tea-cup and cut their stems so that only the heads can be seen above the rim. Also cut the 'Angelique' tulip stems so that only the heads project above the rim of the smaller pitcher. Again, cut the crocus stems so that only their flowerheads are visible above the rim of the larger pitcher. Four tulip heads is sufficient for this small display.

2 Trim the narcissi stems so that the overall height of the flowers is twice the height of the jar. Loosely arrange a mixture of both varieties in each jar. By using a variety of containers the finished display has a good variation of height.

The displays can be grouped together or used individually around the house. They are simple to make, but remember simplicity is often the essence of good design!

EASTER WREATH

· · ·

MATERIALS

· · ·

*plastic foam ring,
30 cm (12 in) diameter*

· · ·

elaeagnus foliage

· · ·

scissors

· · ·

5 polyanthus plants

· · ·

8 pieces of bark

· · ·

.71 wires

· · ·

3 blown eggs

· · ·

2 enamel spoons

· · ·

70 stems daffodils

· · ·

raffia

*Whether in the church or
home, this delightful Easter
decoration will bring pleasure
to all who view it.*

Easter is a time of hope and regeneration and this bright Easter wreath visually captures these feelings. It overflows with the floral symbols of spring with daffodils and polyanthus, and contains eggs, a symbol of birth.

The vibrant colours and the flowers, arranged to look as though they are still growing, give the wreath a fresh, natural glow. There is also a touch of humour in the crossed enamel spoons.

1 Soak the foam ring in water and arrange an even covering of elaeagnus stems, approximately 7.5 cm (3 in) long, in the foam. At five equidistant positions, add groups of three polyanthus leaves.

3 Arrange the polyanthus flowers in single-coloured groups as though they are growing by pushing their stems into the plastic foam. Be sure to leave a section of the ring clear for the eggs and spoons. Cut the daffodils to a stem length of approximately 7.5 cm (3 in) and between four groups of polyanthus arrange groups of 15 daffodils, pushing their stems into the plastic foam.

2 Wire the eight pieces of bark by bending a .71 wire around the middle and twisting to achieve a tight grip. Position the pieces of bark equidistant around the ring by pushing the protruding wires into the plastic foam.

4 Bend .71 wires around the spoons and twist. In the gap left on the ring position one of the spoons, wrapping the wire ends around to the back of the ring. Twist the wires together tightly so that the spoon is embedded in the foam. Do this with both spoons, arranged so that they cross. Wrap raffia around the eggs, crossing it over underneath and tying it on the side. Bend .71 wires around the eggs, twisting the ends together gently. Arrange the remaining daffodils and polyanthus flowers around the eggs and spoons.

WEDDING SWAG

· · ·

MATERIALS

· · ·

knife

· · ·

rope

· · ·

scissors

· · ·

dried nigella

· · ·

dried oregano

· · ·

dried pink larkspur

· · ·

silver reel (rose) wire

· · ·

.91 wires

· · ·

dried lavender

· · ·

dried pink roses

· · ·

wide gauzy ribbon

· · ·

glue gun and glue sticks

*L*avender combines so well with many other flowers, and is combined here with criss-crossing bunches of roses.

This pretty, soft combination is ideal for a summer wedding and can be made any length to fit the particular location. It would look very welcoming placed either side of the church door, or fixed in an arch above it; inside the church, it could be wrapped around a stone pillar. Making a loop at each end of the rope ensures that there is a fixing in the right place.

1 Cut the rope to the required length, with a little extra at each end for the hanging loops. Trim the nigella, oregano and larkspur stems to 15 cm (6 in) in length and make separate piles of each. Start at one end of the rope, tying on a small bunch of nigella with silver reel (rose) wire, to cover the hanging loop.

2 Move along the rope, covering the stems of the nigella with a small bunch of oregano, again tying it in place with wire. Repeat with the larkspur, tying the bunches on to the rope.

3 Continue to alternate these three materials. Check that when the swag is lying on a flat surface, there are no gaps along the side and try to keep the swag to an even thickness along the rope.

4 Bunch and centre-wire the lavender and roses (see Techniques). Add these almost at right angles to the other materials. Push the wires through the centre of the swag and twist the ends together then push the sharp ends back into the swag. Tie a bow in the ribbon and glue it to one end of the swag.

BRIDESMAID'S ROSE CIRCLET

· · ·

MATERIALS

· · ·

*red and pink stemmed paper
rosebuds, with wired leaves*

· · ·

.91 wires

· · ·

*florist's tape (stem-wrap tape),
to match paper rosebud stems*

· · ·

fresh red and pink rosebuds

· · ·

*wire-edged pink-and-white
gingham ribbon*

· · ·

scissors

*The fresh rosebuds will dry
naturally, making the circlet a
permanent keepsake of a
special day.*

This enchanting hair decoration uses dainty rosebuds, so it is perfectly in scale for even the tiniest bridesmaid. Made of fresh and paper flowers, it is very lightweight to wear; if necessary, you can add hair grips, concealed among the flowers and ribbons. Check the size as you work, and keep one side smooth and flat to sit comfortably on the bridesmaid's head.

1 Twist the stems of the red and pink paper rosebuds together to form a circle. Keep all the flowerheads facing in the same direction.

2 Wire and tape the stems of the fresh rosebuds (see Techniques). Attach to the circlet, concealing the joins with tape. Cut the ribbon into three equal lengths and tie in bows. Wire the bows to the circlet, spacing them equally.

BRIDESMAID'S ROSE AND LAVENDER POSY

· · ·

A bunch of carefully selected and beautifully arranged dried flowers not only looks beautiful, but will long outlast fresh blooms, making this posy an enduring reminder of a wedding. The "language of flowers" interprets the meaning of lavender as "devoted attention" and the pink rose as a symbol of affection, so this posy is well-suited for a wedding celebration.

MATERIALS

· · ·

.71 wire

· · ·

12 large artificial or glycerined leaves

· · ·

florist's tape (stem-wrap tape)

· · ·

dried lavender stems

· · ·

bunch dried rosebuds

· · ·

paper ribbon

1 Fold a piece of wire one-third of the way along its length, to form a 15 cm (6 in) stalk. Attach a leaf to the top by its stalk, and bind in place with florist's tape (stem-wrap tape), pulling and wrapping the tape down to the end of the wire. Repeat the process to make 12 leaves.

*M*atch the colour of the roses to the wedding colours, using only the best dried blooms.

2 Divide the lavender into several small bunches. Hold them together loosely, setting the bunches at an angle to give a good shape. This will form the basic structure of the posy. Taking a single rosebud at a time, push the stems into the lavender, spacing them out evenly.

3 If desired, bind the posy with wire so that it will keep its shape while you work. Then edge the posy with the wire-mounted leaves. Bind in place again.

4 Unravel the paper ribbon and use to bind all the stalks together tightly, covering the wire and the stalks completely. Finish off by tying the ends of the ribbon into a bow.

BRIDESMAID'S POSY

• • •

MATERIALS

• • •

dried pink roses

• • •

dried pink larkspur

• • •

.91 wires

• • •

scissors

• • •

raffia

Larkspur looks very summery, especially when combined with roses and tied with raffia.

The great advantage of using dried materials for a wedding is that your displays can be prepared well in advance. Make sure that some of the flowers in this lovely display have interest down the stems and not just at the top; the side of a posy is likely to be seen as much as the top. Remember that too much material will make it uncomfortable to hold.

1 Separate the flowers into two piles. Take a mixed handful of flowers in one hand and add more, criss-crossing the stems to produce a small circular display.

2 Wrap a wire around the middle and twist the ends together, so that the posy keeps its shape.

3 Trim away all the waste material, leaving a bunch of short stems just below the wire. Make sure this is long enough to hold on to, but still looks neat.

4 Tie the posy with plenty of raffia to cover the wire and give a comfortable grip.

Remember that someone will have to carry the posy, so try to keep it light.

OLD-FASHIONED GARDEN ROSE TIED BRIDESMAID'S POSY

• • •

MATERIALS

• • •

*5 deep red and 5 pale apricot
rose heads on stems*

• • •

scissors

• • •

20 stems mint

• • •

6 vine leaves

• • •

twine

• • •

raffia

*Finished with a natural raffia
bow, the posy has a fresh, just-
gathered look. Happily, it is
very simple to make.*

This tiny hand-tied posy of blown red and pale apricot roses and mint is designed to accompany the bridesmaid's circlet headdress. The velvet beauty of the contents gives it charm and impact.

1 Remove all thorns and lower leaves from the rose stems. Starting with a rose in one hand, add alternately two stems of mint and one rose stem until all the materials are used. Keep turning the posy as you build to form the stems into a spiral. Finally add the vine leaves to form an edging to the arrangement and tie with twine at the binding point.

2 Trim the ends of the stems so that they are approximately one-third of the overall height of the posy. Tie raffia around the binding point and form it into a secure bow.

CIRCLET HEADDRESS FOR A YOUNG BRIDESMAID

• • •

Although classic in its design, this bridesmaid's circlet headdress is given a contemporary feel by the use of a rich colour combination not usually associated with traditional wedding flowers.

MATERIALS

• • •

9 individual deep red rose heads

• • •

9 small clusters apricot spray roses

• • •

8 small bunches rosehips

• • •

scissors

• • •

.71 stub wires

• • •

9 small individual vine leaves

• • •

.38 silver wires

• • •

9 small bunches mint

• • •

florist's tape (stem-wrap tape)

The small bunches of orange-red rosehips give a substance to the fabric-like texture of the red and apricot coloured roses.

1 Cut all the flowers to a stem length of approximately 2.5 cm (1 in). Wire the individual rose heads with .71 wires. Stitch wire the vine leaves with .38 silver wire. Tape all the wired items.

    Make the stay wire with .71 wires approximately 4 cm (1½ in) longer than the circumference of the head. Tape the wired flowers and foliage to the stay wire in the following repeating sequence: individual rose, mint, spray rose, vine leaf, rosehips. As you tape materials to the stay wire, form it into a circle. Leave 4 cm (1½ in) of the stay wire undecorated, overlap it behind the beginning of the circlet and tape securely together through the flowers.

TIED BRIDAL BOUQUET

· · ·

MATERIALS

· · ·

10 stems Lilium
longiflorum

· · ·

10 stems cream-coloured
Eustoma grandiflorum

· · ·

10 stems white
Euphorbia fulgens

· · ·

5 stems Molucella laevis

· · ·

10 stems white aster
'Monte Cassino'

· · ·

10 stems dill

· · ·

10 ivy trails

· · ·

twine

· · ·

scissors

· · ·

raffia

*To create a bouquet of this
size requires quite a large
quantity of materials which
may prove expensive, but the
design lends itself to being
scaled down to suit a tighter
budget by using the same
materials in smaller quantities.*

This classic "shower" wedding bouquet has a generous trailing shape and incorporates *Lilium longiflorum* as its focal flowers, using the traditional, fresh bridal colour combination of white, cream and green.

Because the flowers are left on their stems the bouquet is physically quite heavy; however, visually, the arrangement has a natural, loose appearance with the long, elegant stems of *Euphorbia fulgens* and asters emphasizing the flowing effect.

1 Lay out your materials so that they are easily accessible. Hold one stem of *Lilium longiflorum* in your hand about 25 cm (10 in) down from the top of its flower head. Begin adding the other flowers and ivy trails in a regular sequence to get an even distribution of materials throughout the bouquet. As you do this, keep turning the bunch in your hand to make the stems form a spiral.

3 When you have finished the bouquet and are satisfied with the shape, tie it with twine at the binding point, firmly, but not too tightly. Cut the stems so that they are 12 cm (4¾ in) long below the binding point. Any shorter and the weight of the bouquet will not be distributed evenly and it will make it difficult to carry.

2 To one side of the bouquet add materials on longer stems than the central flower – these will form the trailing element of the display. To the opposite side add stems slightly shorter than the central bloom, and this will become the top of the bouquet. Spiralling the stems will enable the short, upper part of the bouquet to come back over the hand when it is being carried. This will ensure a good profile, which is essential to avoid it looking like a shield.

4 Tie raffia around the binding point and form a bow which sits on top of the stems, facing upward towards the person carrying the bouquet.

SCENTED BRIDESMAID'S BASKET

. . .

A very young bridesmaid will find it much easier to carry a basket than clutch a posy throughout what must seem an endless wedding ceremony.

This basket uses simple flowers, in a simple colour combination, simply arranged. The result is a beautiful display appropriate for a child.

MATERIALS

. . .

small basket

. . .

cellophane (plastic wrap)

. . .

scissors

. . .

quarter block plastic foam

. . .

knife

. . .

florist's adhesive tape

. . .

ribbon

. . .

.38 silver wires

. . .

20 10 cm (4 in) stems golden privet

. . .

6 stems tuberose

. . .

20 stems 'Grace' freesias

1 Line the basket with cellophane (plastic wrap) to make it waterproof. Trim the cellophane edges to fit. Soak the quarter block of plastic foam in cold water, trim to fit into the basket and secure in a central position with florist's adhesive tape.

2 Form two small bows from the ribbon. Tie around their centres with .38 silver wires and leave the excess wire projecting at their backs. Bind the handle of the basket with ribbon securing it at either end by tying around with the wire tails of the bows.

3 Build a slightly domed outline throughout the basket with the golden privet, cut to the appropriate length.

4 Cut the tuberose stems to about 9 cm (3½ in) and position in a staggered diagonal across the basket.

5 Cut the freesia stems to approximately 9 cm (3½ in) long and distribute evenly throughout the remainder of the basket. Recess some heads to give greater depth to the finished display.

The wonderful scent of tuberose and freesia is a great bonus to this delightful display.

SCENTED GARLAND HEADDRESS

· · ·

MATERIALS

· · ·

12 small stems golden privet

· · ·

.38 silver wires

· · ·

scissors

· · ·

12 small clusters mimosa

· · ·

12 small clusters crab apples

· · ·

12 heads freesia 'Grace'

· · ·

12 heads tuberose

· · ·

florist's tape (stem-wrap tape)

· · ·

.71 wires

Making the headdress is time consuming and requires a degree of wiring skill, but the result will be well worth the effort. And, of course, it can be kept after the event, although as the flowers are quite fleshy you will need to use the silica gel method of drying.

This garland headdress just oozes the colours and scents of summer: yellows and cream hues mix with the perfumes of tuberose, freesia and mimosa.

The design of the garland allows the headdress simply to sit on the head of the bride or bridesmaid with no need for complex fixing to the hair.

1 Cut the stems of privet to 5 cm (2 in) and double leg mount with .38 silver wire. Cut the mimosa and crab apple stems to 5 cm (2 in) and, grouping them in separate clusters, double leg mount with .38 silver wire. Wire the freesia and tuberose heads on .38 silver wire using the pipping method, and then double leg mount on .38 silver wire. Tape all the wired materials.

2 With .71 wire make a stay wire approximately 4 cm (1 in) longer than the circumference of the bride's or bridesmaid's head – this extra length will remain undecorated.

3 Tape the materials on to the stay wire in the following sequence: privet, tuberose, mimosa, crab apples and freesia. Curve the stay wire into a circle as you proceed.

4 To finish the headdress neatly, overlap the undecorated end of the stay wire with the decorated beginning. Tape the wires together, through the flowers, to secure.

Yellow Rose Buttonhole
• • •

The bold choice of vibrant colours characterizes this stunning buttonhole. The yellow roses and elaeagnus, the orange red rosehips and lime green fennel combine to produce a simple, visually strong decoration suitable for either a man or a woman.

MATERIALS

· · ·

scissors

· · ·

1 yellow rose

· · ·

.71 wires

· · ·

5 elaeagnus leaves, graded in size

· · ·

.38 silver wires

· · ·

15 rosehips and leaves

· · ·

1 head fennel

· · ·

florist's tape (stem-wrap tape)

· · ·

.32 silver reel (rose) wire

· · ·

pin

As with all buttonholes, the construction involves wiring which is, of course, time consuming. Make sure you leave plenty of time to create buttonholes on the morning of the ceremony.

1 Cut the rose stem to 4 cm (1½ in) and wire on .71 wire. Stitch wire all the elaeagnus leaves with .38 silver wires. Group the rosehips, on stems of 4 cm (1½ in), in bunches of five and wire with .38 silver wires. Divide the head of fennel into its component stems and wire in groups with .38 silver wires. Tape all the wired elements.

2 Keeping the rose head central to the display, bind the bunches of fennel and rosehips around it, with .32 silver reel (rose) wire. Bind the elaeagnus leaves to the arrangement with .32 silver reel (rose) wire, placing the largest leaf at the back of the rose, the two smallest at the front, and two medium sized leaves at the side.

3 Trim the wires to approximately 7 cm (2½ in) and tape the wires with florist's tape (stem-wrap tape). Look closely at the completed buttonhole, and, if necessary, bend the leaves down to form a framework for the rose, and adjust the overall shape so that the back of the decoration is flat for pinning to the lapel.

CHURCH PORCH DECORATION

· · ·

MATERIALS

· · ·

gloves

· · ·

secateurs

· · ·

20 bunches long ivy trails

· · ·

twine

· · ·

6 large branches rosehips

· · ·

raffia

· · ·

scissors

This type of decoration is hard work but if you really go for it, the result will be spectacular.

Church festivals, weddings and christenings offer the flower arranger an opportunity to work on a large scale by decorating the church porch. To be successful, the display must have dramatic impact, although it can be simple in its material content.

This porch decoration is designed to look natural, almost as though it is growing out of the structure. Flowers would have been lost in the green mass of ivy, so colour contrast is provided by branches of red rosehips (branches of seasonal blossom would also have the necessary visual strength).

1 Generously drape the ivy trails over the supporting beam of the porch roof starting from the outsides and working towards the centre. As you drape the ivy over the beam, secure at regular intervals with twine.

2 Continue draping the ivy until the beam is evenly covered. Then, again, starting from the outsides, position the branches of rosehips on the top of the ivy trails to hang over the front of the porch.

3 Firmly secure the branches of rosehips in position with twine. Finally form a large bow with the raffia and attach it to the central vertical strut above the rosehips and ivy.

OLD-FASHIONED GARDEN ROSE WEDDING CORSAGE

· · ·

MATERIALS

· · ·

8 stems rose leaves

· · ·

scissors

· · ·

3 rose heads graded thus: in bud, just open, fully open

· · ·

3 small vine leaves

· · ·

38 silver wires

· · ·

florist's tape (stem-wrap tape)

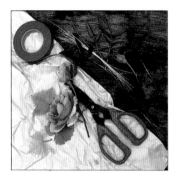

Using just one type of flower with its own foliage and three individual leaves ensures the result is simple yet elegant.

This delicate rose corsage would provide the perfect finishing touch for that special wedding outfit. However, it is best to remember that old-fashioned garden roses are really only available in the summer months.

1 Cut the stems of the rose leaves to length thus: two at 6 cm (2¼ in), two at 4 cm (1½ in), four at 3 cm (1⅛ in). Cut the rose head stems to 4 cm (1½ in) Cut the vine leaf stems to 2.5 cm (1 in) and stitch

wire with .38 silver wire.

Make two "units" of rose leaves each with one 6 cm (2¼ in) stem and one 4 cm (1½ in) stem. Make a "unit" using the two smaller rose heads.

Hold one unit of rose leaves in your hand and place the unit of rose heads on top so that the leaves project slightly above the upper rose head. Bind the units together with .38 silver wire, 6 cm (2¼ in) below the lower rose head.

Add the second unit of rose leaves lower and to

the left of the first. Add the fully opened rose (the focal flower) with the top of its head level with the bottom of the rose above. Bind to the corsage.

Position the vine leaves around the focal flower and bind in place. Position the remaining individual rose leaves slightly recessed around the focal flower and bind in place.

Trim off the ends of the wires approximately 5 cm (2 in) below the focal flower and cover with tape. Adjust as desired.

WEDDING BASKET

. . .

It has long been a tradition that female guests at weddings are given a "gift" to take home with them. These often take the form of a silk tulle bag containing pastel-coloured sugar almonds.

This symbolically romantic heart-shaped basket is decorated with fresh flowers so that it can be used as a container for such gifts.

MATERIALS
. . .
scissors
. . .
10 heads white alstromeria
'Ice cream'
. . .
10 heads white ranunculus
. . .
10 heads white spray rose
'Princess'
. . .
10 clusters small,
white phlox buds
'Rembrandt'
. . .
.38 silver wires
. . .
1 bunch pittosporum
. . .
florist's tape (stem-wrap tape)
. . .
1 heart-shaped basket
(loose weave)
. . .
.32 silver reel (rose) wire

1 Cut all the flowerheads and foliage to a stem length of approximately 2.5 cm (1 in). Double leg mount all the flowers and foliage with one or two .38 silver wires, depending on the weight of each flowerhead. You will need about 25 small, wired stems of pittosporum foliage. Tape all the wired elements with florist's tape (stem-wrap tape). Lay out your materials, ready to decorate the basket one side at a time.

Placed on each table at the wedding reception and filled with sugar almonds, the basket will also make a very attractive decoration in itself.

2 Lay a stem of pittosporum at the basket's centre. Stitch .32 silver reel (rose) wire through the basket and over the pittosporum stem. Stitch a bud of alstromeria over the foliage, followed by a rose head, more pittosporum, a ranunculus head and a cluster of phlox.

3 Repeat this sequence until you reach the bottom point, then stitch .32 silver reel (rose) wire through the basket weave to secure. Decorate the other side of the heart basket, this time working in the opposite direction. Again secure with .32 silver reel (rose) wire.

ORCHID CORSAGE
• • •

MATERIALS
· · ·
*7 orchid flowerheads (spray
orchids)*
· · ·
.38 silver wires
· · ·
*5 small Virginia
creeper leaves*
· · ·
10 stems of bear grass
· · ·
.71 wire
· · ·
*florist's tape
(stem-wrap tape)*
· · ·
scissors

*The corsage is relatively
intricate to make, but the effort
required is rewarded with a
particularly stylish accessory.*

Orchids tend to be naturally ostentatious flowers and as such are perfect for wedding corsages. The grandeur of the spray orchids make them particularly suitable for the mothers of the bride and groom.

1 Double leg mount the orchid heads individually with .38 silver wires. Stitch wire the Virginia creeper leaves by passing a .38 silver wire through the leaflets and bending the wire down to form a false stem, double leg mount this

and whatever natural stem exists with another .38 silver wire. Taking two stems of bear grass, bend them into a loop with a tail, double leg mount this on a .71 wire. Make a total of five bear-grass loops, then tape all of the wired materials.

2 Hold a wired orchid head between your index finger and thumb, add a wired leaf, then bind these together approximately 4 cm (1 in) down the wired stem using the .38 silver wire. Add the rest of the materials creating a very small wired posy, binding them in place with the .38 silver wire. Make sure that the binding point remains in one place.

3 When positioning the materials ensure that the looped bear grass is evenly distributed and that the leaves are also arranged in a regular way through the design so that it is evenly balanced.

4 When everything is wired in place trim the wire stems to about 5 cm (2 in) and cover with florist's tape (stem–wrap tape). Once completed, you may wish to gently manoeuvre the individual elements to achieve the most satisfactory effect.

This stunning corsage can add an element of glamour to even the simplest of clothing.

YELLOW ROSE BRIDESMAID'S BASKETS

· · ·

These arrangements will keep young bridesmaids happy on two counts; first they're easier to carry than posies and second the simple bright colours are such fun – sunshine yellow roses and lime-green fennel in a basket stained orange-red.

MATERIALS
· · ·
FOR EACH BASKET YOU
WILL NEED:

half block plastic foam

· · ·

knife

· · ·

1 small basket (plastic lined)

· · ·

scissors

· · ·

30 stems birch,
approximately 10 cm
(4 in) long

· · ·

10 stems yellow roses

· · ·

5 stems fennel

· · ·

raffia

The flowers are secured in plastic foam and will stay fresh for the bridesmaid to keep after the wedding.

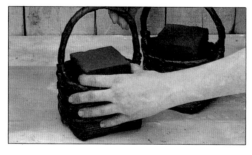

1 Soak the plastic foam in water, cut it to wedge in the basket.(If you are using a shallow basket, you may need to secure the foam in place with florist's adhesive tape.)

2 Clean the leaves from the bottom 3 cm (1½ in) of the birch stems, then arrange them in the plastic foam creating an even domed outline.

3 Cut the roses and fennel to a stem length of 8 cm (3¾ in) and distribute them evenly throughout the birch stems.

4 Tie a raffia bow at the base of the handle on both sides and trim to complete the display.

YELLOW ROSE
BRIDESMAID'S POSY
· · ·

A posy made from slim-stemmed materials has a narrow binding point which makes it easier to carry. This posy uses such materials in a simple but striking combination of yellow roses, lime-green fennel and delicate green birch leaves.

MATERIALS
· · ·
20 stems yellow roses
· · ·
5 stems fennel
· · ·
15 stems birch leaves
· · ·
twine
· · ·
scissors
· · ·
raffia

1 Strip all but the top 15 cm (6 in) of the rose stems clean of leaves and thorns. Split the multi-headed stems of fennel until each stem has one head only. This makes them easier to handle and visually more effective. Strip all but the top 15 cm (6 in) of the birch stems clean of leaves.

Easy to make as a hand-held, spiralled bunch and finished with a natural raffia bow, this posy would be a delight for any bridesmaid to carry and enjoy.

2 Holding one rose in the hand, add individual stems of fennel, birch and rose in a continuing sequence, all the while turning the bunch to spiral the stems. Continue until all the materials are used.

3 Tie the posy with twine at the point where the stems cross – the binding point. Trim the bottom of the stems to leave a stem length of approximately one-third of the overall height of the finished display.

4 Complete the posy by tying raffia around the binding point and finishing with a bow. Finally, trim the ends of raffia.

CELEBRATION TABLE DECORATION

• • •

*The arrangement is based on
a circular, plastic foam ring
with the centre left open to
accommodate the wine cooler.
The splendid silver wine cooler
is enhanced by the beauty of
the flowers, and in turn its
highly polished surface reflects
the flowers to increase their
visual impact.*

A table for any celebratory lunch will not usually have much room to spare on it. In this instance there is no room for the wine cooler, and the answer is to incorporate this large, but necessary piece of catering equipment within the flower arrangement.

The floral decoration is a sumptuous, textural display of gold, yellow and white flowers with green and grey foliage. The spiky surfaces of the chestnuts add a wonderful variation in texture.

1 Soak the plastic foam ring in water. Cut the senecio to a stem length of around 14 cm (5½ in) and distribute evenly around the ring, pushing the stems into the plastic foam, to create an even foliage outline. Leave the centre of the ring clear.

2 Cut the elaeagnus to a length of about 14 cm (5½ in) and distribute evenly throughout the senecio to reinforce the foliage outline, still leaving the centre of the plastic foam ring clear to eventually accomodate the wine cooler.

3 Double leg mount three groups of two chestnuts on .71 wire and cut the wire legs to about 6 cm (2¼ in). Take care, as the chestnuts are extremely prickly and it is advisable to wear heavy duty gardening gloves when handling them.

4 Still wearing your gloves, position the groups of chestnuts at three equidistant points around the circumference of the plastic foam ring, and secure by pushing the wires into the plastic foam.

5 Cut the rose stems to approximately 14 cm (5½ in) in length and arrange in staggered groups of three roses at six points around the ring, equal distances apart, pushing the stems firmly into the plastic foam.

6 Cut stems of eustoma flowerheads 12 cm (4¾ in) long from the main stem. Arrange the stems evenly in the foam. Cut the stems of solidago to a length of about 14 cm (5½ in) and distribute throughout. Finally cut the stems of fennel to about 12 cm (4¾ in) long and add evenly through the display, pushing the stems into the plastic foam.

This magnificent arrangement would make a stunning centrepiece for a wedding table.

DRIED FLOWER GARLAND HEADDRESS

· · ·

An advantage of using dried materials is that they can be made well in advance, which means less to worry about on the big day. There is plenty of wiring involved, but otherwise the construction is relatively straightforward.

This wedding headdress is made from dried materials in beautiful soft pale pinks, greens and lilacs with the interesting addition of apple slices. Apart from being very pretty, it will not wilt during the wedding and can, of course, be kept after the event.

1 Cut the peonies and the roses to a stem length of 2.5 cm (1 in). Double leg mount the peonies with .71 wires and the roses with .38 silver wires. Group the roses into threes and bind together using the .32 silver reel (rose) wire. Group the apple slices into threes and double leg mount them together with .71 wire. Cut the sprigs of ti tree, hydrangea clusters and eucalyptus to lengths of 5 cm (2 in) and double leg mount with .38 silver wires, grouping the ti tree and eucalyptus in twos. Cover all the wired stems with tape.

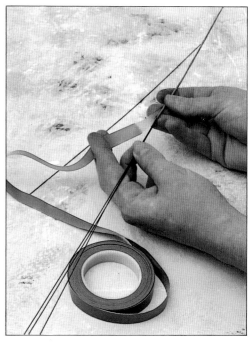

2 Have to hand the bride's head measurements. Make the stay wire on which the headdress will be built with .71 wires, ensuring its final length is approximately 4 cm (1½ in) longer than the circumference of the head.

3 Position a piece of wired eucalyptus on one end of the stay wire and wrap florist's tape (stem-wrap tape) over its stem and the stay wire, to secure them together. Then, in the same way, add in turn a hydrangea cluster, a group of roses, a peony and a group of ti tree, repeating the sequence until the stay wire is covered. Remember to leave the last 4 cm (1½ in) of the stay wire uncovered.

4 To complete the headdress, overlap the uncovered end of the stay wire with the decorated start and tape together with florist's tape (stem-wrap tape), ensuring the tape goes under the flowers so that it is not visible.

The bold nature of this headdress makes it particularly suitable for a bride.

DRIED POMANDER

· · ·

*This pomander is time
consuming to build, but will
last. Sprinkle pot pourri
oil over it to provide a
continuing aroma.*

A pomander is generally defined as a ball of mixed aromatic substances. However, this pomander is designed more for its visual impact than its scent. It would look particularly attractive if carried by a bridesmaid. Alternatively it can be hung in the bedroom, perhaps on the dressing-table.

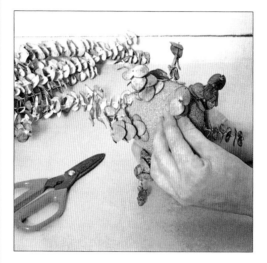

1 Cut the eucalyptus stems into approximately 10 cm (4 in) lengths. Make sure that the stem ends are clean and sharp, and carefully push them into the plastic foam, distributing them evenly over its surface.

2 Cut a length of ribbon long enough to make a looped carrying handle. Make a loop in the ribbon and double leg mount the two cut ends together on .71 wire. Push the wire firmly into the plastic foam ball to form the carrying handle.

3 Cut the stems of the dried roses to approximately 4 cm (1½ in) and wire individually with .71 wire. Group together in threes and bind with .38 silver wire and cover with tape. Cut the dried peony stems to approximately 4 cm (1½ in) and wire them individually on .71 wire, then tape. Wire the dried apple slices individually on .71 wire.

4 Push the wired peonies into the plastic foam, distributing them evenly all over the ball. Push the wired apple slices into the foam, also distributing them evenly over the ball.

5 Push the ten groups of wired roses into the foam, distributing them evenly all over. Cut the ti tree stems into 9 cm (3 in) lengths and push into the foam to fill any gaps around the ball. Once completed you may wish to gently reposition individual elements in order to achieve the most pleasing effect.

Younger bridesmaids may find this charming ball easier to carry than a posy.

DRIED FLOWER CORSAGE

• • •

MATERIALS

• • •

scissors

• • •

2 dried peonies

• • •

3 dried peony leaves

• • •

.71 wire

• • •

.38 silver wire

• • •

3 slices preserved (dried) apple

• • •

3 sprigs dried ti tree

• • •

3 small clusters hydrangea

• • •

8 dried roses

• • •

3 short stems preserved (dried) eucalyptus

• • •

raffia

• • •

florist's tape (stem-wrap tape)

• • •

.32 silver reel (rose) wire

As an alternative to wearing the corsage, it could be attached to a handbag or a prayer book. Of course, it can be kept after the event and perfumed with scented oil.

If dried flowers are the choice for a wedding, a corsage as magnificent as this would be perfect for the mother of the bride. This floral decoration is characterized by softly faded colours in a variety of textures. Dried peonies are used as the focal flowers supported by hydrangeas, roses, ti tree and eucalyptus, and given contrasting textural substance by the unusual addition of preserved apple slices.

1 Cut the peony stems to 4 cm (1½ in) and the three peony leaves to 10 cm (4 in), 8 cm (3¼ in) and 6 cm (2¼ in) respectively. Double leg mount all of these with .71 wire, apart from the shortest peony leaf, which is double leg mounted with .38 silver wire. Double leg mount the apple slices with .71 wire. Cut the sprigs of ti tree to 5 cm (2 in) and form into three small groups, then repeat the process with the hydrangea florets and double leg mount with .38 silver wire.

Cut the rose stems to a length of 2.5 cm (1 in) and the eucalyptus to a length of about 4 cm (1½ in) and double leg mount both on .38 silver wire. Make a small raffia bow and double leg mount on a .38 silver wire around its centre. Tape all of the wired elements with tape ready for making up.

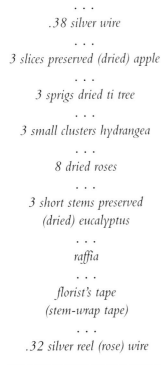

2 Taking the peonies, roses, apple slices and peony leaves, gradually build the arrangement, securing each item individually with .32 silver reel (rose) wire.

3 Position the remaining elements. Attach the raffia bow by its wired stem at the bottom of the arrangement. Secure all materials in place with the .32 silver reel (rose) wire.

4 Trim the ends of the wires to around 6 cm (2¼ in) and cover with tape. You may wish to adjust the wired components to achieve your desired shape.

DRIED ROSE AND APPLE BUTTONHOLE

• • •

There are several reasons why dried flowers are preferred for some weddings. This might be because the bride wishes to keep her flowers after the event or it may be a practical measure for a winter wedding where fresh flowers are unavailable or expensive. This buttonhole is designed for a groom or best man and, unusually, incorporates fruit with the flower and foliage.

MATERIALS
· · ·
3 slices preserved (dried) apples
· · ·
.71 wires
· · ·
scissors
· · ·
6 dried roses
· · ·
.38 silver wire
· · ·
6 short stems glycerined
eucalyptus
· · ·
1 small head
dried hydrangea
· · ·
florist's tape (stem-wrap tape)
· · ·
.32 silver reel (rose) wire

Apple slices give texture and a light touch to the decoration. Add a few drops of rose oil to give scent.

1 Double leg mount the apple slices together on .71 wire. Wire each rose, with a 2.5 cm (1 in) stem, on .71 wire. Double leg mount three roses on .38 silver wire. Leave a 5 cm (2 in) stem on the eucalyptus and hydrangea and double leg mount on .38 silver wire. Tape all the elements.

2 Hold the rose heads in your hand and place the apple slices behind. Then position the hydrangea to the left and bind together all the stems using .32 silver wire. Position the eucalyptus stems to frame the edge of the buttonhole and bind with .32 silver wire.

3 When all these elements are bound securely in place, cut the wired stems to a length of approximately 5 cm (2 in) and bind them with florist's tape (stem-wrap tape). Adjust the wired components to achieve your desired shape, not forgetting the profile.

BRIDE'S VICTORIAN POSY
WITH DRIED FLOWERS
· · ·

Traditionally the Victorian posy, be it dried or fresh, took the form of a series of concentric circles of flowers. Each circle usually contained just one type of flower, with variations only from one circle to the next. Such strict geometry produced very formal-looking arrangements particularly suitable for weddings.

1 Cut the roses and peonies to a stem length of 3 cm (1⅛ in) and individually single leg mount them on .71 wires. Cut the eucalyptus stems to 10 cm (4 in) and remove the leaves from the bottom 3 cm (1⅛ in), then wire as for roses and peonies.

Double leg mount the phalaris grass and honesty heads on .38 silver wire in groups of five. Single leg mount these groups on .71 wires to extend their stem lengths to 25 cm (10 in). Repeat the process with groups of linseed and hydrangea.

All wired elements should be taped with florist's tape (stem-wrap tape).

2 Hold the central flower, a single white rose head, in your hand and arrange the three peony heads around it, then bind together with .32 silver reel (rose) wire, starting 10 cm (4 in) down the extended stems. (Remember that the starting point for binding determines the final size of the posy, and all subsequent flower circles must be bound at the same point.)

3 Rotating the growing posy in your hand, form a circle of pink rose heads around the peonies and bind to the main stem. Around this, form another circle, this time alternating white rose heads and clusters of hydrangea, and bind. Each additional circle of flower heads will be at an increasing angle to the central flower to create a dome shape.

4 Next add a circle of phalaris grass to the posy. followed by a circle of alternating honesty heads and linseed. Bind each circle with .32 silver reel (rose) wire at the binding point.

The design of this bride's posy follows the Victorian method with just a degree of latitude in the content of some circles. Of course, the arrangement is time-consuming to produce, but the reward is a beautiful posy that the bride can keep forever.

5 Finally add a circle of eucalyptus stems and bind. The eucalyptus leaves will form a border to the posy and cover any exposed wires underneath.

6 To form a handle, place the bundle of bound wires diagonally across your hand and trim off any excess wires. Tape with florist's tape (stem-wrap tape) and cover the handle with ribbon.

RUBY WEDDING
DISPLAY
· · ·

Designed as a table arrangement complete with celebratory bow around its container, this display of rich and passionate colours would be a magnificent gift.

Formal looking, but simple in its construction, this Ruby Wedding arrangement is a lavish mass of deep purple tulips and velvet red roses set against the dark glossy green of camellia leaves. A beautiful paper bow completes the effect.

1 Approximately three-quarters fill the bowl with water. Cut the stems of camellia and roses to 7.5 cm (3 in) longer than the depth of the container. Arrange the camellia stems in the bowl to create a low domed foliage outline within which the flowers will be arranged. Arrange half the roses evenly throughout the camellia.

2 Cut the tulip stems to approximately 7cm (3 in) longer than the depth of the bowl and strip away any remaining lower leaves from the stems. Position the tulips in the display, distributing them evenly throughout the roses and camellia. Finally add the remaining roses evenly throughout the arrangement to complete a dense, massed flower effect of deep red hues.

3 Form a festive bow from the paper ribbon. The bow should be substantial but it is important that it is kept in scale with the display. To complete the arrangement tie the bow to the container so that it sits on the front.

GOLDEN WEDDING
BOUQUET
• • •

MATERIALS

• • •

*20 stems golden yellow
ranunculus*

• • •

20 stems mimosa

• • •

gold twine

• • •

scissors

• • •

*2 sheets gold-coloured tissue
paper in 2 shades*

• • •

*piece gold-coloured fabric
approx. 46 cm (18 in) long,
15 cm (6 in) wide*

• • •

gold dust powder

*This arrangement makes a
flamboyant gift but nonetheless
is as simple to create as a
hand-tied bouquet. It can be
unwrapped and placed straight
into a vase of water, with no
need for further arranging.*

This shimmering bouquet makes an unequivocal Golden Wedding statement. Unashamed in its use of yellows and golds, the colours are carried right through the design in the flowers, the wrapping paper, the binding twine and the ribbon, even to a fine sprinkling of gold dust powder.

1 Lay out the stems of ranunculus and mimosa so that they are easily accessible. Clean the stems of leaves from about a third of the way down. Holding a stem of ranunculus in your hand, start to build the bouquet by adding alternate stems of mimosa and ranunculus, turning the flowers in your hand all the while so that the stems form a spiral.

2 When all the flowers have been arranged in your hand, tie the stems together at the binding point with the gold twine. When secured, trim the stems to a length approximately one-third of the overall height of the bouquet.

3 To wrap the bouquet, lay the two shades of tissue on top of each other and lay the bouquet diagonally on top. Pull up the sides of the paper, then the front, and hold these in place by tying the gold twine around the binding point. To complete the display, tie the gold fabric around the binding point and create a bow. Scatter a little gold dust powder over the flowers. Separate the sheets of tissue to give a fuller appearance.

CUT FLOWERS AS A GIFT

· · ·

*Because it is a spiral-tied
bouquet it can be placed
straight into a container
without the need for further
arranging.*

This elegant, long-stemmed bouquet is the gift for a very special occasion. This is a cool and uncluttered arrangement in which the cream colours and soft surfaces of calla lilies and French tulips are brought into focus by the coarse textures and irregular shapes of lichen-covered larch twigs. As a finishing touch, the bouquet is wrapped in cellophane (plastic wrap) and tied with raffia in a bow.

1 Set out all materials for easy access. Remove the lower leaves from the tulip stems and cut the larch twigs to a more manageable length.

Start with a calla lily and add twigs and tulips, all the while turning the growing arrangement so that the stems form a spiral.

2 Continue adding stems and larch twigs until all the materials are used. Tie securely at the binding point with raffia. Trim level the stem ends of the completed bouquet, taking care to avoid cutting them too short.

3 Cut a large square of cellophane (plastic wrap) and lay the bouquet diagonally across it. Wrap the cellophane up around the sides of the bouquet to overlap at the front. Tie securely at the binding point and finish with a raffia bow.

FRESH FLOWERS AS A GIFT-WRAP DECORATION
• • •

This is essentially a corsage used to decorate a wrapped gift. It offers the opportunity to make the gift extra special, and to give flowers at the same time. The colour and form of the gerbera and 'Mona Lisa' lily heads are very bold, and this is contrasted with the small delicate bell heads of lily-of-the-valley and lace-like grey lichen on the larch twigs.

MATERIALS
• • •
1 stem lily 'Mona Lisa'
• • •
scissors
• • •
1 branch lichen-covered larch
• • •
1 small pot lily-of-the-valley
• • •
2 pink gerbera
• • •
raffia
• • •
gift-wrapped present
• • •
ribbon

The decoration is made as a small, tied, flat-based sheaf. This involves no wiring and thus is relatively simple to make, provided you give sufficient thought to the visual balance between the bold and delicate elements.

1 From the lily stem, cut a 20 cm (7¾ in) length with one bud and one open flower on it. Also cut a single open flower on an 8 cm (3¼ in) stem. Cut six twigs from the larch branch, each about 25 cm (10 in) long. Cut three lily-of-the-valley on stems approximately 15cm (6 in) long, each with a leaf.

Cut one gerbera stem to 18 cm (7 in) long and the second to 14 cm (5½ in) long. Create a flat fan-shaped outline with the lichen-covered larch twigs. Position the longer lily stem in the centre of the fan and the single lily head immediately below.

Next arrange the lily-of-the-valley and gerbera flowerheads around the two open lilies. Tie the stems securely with raffia at the point where they all cross (the binding point).

2 Lay the completed decoration diagonally across the wrapped gift and take a long piece of raffia around it, crossing underneath the parcel and bringing it back up to tie off on top of the stems.

Tie the ribbon around the binding point of the decoration and form it into a bow.

DRIED FLOWERS AS A
GIFT-WRAP DECORATION
• • •

MATERIALS
. . .
1 dried sunflower head
. . .
scissors
. . .
.71 wires
. . .
1 small dried pomegranate
. . .
*3 small pieces dried fungi
(graded in size)*
. . .
*3 slices dried orange
(graded in size)*
. . .
.38 silver wires
. . .
*florist's tape
(stem-wrap tape)*
. . .
gift-wrapped present
. . .
raffia

To make a present extra special why not make the wrapping part of the gift? The construction of this display is effectively a dried flower corsage but used to embellish gift wrapping.

It takes a little time to produce but its natural, warm, earthy colours make this a delightful enhancement well worth the effort, and something to keep.

1 Cut the sunflower to a stem length of 2.5 cm (1 in) and double leg mount on a .71 wire. Single leg mount the pomegranates on .71 wire. Double leg mount the small pieces of fungi on .71 wires and the orange slices on .38 silver wires.

2 Wrap all the wired materials with tape, then attach the three orange slices to one side of the sunflower and pomegranate, then attach the three layers of fungi on the other side. Bind all these in place using the .38 silver wire.

3 Trim the wire stems to a length of 5 cm (2 in) and tape together with florist's tape (stem-wrap tape). Tie the raffia around the present and push the wired stem of the decoration under the raffia knot. Secure in place with a .71 wire.

DRIED FLOWERS AS A GIFT
. . .

This is a great way to present dried flowers as a gift. Treat them as you would a tied bunch of cut fresh flowers – make an arranged-in-the-hand, spiral-stemmed bouquet that can be placed straight into a vase.

MATERIALS
. . .
10 small dried pink Protea
compacta *buds*
. . .
10 stems dried pink larkspur
. . .
10 stems dried pink peonies
. . .
*10 stems dried green
amaranthus*
. . .
raffia
. . .
scissors
. . .
2 sheets blue tissue paper
. . .
pink ribbon

The deep pink mixture of exotic and garden flowers – protea and amaranthus with peonies and larkspur – makes this a floral gift anyone would be thrilled to receive.

1 Lay out the dried materials so that they are all easily accessible. Start the bouquet with a dried protea held in your hand, add a stem of larkspur, a stem of peony and a stem of amaranthus, all the while turning the growing bunch.

2 Continue until all the dried materials have been used. Tie with raffia at the binding point – where the stems cross each other. Trim the stem ends so that their length is approximately one-third of the overall height of the bouquet.

3 Lay the sheets of tissue paper on a flat surface and place the bouquet diagonally across the tissue. Wrap the tissue paper around the flowers, overlapping it at the front. Tie securely at the binding point with a ribbon and form a bow.

NERINE HAIR COMB
· · ·

MATERIALS
· · ·

scissors

· · ·

*9 flower heads and buds of
nerine (6 open, 3 buds)*

· · ·

10 hydrangea florets

· · ·

.38 silver wires

· · ·

4 small clusters berries

· · ·

.32 silver reel (rose) wire

· · ·

florist's tape (stem-wrap tape)

· · ·

plastic hair comb

*Quite intricate to construct,
this decoration will take
practice before you get it right.*

This beautiful hair decoration, built on a comb, is suitable for the bride who finds a circlet too cumbersome. Delicate in form, but strong in colour, the comb headdress incorporates a variety of textures and colours; bright pink nerines, pink tinged hydrangeas and berries in shades of pink.

1 "Pip" the flowerheads and buds from the main nerine stem. Wire the open nerine florets by passing a bent .38 silver wire with a loop at its end down the throat of the bloom, so that the loop wedges in the narrowest part. Double leg mount each wired flowerhead, the nerine buds and the individual hydrangea florets with .38 silver wires. Cover the stems of all the wired elements with florist's tape (stem-wrap tape).

2 Make two units of nerine with one bud at the top and one slightly open bloom below it. Make two units of two hydrangea florets.

3 Take the two nerine units and bind them together approximately 2 cm (¾ in) below the junction of the stems using the .32 silver reel (rose) wire. Bind the units of hydrangea florets to the nerine units with the .32 wire. Bend both units back to form a straight line, with the nerines slightly longer than the comb and the hydrangea florets slightly shorter.

4 Position an open nerine bloom at the centre of these bound units, with the top of the flower about 5 cm (2 in) above the binding. This is the focal flower. Add the individual flowers and buds to reinforce the shape. Secure them at the binding point with .32 silver reel (rose) wire. Secure the berries at the binding point with .32 silver reel (rose) wire.

5 When the decoration is complete, separate the wire stems below the binding point into two equal groups and bend them back on themselves parallel to the main stems. Trim the wires at an angle to thin them out, cover each group of wires with tape, to create two prongs.

6 Lay these two wire prongs along the flat back of the comb and tape in position by passing the tape through the teeth in the comb and around the wire prongs. Do this all the way along the length of the comb until the decoration is securely attached.

473

DRIED FLOWER HAIR COMB

· · ·

MATERIALS

· · ·

scissors

· · ·

*7 dried yellow
rose heads*

· · ·

9 dried phalaris heads

· · ·

.38 silver wires

· · ·

3 small dried starfish

· · ·

9 short stems eucalyptus

· · ·

*5 heads dried, bleached
honesty*

· · ·

*florist's tape
(stem-wrap tape)*

· · ·

plastic hair comb

A decorated hair comb is an alternative headdress to the circlet and is particularly useful if the hair is worn up. This decoration in dried flowers is almost monochromatic, with creamy white roses, silvery-grey eucalyptus, silvery-white honesty and soft green phalaris, with the colourful apricot-coloured dried starfish. The starfish also provide strong graphic shapes, which contrast with the softness of the flowers to create a stunning effect.

1 Cut the rose heads and the phalaris to a stem length of 2 cm (¾ in) and double leg mount them with .38 silver wires. Double leg mount the small starfish with .38 silver wire. Cut two of the eucalyptus stems to a length of 6 cm (2¼ in) and the rest to about 4 cm (1½ in). Double leg mount all the eucalyptus and individual heads of honesty with .38 silver wire. Cover the wired stems of all the materials with florist's tape (stem-wrap tape). Create six units, two containing two roses, two with two phalaris and two with two eucalyptus stems, one at 6 cm (2¼ in) and one at 4 cm (1¼ in), with the longer stem at the top of the unit.

2 Take two eucalyptus units and bind them together about 2 cm (¾ in) below the junction of the stems using .38 silver wire. At the binding point, bend each of two wired units away from each other to form a straight line slightly longer than the length of the comb. Take all the units of rose and phalaris heads and bind them individually to the eucalyptus unit at the binding point and bend each of them flat in the same way. Make all of these units slightly shorter than the eucalyptus.

3 Place an individual rose head at the centre of the bound units with the top about 5 cm (2 in) above the binding point. This will be the focal flower. Position the starfish and the honesty around this central rose head and secure at the binding point with .38 silver wire. Position the individual heads of phalaris and short stems of eucalyptus so that they reinforce the shape and profile of the decoration. Bind all items in place with .38 silver wire.

As well as making an attractive hair decoration, this hair comb can be kept as a momento of a very special day.

4 Next, separate the wire stems below the binding point into two equal groups of wires, bend them apart and back on themselves, parallel to the main stems. Trim the wires at an angle to thin them out before covering each group of wires with tape to create two wired prongs.

5 Lay these two wire prongs along the top of the comb and tape into position by passing the tape between the teeth in the comb and around the wire prongs. Do this all the way along the length of the comb until the decoration is securely attached.

BABY BIRTH GIFT

· · ·

MATERIALS

· · ·

1 block plastic foam

· · ·

scissors

· · ·

small galvanized metal bucket

· · ·

1 bunch Pittosporum

· · ·

*15 stems pale pink
'Angelique' tulips*

· · ·

5 stems white spray roses

· · ·

10 stems white ranunculus

· · ·

10 stems white phlox

· · ·

1 bunch dried lavender

· · ·

*ribbon, purple and white check
(plaid)*

*The choice of soft subtle
colours means it is suitable for
either boy or girl. There is also
the added bonus of the
beautiful scents of the phlox
and dried lavender.
Since the arrangement has its
own container it is particularly
convenient for a recipient in
hospital, avoiding, as it does,
the need to find a vase!
Finally, the container can be
kept and used after the life of
the display.*

Celebrate a baby's birth by giving the parents this very pretty arrangement in an unusual but practical container. The display incorporates double tulips, ranunculus, phlox and spray roses, with small leaves of *Pittosporum*. It is the delicacy of the flowers and foliage which make it appropriate for a baby.

1 Soak the plastic foam in water, cut it to fit the small metal bucket and wedge it firmly in place. Cut the *Pittosporum* to a length of 12 cm (4¾ in) and clean the leaves from the lower part of the stems. Push the stems into the plastic foam to create an overall domed foliage outline within which the flowers can be arranged.

2 Cut the 'Angelique' tulips to a stem length of 10 cm (4 in) and distribute them evenly throughout the foliage. Cut individual off-shoots from the main stems of the spray roses to a length of 10 cm (4 in), and arrange throughout the display, with full blooms at the centre and buds around the outside.

3 Cut the ranunculus and phlox to a stem length of 10 cm (4 in) and distribute both throughout the display. Cut the lavender to a stem length of 12 cm (4¾ in) and arrange in groups of three stems evenly throughout the flowers and foliage. Tie the ribbon around the bucket and finish in a generous bow.

PLANTED BASKET FOR BABY
· · ·

This display of pot plants in a basket makes a lovely gift to celebrate the birth of a baby. It is easy to make and quick to prepare, and is a long-lasting alternative to a cut flower arrangement.

MATERIALS
· · ·
1 wire basket
· · ·
2 handfuls Spanish moss
· · ·
cellophane (plastic wrap)
· · ·
scissors
· · ·
*3 pots miniature white
cyclamen*
· · ·
3 pots lily-of-the-valley
· · ·
paper ribbon

*The combination of two
simple and delicate white
plants, baby cyclamen and lily-
of-the-valley, gives the design
charm and purity, indeed
everything about it says
"baby".*

1 Line the wire basket with generous handfuls of Spanish moss, then carefully line the moss with cellophane (plastic wrap). Trim the cellophane to fit around the rim of the basket.

2 Remove the plants from their pots carefully. Loosen the soil and the roots a little before planting them in the basket, alternating the cyclamen with the lily-of-the-valley.

3 Make sure that the plants are firmly bedded in the basket. Make two small bows from the paper ribbon and attach one to each side of the basket at the base of the handle.

DRIED FLOWER HORSESHOE BABY GIFT

· · ·

MATERIALS

· · ·

14 heads dried, white roses

· · ·

42 heads dried, bleached honesty

· · ·

60 heads dried phalaris grass

· · ·

scissors

· · ·

.38 silver wire

· · ·

florist's tape (stem-wrap tape)

· · ·

.71 wires

· · ·

ribbon

What could be nicer for new parents than to receive a floral symbol of good luck on the birth of their baby?

The whites and pale green of this dried flower horseshoe make it a perfect gift or decoration for the nursery.

1 Cut the rose stems, honesty stems and phalaris grass to approximately 2.5 cm (1 in) long. Double leg mount the roses individually on .38 silver wire, then tape. Double leg mount the phalaris heads in groups of five on .38 silver wire, and the honesty in clusters of three on .38 silver wire. Tape each group.

2 Make a stay wire approximately 30 cm (12 in) long from .71 wire on which the horseshoe will be built.

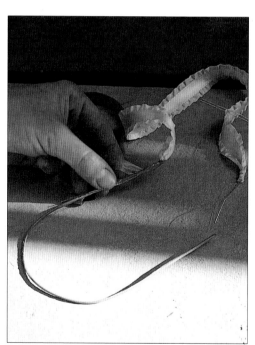

3 Form three small bows approximately 4 cm (1½ in) wide from the ribbon and bind them at their centres with .38 silver wire. Cut a 30 cm (12 in) length of ribbon and double leg mount both ends separately with .38 silver wire. This will form the handle for the horseshoe.

4 Form the stay wire into a horseshoe shape. Tape one wired end of the ribbon to one end of the stay wire. Tape one of the bows over the junction of the ribbon and stay wire, making sure it is securely in place.

5 Starting at the bow, tape the flowers and foliage to the stay wire, to its mid point, in the following repeating sequence: phalaris, rose, honesty. Tape a bow at the centre and tape the last bow and the remaining ribbon end to the other end of the stay wire. Work the flowers in the same sequence back to the centre point.

While making the horseshoe is relatively-time consuming, the effort will no doubt have created something of such sentimental value that it will be kept forever.

DRIED GRASS HARVEST SWAG

· · ·

MATERIALS

· · ·

1 bunch dried, natural
triticale

· · ·

1 bunch dried, natural
linseed

· · ·

1 bunch dried, natural
Nigella orientalis

· · ·

1 bunch dried, natural
phalaris

· · ·

scissors

· · ·

.71 wires

· · ·

1 straw plait, approximately
60 cm (24 in) long

· · ·

twine

· · ·

raffia

Although a good deal of
wiring is required for the
construction of this swag, it is
relatively straightforward and
enjoyable to make.

This harvest swag is a symbolic collection of dried decorative grasses. It relies on the subtlety of colour differences and textural variation in the grasses for its natural, yet splendid, effect.

In a church at harvest time the swag could be hung on a wall, or a series of them could be mounted on the ends of the pews. In the home it could be hung on a wall, or extended to decorate a mantelpiece.

1 Split each bunch of grass into 8 smaller bunches, giving you 32 individual bunches. Cut the stems to approximately 15 cm (6 in) long and double leg mount the individual groups with .71 wires.

3 Repeat this pattern eight times to use all four varieties of grasses, binding each bunch on to the plait with the twine.

4 When all the grasses have been used and the top of the plait reached, tie off with the twine and trim any excess wires.

2 Start by tying a wired bunch of triticale to the bottom of the plait with the twine. Then place a bunch of linseed above, to the left and slightly overlapping the triticale, and bind this on to the plait with the twine. Follow this with a bunch of *Nigella orientalis* above, to the right, and slightly overlapping the triticale. Finish the sequence by positioning a bunch of phalaris directly above the triticale, slightly overlapping, and bind on with the twine.

5 Make a bow from the raffia and tie it on to the top of the decorated plait, covering the wires and the twine.

HARVEST WREATH

• • •

MATERIALS

• • •

27 dried sunflower heads

• • •

.71 wires

• • •

*florist's tape
(stem-wrap tape)*

• • •

scissors

• • •

*30 pieces dried fungus
(various sizes)*

• • •

3 dried corn cobs

• • •

large vine circlet

• • •

raffia

Harvest time conjures up images of fruit, vegetables and ears of corn. This wreath of dried flowers has corn cobs as its harvest time reference point, visually reinforced with fungus, a less obvious autumn crop, and sunflowers, which in this form serve as a reminder of summer days gone by.

1 Single leg mount individual sunflower heads on .71 wires. Tape the stems, then group in threes. Double leg mount these groups with .71 wire and tape the stems. Double leg mount the pieces of fungus with .71 wire. You may need to cut the wire so that it has a sharp end to push through the fungus and twist into a double leg mount. Do not tape these wires.

2 Group the corn cobs at the bottom of the vine circlet and push their stems between the twisted vines, crossing them over each other to form a fan shape. Secure the corn cobs to each other and to the circlet with .71 wire.

3 Attach the groups of sunflowers, evenly spaced, all around the circumference of the circlet by pushing their wires through and wrapping tightly around the vines. These sunflower groups should alternate between the outside and inside edges of the vines.

4 Attach the fungus in groups of twos and threes around the circlet, between the sunflowers and around the corn cobs. The fungus groups should have the largest piece at the bottom with progressively smaller pieces above. Secure the fungus by straddling the vine with the legs of wire and twisting them together at the back.

5 Finally form a large bow from the raffia and tie it to the wreath over the stems of the corn cobs to conceal any remaining visible wires.

The large scale of this simple but unusual combination of materials gives the wreath great visual impact.

HALLOWEEN DISPLAY

· · ·

*This is a fine example of
creating a good shape in a large
display by using the natural
way the material would grow,
and without the support of
plastic foam or wire mesh. The
Halloween atmosphere is
completed by grouping
pumpkins and gourds,
intermingled with candles,
around the base of the
arrangement.*

Make this dramatic arrangement as a decoration for your Halloween party, and, for maximum impact, give it pride of place in a large room or entrance hall. The display is an intriguing mixture of materials in rich autumn colours; long-stemmed, two-coloured antirrhinums, Chinese lanterns, red hot pokers and orange lilies, all set against bright autumn foliage.

1 Cut the ends of the branches of autumn foliage at an angle of 45°, strip the bark from the bottom 5 cm (2 in) and split the branches about 5 cm (2 in) up the stems. Fill the pot with water and arrange the autumn foliage in it to create a fan-shaped outline. This fan must not be flat, and, to give it depth, bring shorter stems of foliage out from the back line into the front and centre of the shape.

2 Strip any leaves from the lower stems of the Chinese lanterns and arrange them throughout the foliage, reinforcing the overall shape. Distribute the red hot pokers throughout the display, again, using taller stems at the rear, and ones getting shorter towards the front.

3 The lilies are the focal flowers in this arrangement. Strip the lower leaves and distribute them throughout the display using taller, less open flowers towards the back and more open blooms on shorter stems around the centre and towards the front. Strip the lower antirrhinum leaves and arrange them evenly throughout the display.

CINNAMON ADVENT CANDLE

. . .

MATERIALS

. . .

*25 medium thickness
cinnamon sticks*

. . .

*1 candle, 7.5 x 23 cm
(3 x 9¼ in)*

. . .

raffia

. . .

scissors

. . .

*plastic foam ring for dried
flowers, 10 cm (4 in) diameter*

. . .

.71 wires

. . .

reindeer moss

. . .

20 red rose heads

. . .

florist's adhesive

*As a bonus, the heat of the
flame releases the spicy aroma
of the cinnamon, and the red
roses completes the festive look
of the candle.
Never leave a burning candle
unattended, and do not allow
the candle to burn down to
within 5 cm (2 in) of the
display height.*

Advent candles often have calibrations along their length to tell you how much to burn each day in the countdown to Christmas. This advent candle has a novel way of marking the passage of time: a spiral of 25 cinnamon sticks of decreasing height. Each day the candle is lit to burn down to the next cinnamon stick until finally on Christmas Day it is level with the shortest.

1 Attach the 25 cinnamon sticks to the outside of the candle by strapping them on with the raffia.

2 Position the cinnamon sticks in equal height reductions so that they spiral around the candle from the tallest at the top to the shortest at the bottom which should be approximately 6 cm (2¼ in) long. The excess lengths of cinnamon will be overhanging the bottom of the candle. Bind the cinnamon securely in place with raffia at two points and cut the excess lengths from the sticks so that they are all flush with the base of the candle.

3 Once the base is level, push the cinnamon-wrapped candle into the centre of the plastic foam ring. Make hairpin shapes from the .71 wires and pin the reindeer moss on to the foam to cover the ring completely.

4 Cut the stems of the dried roses to a length of approximately 2.5 cm (1 in). Add a little glue to the bases and stems of the roses. Push them into the plastic foam through the reindeer moss, to create a ring of rose heads around the candle.

CHRISTMAS ANEMONE URN

• • •

MATERIALS

. . .

1 small cast-iron urn

. . .

cellophane (plastic wrap)

. . .

1 block plastic foam

. . .

florist's adhesive tape

. . .

scissors

. . .

*1 bunch laurustinus
with berries*

. . .

10 stems bright orange roses

. . .

*20 stems anemones
('Mona Lisa' blue)*

The classic feel of a Christmas arrangement is retained by the use of the rusting cast-iron urn in which this spectacular display is set.

This vibrant display uses fabulously rich colours as an alternative to the traditional reds and greens of Christmas. An audacious combination of shocking orange roses set against the vivid purple anemones and the metallic blue berries of laurustinus makes an unforgettable impression.

1 Line the urn with the cellophane (plastic wrap). Soak the plastic foam in water and fit it into the lined urn, securing with the adhesive tape. Trim the cellophane around the rim of the urn.

2 Clean the stems of laurustinus and evenly arrange in the plastic foam to create a domed, all-round foliage framework within which the flowers will be positioned.

3 Distribute the roses, the focal flowers, evenly throughout the foliage, placing those with the most open blooms about two-thirds of the way up the arrangement, and more closed blooms towards the top.

4 Push the stems of anemones into the plastic foam amongst the roses, spreading them evenly throughout the arrangement so that a domed and regular shape is achieved.

TULIP AND HOLLY WREATH

. . .

MATERIALS

. . .

*plastic foam ring,
25 cm (10 in) diameter*

. . .

100 stems white tulips

. . .

scissors

. . .

holly with berries

*The tulip stems are pushed
fully into the foam in tight
masses, so that only their heads
are visible.*

The extravagant use of white tulips achieves a sophisticated purity in this Christmas decoration. A cushion of white blooms interspersed with glossy dark green leaves and vibrant red berries produces a wreath that can be used either on a door or, with candles, as a table centrepiece.

1 Soak the plastic foam ring in water. Cut the tulips to a stem length of approximately 3 cm (1⅛ in). Starting at the centre, work outwards in concentric circles to cover the whole surface of the plastic foam with the tulip heads.

2 Cover any exposed foam and the outside of the ring with holly leaves by pushing their stems into the foam and overlapping them flat against the edge of the ring. (You may wish to secure the leaves with .71 wire.)

3 Cut 12 stems of berries approximately 4 cm (1½ in) long and push them into the foam in two concentric circles around the ring, one towards the inside and the other towards the outside. Make sure no foam is still visible.

CHRISTMAS CAKE DECORATION

· · ·

If you're tired of decorating your Christmas cake in the same old way, with tinsel-edged paper, robins and snowmen stuck on top, be brave and go all out for a whole new look using natural materials! Combined with night-lights (tealights), this arrangement forms a memorable Christmas display.

MATERIALS

· · ·

ribbon (width approximately 7.5 cm/3 in) in 2 patterns

· · ·

3 10 cm (4 in) diameter Christmas cakes

· · ·

clear adhesive (sticky) tape

· · ·

scissors

· · ·

gold twine

· · ·

1 glass cake stand

· · ·

1 handful cranberries

· · ·

1 handful small cones

· · ·

4 purple tulip heads

· · ·

7 red rose heads

· · ·

1 stem small camellia leaves

· · ·

gold dust powder

· · ·

3 night-lights (tea-lights)

1 Wrap the ribbon around the outside of each of the cakes and secure with a piece of clear adhesive tape. Tie the gold twine around the middle of each cake, over the ribbon, finishing with a bow at the front. This is both decorative and useful as it will hold the ribbon in place until the cakes are to be eaten.

2 Position the cakes on the stand and scatter cranberries and cones between them. Pull the petals from the tulips and the roses and scatter them among the cranberries and cones. Scatter camellia leaves similarly. Sprinkle a little gold dust powder over the petals and place the three night-lights (tea-lights) between the cakes.

Rather than one large cake this display uses a group of three small cakes which themselves become part of the decoration. The rich reds and purples of the flowers and fruit with green and gold trimmings combine lusciously with the night-lights (tea-lights). Never leave burning candles unattended.

491

CLEMENTINE WREATH

. . .

MATERIALS

. . .

.71 wires

. . .

27 clementines

. . .

*plastic foam ring, approximately
30 cm (12 in) diameter*

. . .

pyracanthus berries and foliage

. . .

ivy leaves

*The wreath will look
spectacular hung on a door or
wall, and can also be used as a
table decoration with a large
candle at its centre, or perhaps
a cluster of smaller candles of
staggered heights. The wreath
is very easy to make, but it is
heavy and if it is to be hung
on a wall or door, be sure to fix
it securely.*

This festive Christmas wreath is contemporary in its regular geometry and its bold use of materials and colours. Tightly-grouped seasonal clementines, berries and leaves are substituted for the traditional holly, mistletoe and pine. The wreath has a citrus smell, but can be made more aromatic by using bay leaves and other herbs instead of ivy.

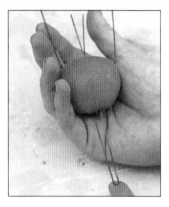

1 Push a .71 wire across and through the base of the clementine from one side to the other, and bend the two projected ends down. Bend another .71 wire to form a hairpin shape and push the ends right through the middle of the clementine so that the bend in the wire is sitting flush with the top of the fruit. Do the same to all the clementines. Cut all the projecting wires to a length of approximately 4 cm (1½ in).

2 Soak the plastic foam ring in water. Arrange the wired clementines in a tight circle on the top of the plastic ring by pushing their four projecting wire legs into the foam. Form a second ring of clementines within the first ring.

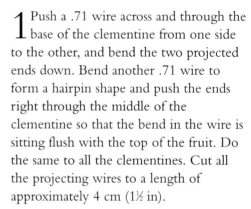

3 Cut the pyracanthus into small stems of berry clusters and foliage approximately 6 cm (2¼ in) long. Push the stems into the outer side of the plastic ring and between the two rings of clementines, making sure it is evenly distributed.

4 Cut the ivy leaves into individual stems measuring approximately 7 cm (2¾ in) in length. Push the stems of the individual leaves into the plastic ring, positioning a leaf between each clementine.

MISTLETOE KISSING RING

. . .

MATERIALS

. . .

scissors

. . .

*7 berries-only stems of
winterberry*

. . .

large bunch mistletoe

. . .

twine

. . .

1 twisted cane ring

. . .

*1 roll tartan
(plaid) ribbon*

*Very simple in its construction
this design does require a
reasonable quantity of good
quality, fresh mistletoe for it to
survive the full festive season.*

Instead of just tying a bunch of mistletoe to some strategically placed light-fitting in the hall, be creative and make a traditional kissing ring. This can be hung up as a Christmas decoration and still serve as a focal point for a seasonal kiss!

1 Cut the stems of the winterberry into 18 cm (7 in) lengths. Divide the mistletoe into 14 substantial stems and make the smaller sprigs into bunches by tying with twine. Attach a branch of winterberry on to the outside of the ring with the twine. Add a stem, or bunch, of mistletoe so that it overlaps about one-third of the length of winterberry, and bind in place. Bind on another stem of winterberry, overlapping the mistletoe.

2 Repeat the sequence until the outside of the cane ring is covered in a "herringbone" pattern of materials. Cut four lengths of ribbon of approximately 60 cm (24 in) each. Tie one end of each of the pieces of ribbon to the decorated ring at four equidistant points around its circumference. Bring the four ends of the ribbon up above the ring and tie into a bow; this will enable you to suspend the finished kissing ring.

CHRISTMAS CANDLE TABLE DECORATION

• • •

What could be more pleasing at Christmas, when the table is groaning under the weight of festive fare, than to complete the picture with a Christmas candle table decoration?

This rich display is a visual feast of the seasonal reds and greens of anemones, ranunculus and holly, softened by the grey of lichen on larch twigs and aromatic rosemary. The simple white candles are given a festive lift with their individual bows.

MATERIALS

• • •

plastic foam ring,
25 cm (10 in) diameter

• • •

25 cm (10 in) wire basket
with candleholders

• • •

10 stems rosemary

• • •

10 small stems lichen-covered
larch

• • •

10 small stems holly

• • •

scissors

• • •

30 stems red anemones
('Mona Lisa')

• • •

30 stems red ranunculus

• • •

roll paper ribbon

• • •

4 candles

The space at the centre of the design is the perfect spot for hiding those little, last-minute, surprise presents!
Never leave burning candles unattended and do not allow the candles to burn below 5 cm (2 in) of the display height.

1 Soak the plastic foam ring in water and wedge it snugly into the wire basket. You may need to trim the ring slightly, but make sure that you do not cut too much off by mistake.

2 Using a combination of rosemary, larch and holly, create an even but textured foliage and twig outline, all around the plastic foam ring. Make sure that the various foliages towards the outside edge of the display are shorter than those towards the centre.

3 Cut the stems of the anemones and ranunculus to 7.5 cm (3 in). Arrange them evenly throughout the display, leaving a little space around the candleholders. Make four ribbon bows and attach them to the candles. Position the candles in the holders.

CHRISTMAS TREE DECORATIONS

· · ·

MATERIALS
· · ·
*FOR STARS AND
CHRISTMAS TREES*
*1 block plastic foam
(for dried flowers)*
· · ·
knife
· · ·
shaped pastry cutters
· · ·
plastic bag
· · ·
loose, dried lavender
· · ·
gold dust powder
· · ·
florist's adhesive
· · ·
*loose, dried tulip and rose
petals*
· · ·
cranberries
· · ·
gold cord
· · ·
scissors
· · ·
*FOR DRIED FRUIT
DECORATIONS*
gold cord
· · ·
dried oranges and limes
· · ·
florist's adhesive
· · ·
dried red and yellow rose heads
· · ·
cinnamon sticks

As an alternative to commercially available Christmas tree decorations why not make your own? The decorations illustrated here use dried flower-arranging materials supplemented with some gold dust powder and seasonal cord and they are so easy to make you can even let the children help you.

1 For the stars and Christmas tree decorations, cut the block of plastic foam into approximately 3 cm (1 in) thick slices. Using the pastry cutters, press star and tree shapes from the plastic foam. Mix the dried loose lavender with two tablespoons of gold dust powder in a plastic bag (first making sure the bag has no holes in it), and shake together. Liberally coat all the surfaces of the plastic foam shapes with florist's adhesive.

2 Place the adhesive-covered shapes in the bag of lavender and gold dust powder, and shake. The shape will be coated with the lavender heads and powder. As a variation, press some of the dried tulip and rose petals on to the glue-covered shapes before putting them into the bag. Only the remaining exposed glued areas will then pick up the lavender. As a further variation, glue a cranberry to the centre of some of the stars. Make a small hole in the shape, pass gold cord through and make a loop with which to hang the decoration.

3 To make the dried fruit decorations, first tie the gold cord around the fruit, crossing it over at the bottom and knotting it on the top to make a hanging loop. Dab a blob of florist's adhesive on to the base of a rose head and stick it to the fruit next to the knotted gold cord at the top. Dab some adhesive on to two or three short pieces of cinnamon stick and glue these on to the dried fruit, grouping them with the rose head.

CHRISTMAS WIRE-MESH URN

• • •

MATERIALS

· · ·

scissors

· · ·

15 dried red rose heads

· · ·

.38 silver wire

· · ·

15 heads
Nigella orientalis

· · ·

15 small glycerined beech
leaves

· · ·

75 small pieces cinnamon
stick, approximately 5 cm
(2 in) long

· · ·

gold-coloured cord

· · ·

15 small bunches dried linseed

· · ·

.71 wire

· · ·

florist's tape
(stem-wrap tape)

· · ·

1 wire-mesh urn

· · ·

.32 silver reel (rose) wire

· · ·

dried oranges and limes

· · ·

gold dust powder

The urn could be used for all
sorts of Christmas goodies to
brighten a table or sideboard
during the festive season.

Sometimes we find odd things around the house which, with a little imagination, could be given a new lease of life. In this case an old wire-mesh urn has been turned into a seasonally decorated container for dried fruits.

1 Cut the rose stems and *Nigella orientalis* heads to 2.5 cm (1 in) and individually double leg mount them on .38 silver wires. Stitch wire the beech leaves with .38 silver wires. Tie the cinnamon into groups of five with the gold cord. Push a .38 silver wire around the cinnamon and under the cord. Make 15 bunches of linseed and double leg mount on .71 wires. Tape all the wired materials.

2 Take a bunch of linseed and lay it on the rim of the urn and bind on with .32 silver reel (rose) wire, passing the wire through the gaps in the mesh and pulling it tightly over the wired stem of the linseed and again through the mesh. Attach a rose head in the same way but slightly overlapping the linseed, and repeat this process with the grass head, the beech leaves and the cinnamon bundles.

3 Work continuously around the rim of the urn, always slightly overlapping the materials, until it is covered. Make sure that the materials come together neatly and there is no gap, then stitch the .32 silver reel (rose) wire through the mesh several times to secure finally. Fill the urn with the dried oranges and limes and scatter a little gold dust powder over the whole decoration.

ADVENT CANDLE WREATH
• • •

An Advent wreath has four candles, one to be lit on each of the four Sundays leading up to Christmas Day.

This one is built on a pine foliage ring and uses fruits and spices for its decoration.

1 Attach the four candles at equal distances around the circumference of the ring by cutting away some of the pine needles, putting hot glue on both the base of the candle and on the ring and pressing the two surfaces together for a few seconds. At the base of each candle glue an arrangement of the various materials. The orange slices and cinnamon sticks should be used in groups for the greatest effect.

2 Make sure each candle has a selection of the materials at its base, spreading out around the ring.

3 Make four bows from the ribbon and bind with .71 wires at their centres. Attach these to the Advent wreath by pulling the two tails of .71 wire around the width of the ring, twisting them together underneath and returning the cut ends into the moss. Position one bow at each of the four central points between the candles. Make sure that the bows do not touch the candles.

MATERIALS
• • •
30 cm (12 in) blue pine foliage ring
• • •
45 x 30 cm (2 x 12 in) candles
• • •
scissors
• • •
glue gun and glue sticks
• • •
12 slices dried orange
• • •
4 fresh clementines
• • •
6 dried cut lemons
• • •
5 dried whole oranges
• • •
4 fir cones
• • •
4 physallis heads
• • •
16 short pieces cinnamon stick
• • •
ribbon
• • •
.71 wires

This wreath is not complicated to make and can be used as a table decoration or, with ribbons, it could be hung in your hall.
Never leave burning candles unattended.

CHRISTMAS WREATH

· · ·

MATERIALS

· · ·

ball of string

· · ·

copper or steel garland ring

· · ·

sphagnum moss

· · ·

scissors

· · ·

silver reel (rose) wire

· · ·

secateurs

· · ·

blue pine (spruce)

· · ·

birch twigs

· · ·

.91 wires

· · ·

freeze-dried artichokes

· · ·

dried red chillies

· · ·

dried pomegranates

· · ·

fir cones

· · ·

glue gun and glue sticks

· · ·

dried lichen

· · ·

rope or ribbon

The artichokes provide dramatic shapes and texture, but you can use another dried material if they are not readily available.

This luxurious Christmas wreath combines the rich colours and textures of pomegranates, artichokes and chillies with traditional evergreen foliage and fir cones. It can be hung on a door or placed in the centre of the dining table.

1 Attach the end of the string to the larger of the two rings. Attach the moss to both sides evenly, winding the string tightly around the ring. Continue until the whole ring is covered, then tie the string firmly and trim the ends.

2 Tie the end of the silver reel (rose) wire to the ring. Snip off several sprigs of blue pine (spruce) and build up a thick garland by staggering them evenly around the ring. Secure each sprig in place by winding the wire tightly around the stem.

3 Continue to build up the blue pine (spruce) base until the whole ring is covered. Cut off the wire and twist it around itself several times on the underside of the wreath.

4 Make large loops out of birch twigs and place diagonally at intervals around the wreath. Secure with lengths of wire bent into U-shaped pins pushed firmly through the middle of the wreath.

5 Wire the larger dried materials individually (see Techniques). Begin with a group of artichokes. Push the wired stems firmly through the body of the wreath.

6 Wire the chillies in threes (see Techniques). Group them together between the artichokes in large clusters.

This full-bodied wreath makes a perfect decoration for the festive season.

7 Insert the pomegranates in clusters of at least five to balance the artichoke and chilli groups. Fill in the gaps with smaller clusters of fir cones.

8 Glue the lichen to the wreath. It is very delicate and cannot be wired. Intertwine rope or ribbon between the dried materials. Anchor it with wires folded in half to form U–shaped pins.

GILDED FIG PYRAMID
· · ·

MATERIALS
· · ·
gilded terracotta plant pot
· · ·
*plastic foam cone for dried
flowers, approximately 25 cm
(10 in) high*
· · ·
40 black figs
· · ·
gilding paint
· · ·
.71 wires
· · ·
scissors
· · ·
50 ivy leaves

*This display has a powerful
impact that is disproportionate
to the simplicity of its
construction.*

This abundant use of figs produces a gloriously decadent decoration for a festive table. The deep purple figs with their dusting of gold, arranged with geometric precision, create an opulent yet architectural focal point for the most indulgent of occasions.

1 Make sure that the plastic foam cone sits comfortably in the pot. To ensure stability, you may wish to put a drop of adhesive around the edge of the cone base. Gild the figs slightly on one side of the fruit only, by rubbing the gilding paint on to the skin with your fingers.

2 Wire the gilded figs by pushing a .71 wire horizontally through the flesh approximately 2.5 cm (1 in) above the base of the fruit. Carefully bend the two protruding pieces of wire so that they point downwards. Do take care when wiring the figs or you could tear their skins.

3 Attach the figs to the cone by pushing their wires into the plastic foam. Work in concentric circles around the cone upwards from the bottom.

4 When the cone is covered, position the last fig on the tip of the plastic foam cone, with its stem pointing upwards to create a point.

5 Make hairpin shapes out of the .71 wires and pin the ivy leaves in to the cone between the gilded figs, covering any exposed foam.

SUPPLIERS

· · ·

Most of the materials needed in this book can be obtained from Terence Moore Designs, which also undertakes special commissions and runs one-day workshops for individuals and groups. There are many stockists of floral materials, and since dried materials are more difficult to find, the following suppliers are particularly recommended. When buying dried stock, make sure that it is as fresh as possible and has plenty of colour. If the material looks muddy or is brittle to touch, then it has been in stock for a long time and should be avoided. Suppliers with only a small range of dried materials will probably have a slow turnover, so avoid buying from them.

UNITED KINGDOM

Terence Moore Designs
The Barn Workshop
Burleigh Lane, Crawley Down
West Sussex RH10 4LF
Tel/Fax: (01342) 717944.

The Bay Tree Florist
19 Upper High Street, Thame
Oxon OX9 3EX
Tel: (01844) 217993.

Bright Ideas
38 High Street, Lewes
East Sussex BN7 2LU
Tel: (01273) 474395.

Country Style
358 Fulwood Road, Ranmoor
Sheffield S10 3GD
Tel: (01742) 309067.

De La Mares Florist
Rue A Don, Grouville
Jersey
Channel Islands
Tel: (01534) 851538.

Forsyths
7 Market Place, St Albans
Herts AL3 5DK
Tel: (01727) 839702.

Hilliers Garden Centre
London Road (A30)
Windlesham
Surrey GU20 6LN
Tel: (01344) 23166.

Hilliers Garden Centre
Woodhouse Lane, Botley
Southampton S03 2EZ
Tel: (01489) 782306.

Lesley Hart Dried Flowers
37 Smith Street, Warwick
CV34 4JA
Tel: (01926) 490356.

Mews Gallery
Old Stone House
23 Killenchy Comber
Co. Down, Northern Ireland
BT23 5AP
Tel: (01247) 874044.

Page and Bolland
Denscombe Mill, Shillingford
Tiverton, Devon EX16 9BH
Tel: (01398) 6283.

Three French Hens
Home Farm, Swinfern
Nr Lichfield
Staffs WS14 9QR
Tel: (01543) 481613.

UNITED STATES

American Oaks Preserving
Company, Inc.
601 Mulberry Street
North Judson
Indiana, 46366
Tel: (800) 348 5008.

Earthstar Herb Gardens
438 West Perkinsville Road
China Valley, Arizona, 86323
Tel: (602) 636 2565.

Fischer & Page, Ltd.
134 West 28th Street,
New York, New York 10001.

Gold Mine Catalog
W10635, Highway 1
Reeseville
Wisconsin, 53579
Tel:(414) 927 3603.

Herb Gathering
5742 Kenwood, Kansas City
Missouri, 64110
Tel: (816) 523 2653.

J&T Imports
PO Box 642, Solana Beach
California, 92075 (wholesale).

Lee Wards
Main Office, Elgin
Illinois, 60120.

Meadow Everlasting
RR 1, 149 Shabbona Road
Malta, Illinois, 60150
Tel: (815) 825 2539.

Patchogue Florals Fantasyland
10 Robinson Avenue
East Patchogue
New York, 11772
Tel: (516) 475 2059.

Stamens & Pistils
875 Third Avenue, New York
New York, 10022
Tel: (212) 593 1888.

Sun Kempt
PO Box 231, Yorkviller
New York, 13495
Tel: (315) 797 9618.

Tom Thumb Workshop
Rt. 13, Box 357, Mappsville
Virginia, 23407
Tel: (804) 824 3507.

Wayside Gardens
1 Garden Lane, Hodges
South Carolina, 29695–0001
Tel: (800) 845 1124.

Well-sweep Herb Farm
317 Mount Bethel Road,
Port Murray
New Jersey, 07865
Tel: (201) 852 5390.

CANADA

Crafts Canada
440–28 Street, NE,
Calgary
Alberta T2A 6T3
Tel: (403) 569 2355.

Multi-crafts and Gifts
2210 Thurston Drive, Ottawa
Ontario, K1G 5L5.

INDEX
· · ·